HEARING PAUL'S VOICE

Hearing Paul's Voice

Insights for Teaching and Preaching

M. Eugene Boring

WILLIAM B. EERDMANS PUBLISHING COMPANY
GRAND RAPIDS, MICHIGAN

Wm. B. Eerdmans Publishing Co.
4035 Park East Court SE, Grand Rapids, Michigan 49546
www.eerdmans.com

26 25 24 23 22 21 20   1 2 3 4 5 6 7

ISBN 978-0-8028-7750-5

Library of Congress Cataloging-in-Publication Data

Names: Boring, M. Eugene, author.
Title: Hearing Paul's voice : insights for teaching and preaching / M. Eugene Boring.
Description: Grand Rapids, Michigan : William B. Eerdmans Publishing Company,
    2020. | Includes bibliographical references and index. | Summary: "Boring offers a
    historically informed and pastorally sensitive reading of the Pauline voices in the New
    Testament for contemporary preachers and teachers"— Provided by publisher.
Identifiers: LCCN 2019047938 | ISBN 9780802877505 (paperback)
Subjects: LCSH: Bible. Epistles of Paul—Study and teaching. | Bible. Epistles of Paul—
    Homiletical use.
Classification: LCC BS2650.55 .B67 2020 | DDC 227/.06—dc23
LC record available at https://lccn.loc.gov/2019047938

Unless otherwise noted, biblical quotations are from the New Revised Standard Version.

שְׁמַע יִשְׂרָאֵל

Hear, O Israel

— DEUTERONOMY 6:4

ὁ ἔχων ὦτα ἀκουέτω

Let anyone with ears listen!

— MARK 4:9

Μακάριος ὁ ἀναγινώσκων
καὶ οἱ ἀκούοντες τοὺς λόγους
τῆς προφητείας

Blessed is the one who reads
aloud and blessed are those
who hear the words of this
prophecy.

— REVELATION 1:3

Prayers and confessions
of those who interpret the Scriptures
for the people of God

אֲדֹנָי יְהוִֹה נָתַן לִי לְשׁוֹן לִמּוּדִים
לָדַעַת לָעוּת אֶת־יָעֵף דָּבָר
יָעִיר בַּבֹּקֶר בַּבֹּקֶר
יָעִיר לִי אֹזֶן לִשְׁמֹעַ כַּלִּמּוּדִים:

The Lord God has given me the tongue of a teacher,
that I may know how to sustain the weary with a word.
Morning by morning he wakens—
wakens my ear to listen as those who are taught.

        —Isaiah 50:4, an interpreter of the prophet

Πολλοὶ οὖν ἀκούσαντες ἐκ τῶν μαθητῶν αὐτοῦ εἶπαν·
σκληρός ἐστιν ὁ λόγος οὗτος· τίς δύναται αὐτοῦ ἀκούειν;

Many therefore of his disciples,
when they had heard this, said,
This is an hard saying; who can hear it?

        —John 6:60 KJV, an interpreter of Jesus

προσευχόμενοι ἅμα καὶ περὶ ἡμῶν,
ἵνα ὁ θεὸς ἀνοίξῃ ἡμῖν θύραν τοῦ λόγου
λαλῆσαι τὸ μυστήριον τοῦ Χριστοῦ . . .
ἵνα φανερώσω αὐτὸ ὡς δεῖ με λαλῆσαι

. . . pray for us also,
that God may open to us a door for the word,
to declare the mystery of Christ . . .
that I may make it clear, as I ought to speak.

        —Colossians 4:3–4, an interpreter of the apostle

Contents

Foreword

In his *What's Good about This News? Preaching from the Gospel and Galatians*, the noted New Testament scholar and preacher David L. Bartlett remembers that, in the early days of his parish ministry, he was devoted to the teachings of the apostle Paul. Almost every week, his sermons were based not on a Gospel reading but on an Epistle text, "where," he writes, "I have long suspected gospel is more explicit than in the Gospels."[1]

One Sunday, after one of Bartlett's more impassioned Pauline sermons, a parishioner, who happened to be a distinguished theologian and ethicist, stopped at the church door long enough to observe, "There's no question where the center of the canon lies with you."

Taking this as at least a mild criticism, a somewhat chastened Bartlett went back to his study and took out his Bible to think about what text he might preach on the following Sunday. "As I picked up the aging Revised Standard Version of the Bible," he recalls, "there fluttered forth from the binding and landed on the desk exactly seven pages—the entirety of Galatians, the poor epistle worn out from overuse."[2]

I, too, can remember the days, in a time before narrative preaching and self-confession became all the rage, when Paul reigned supreme in many pulpits, at least in the Protestant world. Paul was seen as the great architect of Christian systematic theology, one who articulated the framework for understanding the broad sweep of salvation in Christ, from the sinfulness that leaves humanity confused, not understanding its own actions, doing not what we desire but the very thing we hate (Rom 7:15), to the gift of redemption given by grace and held onto by faith.

But I can also remember when the polls began to turn against Paul. By the time I was a young seminary professor, Paul had been framed by many as the "inventor" of hidebound institutional Christianity, the doctrinaire corrupter of the simple and pure religion of Jesus. Paul was seen as a gloomy misogynist, a scowling presence who patrolled the halls of the church like an assistant principal at the high school, eager to hand out demerits and sentence people to detention hall.

"St. Paul's got a bloody lot to answer for," quipped 1960s comedian Peter Cook. In one of his skits, Cook imagines a happy family sitting down to a fabulous breakfast of fried mussels and coffee. It's a lovely day, and, since the sun is shining and the birds are chirping merrily, the family is thinking perhaps of a nice seaside picnic. Suddenly there is a knock at the door. It's a messenger bearing a letter from the apostle Paul:

> *Dear George and Deirdre and family,*
>
> *Stop having a good time, resign yourself to not having a picnic, cover yourself with ashes and start flaying yourselves, until further notice.*
>
> *Signed Paul*[3]

In the light of all this, it is refreshing, even surprising, to encounter the Paul that Eugene Boring portrays in this volume. In clear and engaging terms, Boring introduces us to a Paul quite different from the master theological architect, on the one hand, and from the glum moralist, on the other. As Boring sees him, Paul might be systematic in thought, but he was no systematic theologian. He was a missionary and a working pastor, a person with deep convictions about what God had done in Christ but one who "doesn't always know what his theology is until what he brings to the situation interacts with it." While deeply concerned about the church, Paul did not travel the ancient world trying to persuade people to join a new group or support some institution. For Paul, the church is not a structure organized around a cause. It is, rather, those "called out" by the dramatic act of God in Christ. This Paul doesn't have ready-made answers to life's dilemmas, but, rather, is one who allows the practical, concrete situations he encountered to summon forth his insights. This makes Paul a friend and companion of pastors today. As Boring says, "Preachers who struggle to bring text and congregation together understand this."

Contrary to the notion that Paul tamped down the free-flowing, open-ended gospel of Jesus, Boring understands Paul as the one who grasped the universal implications of what God had done in and through Jesus. "The Bible," he says, "does not present a 'universal' Jesus who was then obscured by a 'narrow' Paul." Indeed, many may think that Jesus was the first to preach the radical inclusiveness of the gospel, but it was actually Paul who gave voice to the gospel's full breadth. "There is nothing in the Gospels," Boring writes, "like Galatians 3:28: 'There is no longer Jew or Greek, there is no longer slave or free, there is no longer male and female; for all of you are one in Christ Jesus.' There is nothing in the Gospels that suggests that when Jesus called twelve disciples as the core of the renewed Israel, the people of God that would become the inclusive church, he included women, slaves, or Africans."

In masterly fashion, Boring guides us through Paul's witness, from the beginnings in the Thessalonian correspondence to the mature and full thought of Romans and on to the elaboration of Pauline trajectories in the deutero-Pauline letters and other post-Pauline literature. He sees strong continuities here, that what was present at the beginning of Paul's ministry still shimmered at the end and that what followed in Paul's wake was mainly not a step backward but a step forward, not a decline in Pauline urgency but a necessary extension of Paul's thought into different social and ecclesial contexts.

Most of all, though, this book comes as a stimulation to preachers and teachers in the church to recognize that the gospel as envisioned by Paul is not essentially a sequential argument. Point one: idolatry and polytheism are wrong. Point two: we are all sinners. Point three. . . . No, the gospel begins, as it did for Paul, with an astonished cry, "The living God of Israel has done it again! God has raised Jesus from the dead!"

Thomas G. Long

Bandy Professor Emeritus of Preaching
Candler School of Theology
Emory University
Atlanta, Georgia

Preface

This book is the second volume of an informal series, the first of which is *Hearing John's Voice: Insights for Teaching and Preaching*, published by Eerdmans in 2019. In *HJV* I began with Revelation, regarded by many of us as the strangest and most difficult book in the Bible, presenting a worldview and theology the most distant from our own. The premise: the strangeness of Revelation makes it difficult to read in our own agenda and theology, compelling us to work at listening to the text on its own terms. The flip side of this: if we can hear the voice of God speaking through John in Revelation, we will improve our competence in hearing other Bible texts. The book then explores, with listening ears, some of the theological depths of the Johannine Letters and the Gospel of John.

The constant goal of this series is to approach within hearing distance of the Bible's own message. The following pages aim to encourage and facilitate *drinking directly from the generative springs from which biblical theology emerges, wading in them, even submerging and perhaps being overwhelmed by them.* These pages do not attempt to survey the whole of Pauline theology, but to offer probes and soundings that hopefully both facilitate and illustrate serious, in-depth engagement with the Bible, with ears always open to being taught from the Scriptures, with eyes on communication of its manifold message in Christian proclamation and instruction.

My sincere thanks to the capable Eerdmans editorial staff for encouraging and helping to shape this project, whose combination of professional competence and friendly helpfulness have both gladdened the way and enhanced the result: James Ernest, Trevor Thompson, Jenny Hoffman, Tom Raabe, William Michael Beachy, and Amy Kent.

My deepest gratitude goes to a rather large group of preachers and teachers, most of whom do not know each other, but who have read and responded to various parts and stages of this developing project. The group includes congregational pastors and teachers, college and seminary professors of Bible and homiletics, denominational executives, clergy and laypersons, representing several denominations. They have responded by email and met with me in groups and one-on-one. They sometimes disagree with each other and with me. They have been my students and teachers. All are active members of congregations; virtually all preach and/or teach regularly in congregations. The common denominator is commitment to the church and the desire to be vehicles of the *Verbum Dei* through which the church is called into being and nourished for its witness and mission in the world. I am profoundly grateful to each of them. Special thanks to Thomas G. Long for help, extending from his counsel, which began in the course of a long breakfast in Atlanta some years ago in the prenatal stage of this project, to his encouraging words in the foreword of this book. I also remember with great appreciation the two series of lectures in which I presented a preliminary form of *Hearing John's Voice* and *Hearing Paul's Voice*, inaugurating the Izola Jones Lectureship at First Christian Church of Boonville, Missouri. The lectureship was made possible by Joyce Lake, as a memorial to her mother. I have warm memories of the hospitality of the pastor, Roger McMurry, Elzan McMurry, and the whole congregation. I dedicate this book to this group of colleagues, brothers and sisters in ministry, and to all faithful preachers and teachers who continue to nourish the church in the biblical faith:

David Artman, Bobby Cook, Miles Cook, Charlotte Coyle, Jerry Coyle, Bryan Feille, Laurie Feille, Jeff Gehle, Kim Hames, Thomas G. Long, Andy Mangum, Roger McMurry, Sammie Maxwell, Lance Pape, Ryan Pfeiffer, Russell Pregeant, Jim L. Robinson, Walter Rogero, Irwin Sentilles, Dawn Weaks, Newell Williams, Raymond B. Williams, Christopher Wilson.

M. Eugene Boring
Fort Worth, TX
October 16, 2019

Prologue

Two travelers walk along the road, engaged in serious and friendly conversation. It's a familiar road. We know it well. On this road, there is no stopping, no turning back. We can remember some of the road behind us, with its joys, sorrows, and things we might do differently now, but there are no do-overs, no Undo command. Even if we try to stop, the road itself, an ever-flowing stream, moves relentlessly on. Even if we think we remain the same, our world is different every day, leaving yesterday behind and moving on to who-knows-where. It's a one-way road; we meet no oncoming traffic, no one who has been there and back.

This is just the way the road is, and it does not interfere with the conversation between the two travelers, which is about where the road leads. One believes the road leads nowhere; it either goes on forever or gradually becomes smaller and less distinct, and then fizzles out into nothingness. Fade to black.

The other believes the road leads to the city of God.

There are other people on the road. A lot of them. Some are like us; they speak the same language, call the same country their home. Others are different. It is sometimes scary, and we tend to huddle together with those who are like us.

The conversation repeatedly returns to the main question: "Where does the road go?" Some people on the road say, "I don't know where the road is going. I don't think anybody knows. I haven't thought about it much." Some say, "I know where I am going. When my body dies, the road may go on and on, but my soul goes to heaven."

But that's not the question. It's not about me; it's about the road, the world, and all those other people. If we knew where the road and the world itself were headed, we might do some things differently, might even see the bad things that happen along the road in a different light. If the road is actually going someplace, are we all going to the same place, or does it finally divide—some to the right, some to the left? Is there only one road, or are different groups of people on different roads? Are there interchanges, or are we stuck on the road we're on?

All along the road, the two travelers experience the same things, a mixture of good and evil. They have different attitudes, different feelings, about the trip itself. The difference between them is a matter of faith. Not that one has faith and the other does not; they each have their faith. The one who believes the road leads to the city of God did not figure this out on her own, nor is it a matter of wishful thinking. She believes that the goal and meaning of the road have been revealed. Not that she has had some personal revelatory experience, but she belongs to a community of pilgrims on the road who believe that the Creator has revealed the ultimate goal and meaning of things, including our own little lives.

Neither, of course, can prove his view about the road. But the two can't resolve their differences by agreeing that, after all, it's just the way they feel about it, that each should respect other people's opinions but no one should claim that his view is really true. Though the world is sufficiently ambiguous to be interpreted theistically or atheistically, at the last turn of the road, one of them will turn out to be right about the objective reality, and to have been right all along. Their conversation is not about their feelings but about truth.[1]

Chapter 1

Paul's Theology: Grasping and Being Grasped

When, about 50 CE, Paul, Silvanus, and Timothy turned off the Via Egnatia and walked into the bustling city of Thessalonica, they were the first Christians in town. The members of the church they founded there were all new converts. Paul's letter to them a few months after the beginning of the church is our earliest extant Christian text.

By contrast, the congregations represented by Revelation, 1–3 John, and the Fourth Gospel were already in their third generation of church life when those books were written. They were looking back on an extensive and conflicted history and looking out on a multicultural world with a variety of religious traditions. Most of the Johannine Christians had grown up in the context of church life and were steeped in its traditions. Many of us share this experience—the only church we have ever known has been around for a lot longer than we have—and we have much to learn from the spectrum of Johannine texts about communicating and interpreting the good news of Christian faith in our own time.

We also have much to learn from this earliest text in the New Testament. In 1 Thessalonians, Paul gives us a glimpse of his struggle to communicate the faith to newcomers who had become Christian believers with no Jewish or biblical background. For many of us who share Paul's struggle to speak to sincere but secularized hearers and nurture them in the faith, 1 Thessalonians is nearer our own situation than any of the Johannine texts.

Theology: Faith Seeking Understanding

Paul is a theologian, and so are we preachers and teachers, every one of us, and so are most of the people in the congregations to which we belong. They may be hesitant to think of themselves as theologians, and we preachers—to curry favor with such good people—may sometimes be hesitant as well. All the same, we are theologians, and so is Paul, though he, too, never explicitly talks about "theology." The church members who listen to us on Sunday mornings may need to be encouraged to think of their minister, their church school teacher, and themselves as theologians.

The noun "theology" (*theologia*) and the verb "theologize" (*theologeō*) were available to Paul. They had been used for centuries before Paul (e.g., by Aristotle) and were current in first-century religious discourse (see, e.g., Plutarch), but it is no accident that neither Paul nor any other New Testament writer uses any of the available vocabulary for "theology." The author of Revelation is labeled "St. John the Theologian" in the title of later manuscripts of the New Testament, but otherwise *theologia*, *theologeō*, and related words are entirely absent from the New Testament.

Paul claimed to preach the gospel (the verb *euangelizomai* is used nineteen times, the noun *euangelion* forty-eight times, in the undisputed letters). He does not describe himself as conducting theological discussions. He rejected "lofty words . . . [of] human wisdom" in order, by the power of the Holy Spirit, to proclaim the crucified Jesus as representing the wisdom and power of God (1 Cor 2:1–5).[1] This datum has allowed some preachers and teachers to disdain theology as "human tradition" and "vain philosophy" and "wrangling over words, which does no good but only ruins those who are listening." The Bible warns us against such people (Matt 15:6; Col 2:8; 2 Tim 2:14). It depends, of course, on what one means by "theology."

"How many angels can dance on the head of a pin?," a question supposedly debated by medieval scholastics, is often used to illustrate "theology" as inane frivolity or merely an irrelevant indoor sport. The illustration is not apt. The issue was whether the realities of the transcendent world of God can be thought of in terms of the space-time continuum of this world, which makes God a part of the universe rather than the transcendent Creator. Such questions that ponder angels in terms of "How much space does an angel occupy?" and "How much does God weigh?" were not posed in order to obtain answers but to point out the fallacy of reducing the world of God to the space-time categories of our mundane world.

We are using the term here in the classic sense of Anselm of Canterbury (eleventh century), *fides quaerens intellectum*, "faith seeking understanding." So understood, theology includes the serious intellectual effort of believing scholars to examine the faith, an ongoing quest for a broader and deeper grasp of (or, rather, being grasped by) the truth of God made known in Jesus Christ. But theology is much more than the critical re-flection on the faith by academic theologians. Theology is necessary in order to state what we believe in the first place, even to ourselves. Faith as trust is exercised by babies, but faith that is thought about and stated requires concepts and language, and is already theology. Thus, for adults, "faith" and "theology" are not alternatives but require each other. Primal faith is that personal elemental trust in God that calls forth the preconcep-tual, prelinguistic response of love and obedience to God, obedience-in-personal-trust. But as soon as one *thinks* about this faith and attempts to express its content in thoughts and words, faith is seeking understanding, and the result is theology. So understood, theology is not only intentional reflection on religious truth, not only philosophical and academic discus-sions of divine and ultimate things. Every *statement* of faith is and must be theological, for faith cannot express itself without having some conceptual and linguistic content. The church member, preacher, or teacher who may claim a bit smugly that "I'm just a simple believer; I don't go in for all that fancy theology" may actually be articulating a true insight, expressing an authentic disdain for frivolous academic abstractions, but this cannot be a rejection of theology as such, whatever it be called. Whether believers are simple or sophisticated, every statement expressing faith is necessar-ily faith seeking understanding, that is, a theological statement. When one responds to the question of what one means by God, even if only in an internal monologue to clarify one's own thinking, one is making a theological statement. Thus theology is not only the discipline that tests our preaching and teaching for its conformity and appropriateness to the gospel. The preaching being tested by critical, reflective theological think-ing is already theology and, as the conceptual and linguistic expression of the faith, cannot be anything else. This is what I mean by claiming that all Paul's statements expressing his faith, and all our sermons and church-school lessons, are theology. Whoever believes anything and attempts to articulate that belief in concepts and language is doing theology. This is first-level, primary theology. Only rarely does Paul indulge in second-level theology, which reflects on and attempts to explain the theological affirmations made at this primary level. Paul's affirmation of the resurrec-tion in the traditional creed of 1 Corinthians 15:3–5 is first-level, primary theology; his *discussion* of the resurrection in the paragraphs that follow ventures into second-level theology. Every sermon, good or bad, simplis-tic or profound, is theology of one or the other sort. The only way to avoid theology is not to believe or not to think. To be sure, while faith causes us to think, faith generates more than thought—faith sings, confesses, rejoices, and suffers. Faith acts.[2]

We are not here attempting to reconstruct the "theology of Paul" in any comprehensive sense. Paul was not a systematic theologian. Not only does he not send theological essays on particular themes to his churches, but he does not have this worked out in his own mind in a systematic way. "Systematic theology," in the sense of a comprehensive way of thinking about and stating the faith in ways that make some kind of sense in one's own categories, is a necessary and valuable discipline. Theology is what we thinking believers, believing thinkers, do and must do, whether systematically or willy-nilly, in expressing the faith in our own categories: what we mean by "God," "Christ," "salvation," "church," "the meaning of history," "the meaning and purpose of my own life," and such. In this sense, everyone has a "systematic" theology, even if it is implicit, inchoate, undeveloped, contradictory, fragmentary, tentative. In this sense, it means simply "thinking about our faith, expressing its meaning as coherently as we know how or feel the need to." In this elemental sense, Paul did have a "systematic theology"; if you had stopped him on the street in Thessalonica and asked him what he meant by "Christ," "church," and the "parousia," he would not have been tongue-tied. Perhaps after a minute to collect his thoughts, he could have given a reasonable response. Though Paul was not a systematic theologian, his theology does have a systematic quality; it is not a hodgepodge of random or arbitrary ideas. Throughout the history of the church, Paul has been recognized as a theologian of great depth. But he does not have a comprehensive, consistent theological system always ready to hand, upon which he can draw and trot out particular segments to address each concrete situation as it emerges. He does not respond ad hoc but draws upon his core theological convictions. What these in fact mean sometimes first becomes clear as he thinks through the meaning of the faith for the particular situation. As we make some soundings in the "theology" of 1 Thessalonians, we are not attempting to reconstruct the "theology of Paul" the person, the growing and changing collection of ideas he carried around with him that expressed his faith. In preaching or teaching from a New Testament text, or merely trying to hear and understand it for our own edification, we want to get within hearing distance of a *text* in our (= the church's) Bible, not reconstruct the whole theology of the person or community behind the text.

In the generations after Paul's death, the church accepted and affirmed the extant Pauline letters as Holy Scripture. We preachers and teachers in the church want to shape our own theology in dialogue with the Bible, which means listening to its message in its own theological terms. In dealing with any text from a Pauline letter, we want to get a handle on Paul's theology as a whole. But how can people today get their minds around this disparate collection of letters, which embed the gospel and Christian nurture in profound theology, combined with practical instruction, passion, politics, and autobiography? This can be done in two basic ways, each of which is both valuable and problematical. One can strive for a holistic, bird's-eye view, assembling Paul's statements on God, Christ, Holy Spirit, church, sin, salvation, faith, love, ethics, and the like into some sort of topical systematic statement. Or one can approach the letters one at a time in their presumed historical order, concentrating on the particular facets of Paul's theology that surface in each letter. The *synchronic-systematic* approach attempts to summarize Paul's theology as an organized whole; the *diachronic-historical* perspective aims at understanding the theology expressed in each letter as the context for preaching or teaching from a text in that letter. Needless to say, neither approach can be implemented afresh each time one studies a particular text; acquiring such a perspective must be part of the preacher's or teacher's overall long-term strategy of continuing theological study. Helpful books that adopt each approach, or combine them, are suggested at the end of this volume.

Paul's theology is a work in progress, as is ours and that of the people who receive our preaching and teaching. His letters allow us to overhear the intense dialogues in which his theology is forged and shared. To each situation he brings the Scripture—the revelation of God in Torah, Prophets, and Writings—in which his mind is steeped and which he now seeks to understand in the light of God's definitive revelation in the event of Jesus Christ. He brings tradition—creeds, songs, insights, and convictions from previous experience, contacts with other apostolic missionaries and teachers, including his own colleagues and associates, men and women who are his coworkers. He brings his conviction that his theological work as missionary preacher is guided and empowered by the Holy Spirit. Paul's sense of his ministry is analogous to the preacher's task today. Each situation tailors and reshapes what Paul brings and, in this matrix, also generates new insights, new content, so that he does not merely "apply" previous traditions and insights. Paul doesn't always know what his theology is until what he brings to the situation interacts with it. He doesn't always know what the answer is until the situational question brings it into being. Preachers who struggle to bring text and congregation together understand this.

Our procedure will be to adopt a historical perspective, beginning with 1 Thessalonians as the earliest extant Pauline letter, then working through Romans as Paul's last and longest letter that summarizes the major themes of his theology. In each case we will ask how the readers would have understood the text of that letter, without importing all that we later interpreters might know from reading the rest of the Pauline corpus and other New Testament documents not available to them. Preaching or teaching on Christian hope in 1 Thessalonians 4:13–18, for example, would not use this text as a launching pad for a topical sermon or lesson about hope in general, a presentation, perhaps with good and helpful thoughts that could be attached to any biblical text containing the word or idea "hope." Nor should a sermon or lesson on this text become a comprehensive treatment of Paul's eschatology compiled from all his letters. The approach we adopt here is in step with Paul's own preaching, the composition of his letters, and their formation into the New Testament canon, and is historical and particular rather than general and systematic. This is also the goal of our preaching and teaching, which aims at allowing the congregation or class to hear the testimony of a particular text. This does not mean, however, that we artificially and mechanically limit our reflection to the words on the pages of the letter before us, pretending when we read 1 Thessalonians that we have never read 1 Corinthians or Romans, as though we do not live in a church with nineteen centuries of experience or have never thought about the subject ourselves. Our preaching from a particular text can be authentically informed by what we understand of Paul's theology as a whole. There are, in fact, items of information and insight not found in 1 Thessalonians that were known by the original readers that facilitated their understanding of the letter. We also are aware of some of these from our critical reading of other New Testament texts.

For example, in 1 Thessalonians, Paul never explicitly refers to baptism, the Eucharist, or creedal statements. However, in a letter to Corinth written four or five years later, he refers to baptism as presupposed for all Christians (1 Cor 1:13–17; 10:2; 12:13; 15:29), includes the eucharistic tradition he had received and passed on to the Corinthians (11:23–26), and cites the basic creedal statement he had presumably taught them when the church was founded, just after the church-founding visit in Thessalonica. None of this appears in 1 Thessalonians, but Paul does refer to having passed on traditional teaching to the new church in Thessalonica (1 Thess 4:1; cf. 2:13), and we have every reason to believe he delivered the same traditions in all his churches (1 Cor 1:2; 4:17; 7:17; 15:11). It seems we can and should read

1 Thessalonians with the assumption that the new congregation in Thessalonica understood the letter in the light of these traditions and practices Paul had established when the church was founded, traditions we can engage in 1 Corinthians or other letters of Paul.

On the other hand, 1 Thessalonians makes no reference to justification by grace through faith in contrast to "works of the law," a matter that became crucial in his later letters to the Galatians and Romans. Nor is there any indication of the "body of Christ" imagery for the church that is central to the ecclesiology of 1 Corinthians and Romans, continued in different ways in the post-Pauline Colossians and Ephesians. We know these as important Pauline teachings in later letters. We should be hesitant to read them into 1 Thessalonians.

Theology as Personal: Paul, "Julia," and Ourselves

Authentic preaching is not only theological but also intensely personal. The New Testament is not, of course, a book of abstract ideas and principles but deals with particular people—423 different persons are explicitly named, in addition to numerous individuals whose names are not given. Paul's letters are addressed to churches—not to the church in general but to particular congregations composed of individuals whose names he knows, whose faces he sees as he writes. We will approach 1 Thessalonians as expressing the personal theology of Paul and ask how it would have been heard by a representative member of the congregation, whom we will call "Julia."

Paul

"So deeply do we care for you that we are determined to share with you not only the gospel of God but also our own selves, because you have become very dear to us" (1 Thess 2:8). Paul's theology bears this personal stamp throughout. God's revelation is supremely and definitively not in a book but in a personal life: that of Jesus of Nazareth (2 Cor 4:4). The revelation of God continues in and through the lives of those God calls, both Paul himself and the church people to whom he writes. Paul does not merely illustrate the gospel by anecdotes from his personal life; he believes the gospel itself has changed his life and is embodied in his own being, and he does not hesitate to recount his own experience as communication of the gospel (e.g., 1 Thess 1:5–3:13; virtually all of Philippians and Philemon; 1 Cor 1:4–4:20; 9:1–27; 15:1–11; 16:5–20; 2 Cor 1:3–2:17; 4:1–12; 7:5–15; Gal 1:1–2:21; 6:1–17). Even Paul's last and longest letter, the profoundly theological letter to the Romans, the only letter written to a church he had not founded or visited, concludes with greetings to and from real people, a list of thirty-five persons.

Theology is personal not only for the apostle but also for the churches to whom he writes. Paul writes letters that became Scripture, yet he claims that God's letter is not the pen and ink of his letters but the message embodied in the Christian community (2 Cor 3:2–3). So also, Christian ethics is not a matter of philosophical reflection on the nature of morality or conformity to a transcendent abstract standard, but it consists of personal relationships among fellow human beings and between human beings and God. Just as the definitive revelation of God was a person, so for Christian faith God himself is conceived personally. Such language is necessarily metaphorical. All the persons we know have brains, hearts, eyes, ears, hands, digestive and reproductive systems. God has none of these, yet the Bible unreflectively (not "naively") speaks of God in personal, male and female imagery, as one who wills and thinks, sees and hears, acts in history. And loves. Theology, language about God expressing trust in God, is necessarily personal; God's call to us in Scripture and preaching is a person-to-person call.

"Julia"

Julia is an imaginary figure who represents real people, the members of the new church in Thessalonica in the year 50 CE. Julia is on her way to a meeting of the small congregation that gathers in the dining room and atrium of an affluent neighbor's home. Like every other member of the little group, Julia is a recent convert to the new faith. A few months before, a transient tentmaker and part-time preacher named Paul had come to town with two of his coworkers; they were barely noticed in the large seaport city on the main east-west highway, accustomed as it was to being lectured to and harangued by traveling philosophers, teachers, entertainers, and con artists. Julia did not get to know Paul personally, but her neighbor was among those who had heard him and, along with a few others, had been convinced by his message, had been baptized, and had become a promoter of the new faith. After a couple of months, the transient preachers and their little flock of "believers," as they called themselves, began to attract unfavorable public attention; there was some kind of trouble in which people were hurt; and the preachers left town (1 Thess 1:6; 2:2, 14; 3:4, 7; Acts 17:1–9).

A few weeks later, Julia herself became a believer. The group met weekly, shared a meal together, sang and prayed, listened to readings from the sacred scrolls, were moved (or put off) by some of the group who claimed spiritual experiences, including making speeches inspired by the power of the "Holy Spirit." Things had not gone smoothly. Members of the group were suspect in the eyes of their neighbors, who were inclined to believe the rumors circulating about them—that they ate flesh and drank blood, had "love feasts" in which men and women participated on equal terms, and worshiped a criminal executed for attempting to overthrow the government. The little group spoke of themselves as an *ekklēsia*, which means "assembly"—the same word used by the legally constituted assembly of local citizens. Most of them, however, no longer participated in the city's patriotic and religious occasions. While Julia had not experienced major difficulties herself, some in the group had been snubbed at work and sometimes publicly ridiculed, and a few had been physically attacked. The congregation had been startled at the deaths of some of its members, for they had understood that they would all live until Jesus came from heaven to save them. For the most part, their troubles had drawn the group closer together, but a few were wondering if being baptized had been a mistake, and some had already abandoned the group. Julia was among the majority that had persevered, and was especially interested in the meeting that evening—they met after work on Sundays—for the little group had received a letter from Paul. In the months since the traveling missionaries ("apostles" they called themselves) had founded the church and moved on, they had been visited once by Timothy, Paul's helper, but this letter was the first they had heard from Paul himself. She wanted to hear the letter herself, and she wanted to know what the others would think of it. We are both like and unlike Julia.

We are like Julia. Like us, she had not known Paul personally. Nonetheless, she knows that when the letter is read aloud in the group's worship service that evening, she will hear the letter as addressed to her too, though she was not among the "founding members" baptized during the initial mission (1 Thess 5:27!). Paul writes to the church, and Julia belongs to the church, which includes those who had been converted by the preaching and teaching of the new congregation after his departure, people who had been trained and commissioned to carry on the work (5:12). Julia is still learning what it means to belong to the church; the other members will bring Julia up to speed, will interpret the meaning of the obscure parts of Paul's letter and the other sacred writings the congregation repeatedly hears read in their worship—the same Scriptures, so she understands, that Jewish worshipers hear every week in their synagogue services.

Our earliest New Testament document already poses the issue present in every biblical text, which is both not-written-to-us and written-to-us. When we read 1 Thessalonians, we are aware that it was not written to us, and that to understand it we must imaginatively enter the thought world of its author and first hearers/readers. We are also aware that from the beginning some who heard 1 Thessalonians did not know the author personally and had not experienced the founding events of the church to which they belonged, events presupposed by the letter itself. The church, then and now, brings newcomers within hearing distance of the letter that is also addressed to them, by interpreting elements of the letter they do not understand or misunderstand. From its earliest days, the church has always found it necessary to interpret its foundational texts to those who later became members of the Christian community. We, too, belong to this church. When we read 1 Thessalonians, we need those who were in Christ before we were (cf. Rom 16:7) to help us understand our Bible. But when we read 1 Thessalonians, we are not reading someone else's mail.

Julia, like us, hears Paul's letter as addressed to her as a member of the church. Understanding it means identifying herself as addressee. She does not hear it as though she were the writer, but as the hearer to whom it is addressed. In later times such as our own, the goal of the good reader is to identify with the text's addressees, not with its author. We later readers identify with Julia, not with Paul. We preachers and teachers do not stand with Paul over against the congregation—"Paul and I have something to say to you"—but with the reader—"Paul's letter has something it wants to say to us." We preachers must first become hearers, then help the congregation or class to hear what the text has to say. It is addressed to us, preacher and congregation. We are like Julia.

We are also unlike Julia. We have helpful information about Paul and the early church that Julia did not have and could not have had. We have several of Paul's later writings in which he spells out his teaching on various subjects, and we have Acts, which informs us about Paul's life and work. Julia had belonged to the church for a few weeks; the church to which she belonged had existed for only a few months. We may have belonged to the church since childhood; the church to which we belong has nearly two thousand years of experience in formulating its message and mission in an enormous variety of times and places. We modern readers look back on a long history of the church, some of it heroic and venerable, some of it embarrassing and shameful. The Thessalonians did not have either this baggage or this appreciation. They themselves are the only church they had ever experienced. Our un-Julia aspects can be both pluses and minuses. The church we belong to has learned much over the centuries and across the continents, and it has much to offer us. But in preaching or teaching from 1 Thessalonians, our goal must first be the same as Julia's: to hear what this *text* has to say to *us*.

We thus have both more and less than Julia had. We have all Paul's letters to illuminate this one. But she had Paul's letter as a whole, repeatedly read forth orally in the assembled congregation. She had no personal copy in which she could "look up" verses. It was an oral/aural society in which few people had personal copies of texts—and it would be generations before Paul's letters were collected, edited, bound together as Scripture, and divided into chapters and verses for ready reference. We *can* have Paul's letter in the same way Julia did, but we have to work at it. We have probably never heard the letter as a whole read aloud in the church's worship, but we can do this ourselves, can read or listen to it all at one sitting, and can get our minds around what it has to say in a way that does not reduce it to bits and pieces of inspirational confetti.

Julia had been converted by hearing the word of God that came through the testimony of a fellow member of the church, a neighbor who had been converted only a few weeks prior to Julia's own conversion. Every syllable of the sermon, lesson, or conversation that had led to her conversion had been in the neighbor's own language, vocabulary, and thought forms. This neighbor's testimony that had been instrumental in Julia's conversion was itself in the process of being reshaped by his Christian faith; that is, the transforming word had been shaped and reshaped by the neighbor's theology, itself already shaped by Paul's theology. The word of God is not identical with any human theology—not Paul's, not the modern preacher's—but it is inseparable from it: no theology, no preaching the gospel. The word of God always has a content, always takes on human linguistic and thought forms.

We are unlike Julia in that she knew her life was inseparably bound up with the life of the church to which she now belonged. She had no Bible of her own, no local Christian bookstore, no religious marketplace on TV or the Internet, no friends of other denominations to discuss religion with while keeping her own counsel and making up her own mind. If she didn't like what was going on at church, she could not go to another congregation down the street. We may think we can have our own personal brand of Christianity or of following Jesus. Julia knew God had chosen and called a people to be his witnesses in the world and had given the Holy Spirit to them, that, as Paul would explain in later writings, she belonged to a living body of Christ and was not a separate cell that could decide to make it on her own. She knew she needed to hear the word of God that came through Paul's letter addressed to the church. She knew she belonged to the church, and that she needed to deepen her understanding of what that meant.

Conversion, the Living God, and the New World I Already Live In

Listening along with Julia, we hear, on the very first page, Paul summarize his message as the story that weaves together God's cosmic act in Christ and God's personal act in Julia's conversion and ours: "how you turned to God from idols, to serve a living and true God, and to wait for his Son from heaven, whom he raised from the dead—Jesus, who rescues us from the wrath that is coming" (1 Thess 1:9–10).

If we ever found it necessary to formulate a one-sentence summary of what it means to belong to the church, could we come up with anything even close to Paul's summary here? Though Julia is still learning, she recognizes all three elements of this compressed outline of the meaning of Christian discipleship as real, life-changing events: (1) she herself has acted and been acted upon—she has been converted; (2) the one true God has acted definitively in raising Jesus from the dead; and (3) she lives in a new world, an in-between time bracketed by the first and second advents of Jesus. Since these three dimensions of Christian faith are basic to all Paul's theology, we will explore them here, as represented in 1 Thessalonians, as our entrée into the study of Paul's theology common to all his letters.

Conversion

Believing the gospel preached by Paul does not add on new insights and responsibilities to the life, mind-set, and worldview I already have; it is not a new worthy cause to which I can contribute, a new support group in which I can find spiritual resources to cope with myself and the world—not "one more thing" but "this one thing" (cf. Phil 3:13). If what Paul proclaimed was true, then something has *happened* that makes *all* the difference. The world

I live in, the road I am on, is different from what I had always assumed. And *I* am different, my life, my understanding of who I am and what my life is about, what's important and what's not, what is the center and what is on the margins—all this is different. This is not merely a psychological change. In conversion one enters into a new world, a new symbolic universe, the world as it really is, not just a new way of thinking about the old world, as though it continues as the "real," objective world that is merely thought about more "religiously" or "spiritually." Conversion is a matter of reorientation that goes to the root of our being; it's not just inserting increments of new information into the old framework. The contrast is not merely between past bad behavior and future good behavior, a resolution to try a little harder to be a little nicer. The contrast is between thinking the things of God and thinking the things of human things, thinking as God does rather than as human beings do (see below on Rom 8:1–33). When Julia and her brothers and sisters in the new little community in Thessalonica converted, Paul says they "turned," repented, reoriented, entered a new symbolic universe, a new narrative world, a new creation; they did not just accept a new idea within their old frame of reference.

The classical definition of "conversion" in the Hellenistic world, in Arthur Darby Nock, *Conversion: The Old and New in Religion from Alexander the Great to Augustine of Hippo* (London: Oxford University Press, 1961), 7: "By conversion we mean the reorientation of the soul of an individual, the deliberate turning from indifference or from an earlier form of piety to another, a turning which implies a consciousness that a great change is involved, that the old was wrong and the new is right." Nock gives numerous examples. See also M. Eugene Boring, Klaus Berger, and Carsten Colpe, *Hellenistic Commentary to the New Testament* (Nashville: Abingdon, 1995), index under "conversion," "rebirth."

This world- and life-changing event did not just happen—the one true God had done something in Judea twenty years before Julia heard the message, and this same God had acted in Julia's own experience a few weeks before, when she heard and believed this message. God's act and Julia's act were interwoven; God had acted and Julia had acted. She both converted—her own decision—and *was* converted—the act of God. As in 1 Thessalonians 1:9, so Paul in his later letters frequently points his readers back to the decisive event of their own beginnings, the radical turn in their lives, the initial experience of grace and their response (e.g., 1 Cor 6:11; Gal 3:1–3; Rom 6:3–4, 17–18).

These words in which Paul calls his readers to remember their own conversion can be heard only with difficulty by many twenty-first-century mainliners, who tend to identify the language of conversion with stories of I-used-to-get-drunk-and-beat-my-wife-and-kids-but-then-I-found-the-Lord. This does not mean serious mainline Christians have not been converted. For some, the event may have been sudden and dramatic, and they can tell you the time and place, and it need not be of the from-lowlife-to-respectable genre. For others, probably the vast majority of those who hear our sermons and teaching, conversion is thought of, if at all, as a gradual process, perhaps still under way.

Fire

Blaise Pascal (1623–1662), French philosopher and mathematician, had been a baptized believer and church member since childhood, along with his family a respectable upper middle-class Roman Catholic. In his twenties, he adopted the teachings and practice of a strict Augustinian community, the Jansenists, which he saw as his adult reaffirmation of the truth of the Christian faith. In his early thirties, the event and meaning of Jesus's crucifixion became vividly, intensely real to him. He later called this his "definitive conversion," which he recorded on a piece of parchment that he carried with him the rest of his life, sewed inside his coat. He never expected anyone else to see it. I trust I do not profane it or violate his personal piety by citing it here:

> The year of grace 1654, Monday, 23 November, feast of Saint Clement
> . . . from about half-past ten in the evening until about half-past twelve
> . . . FIRE . . . God of Abraham, the God of Isaac, the God of Jacob, and
> not of the philosophers and savants. . . . Certitude. Certitude. Feeling. Joy.
> Peace. . . . Joy, joy, joy, tears of joy.
> I have cut myself off from him, shunned him, denied him, crucified
> him.
> Let me never be cut off from him!
> He can only be kept by the ways taught in the Gospel.
> Sweet and total renunciation.
> Total submission to Jesus Christ and my director.
> Everlasting joy in return for one day's effort on earth.
> I will not forget thy word. Amen.

None of us, however, can understand the New Testament's language of conversion in the way Julia and her contemporaries understood it. None of them, nor anyone they knew, had grown up in the church, nor in a community of churches. Unencumbered by nineteen centuries of tradition and acculturation, she and her fellow church members experienced conversion in its raw reality.

Precisely for this reason—they were clear that they had been converted—we (post)moderns may learn something of the meaning of conversion from them. They had not been converted from irreligion to religion—they and all their friends and neighbors had already been religious people. They had been grasped by the message of some traveling preachers, and had made a fundamental break with the life they had always known. Such conversions were not unknown in the first-century Hellenistic world. The mystery cults, for example, offered richly satisfying personal experiences of leaving the old life behind and the joyful re-birth to a new self. The call to conversion is not unique to Christianity, then or now. Converted *from* what *to* what (or whom)—that is the crucial issue.

Learning to See What Is Hiding in Plain View

"My life has been defined largely by two events in my early years. The first was a flash of insight that came in church one Sunday. The minister, Ira Flowers, said something in his sermon that jolted my consciousness with this thought: What we talk about in church is either the most important thing in life or of no impor-tance at all. Deeply moved by this realization, I decided in that moment that my Christian faith was the center of my life and that I would live out my days on that basis. I was, of course, simply echoing the first commandment: 'you shall have no other gods before me' (Exod 20:3). And one of the themes of this book is my perception of violations of that commandment—which is to say, idolatries—that have infected my home state, my country, and even the church."

—Russell Pregeant, *For the Healing of the Nation*
(Eugene, OR: Cascade, 2016), 11

One Living God, Not Many Dead Idols

As his letter to the church is read aloud in worship, Julia and her fellow converts hear the voice of Paul summarize what had happened to them: "you turned to God from idols, to serve a living and true God." They knew that a glorious/ threatening/painful transformation had occurred in their lives, but this was not the way they would have said it. "Turn" represents Paul's Jewish understanding of repentance, an about-face, a reversal of directions on the road of life, from going away from God to going toward God and the city of God at the end of the road. Turning "from dead idols" was also Paul's Jewish way of talking about pagan religion, in a way Julia would never have spoken of her previous life. Julia and her fellow church members had not thought of themselves as "worshiping dead idols" prior to Paul's arrival in town, waiting and hoping that someone would come and tell them about the real God. Especially in a center of Roman power such as Thessalonica, public religious and patriotic celebrations would feature performances such as recitations of Virgil's *Aeneid*, the "national epic" of Roman origins, in which the gods were alive and active, guiding history to the founding of Rome, intervening for the salvation of the empire and heroic individuals. The statues and images of the gods were ways of representing their divine reality, but the gods lived in the heavenly, spiritual world, not in the statues that represented them. Julia had believed in this world of gods that af-

"Desiderata" as Pop Stoicism

Written in 1926 by Max Ehrmann, a lawyer of Terre Haute, Indiana, the prose poem "Desiderata" is often supposed to be ancient "Eastern" wisdom.

Go placidly amid the noise and haste, and remember what peace there may be in silence. As far as possible, without surrender, be on good terms with all persons. Speak your truth quietly and clearly; and listen to others, even to the dull and ignorant; they too have their story. Avoid loud and aggressive persons; they are vexations to the spirit. If you compare yourself with others, you may become vain or bitter, for always there will be greater and lesser persons than yourself. Enjoy your achievements as well as your plans. Keep interested in your own career, however humble, it's a real possession in the changing fortunes of time. Exercise caution in your business affairs, for the world is full of trickery. But let this not blind you to what virtue there is; many persons strive for high ideals, and everywhere life is full of heroism. Be yourself. Especially do not feign affection. Neither be cynical about love; for in the face of all aridity and disenchantment, it is as perennial as the grass. Take kindly the counsel of the years, gracefully surrendering the things of youth. Nurture strength of spirit to shield you in sudden misfortune. But do not distress yourself with dark imaginings. Many fears are born of fatigue and loneliness. Beyond a wholesome discipline, be gentle with yourself. You are a child of the universe no less than the trees and the stars; you have a right to be here. And whether or not it is clear to you, no doubt the universe is unfolding as it should. Therefore be at peace with God, whatever you conceive him to be. And whatever your labors and aspirations, in the noisy confusion of life, keep peace in your soul. With all its sham, drudgery and broken dreams, it is still a beautiful world. Be cheerful. Strive to be happy.

Christian believers give thanks to the one God revealed in Jesus Christ for the gift of life, do not claim "a right to be here," and rejoice in being children of God who are part of God's eternal plan for the universe (see below on Ephesians).

fected everyone's personal life and the welfare of society as a whole. The gods presented in the *Aeneid* and honored by community festivals were arbitrary, fickle, swayed by flattery and the massive number of sacrifices constantly being offered to preserve the welfare of the state and secure the good fortune of individuals. Success in life included learning how to negotiate one's course through a world with a number of competing, sometimes hostile powers. This is what public and patriotic cultural religion was for.

For many people in the first century, such a view of the world and life was not problematical but simply the normal way of fitting into the world, the way things are and always have been, and they hardly gave it a thought. A minority of serious and thoughtful people found traditional religion oppressive and sought relief from a view of the world in which "human life . . . lay foully prostrate upon earth crushed down under the weight of religion" (Lucretius, *On the Nature of Things* 1.62). Lucretius and like-minded souls welcomed the philosophy of Epicurus, who did not deny the reality of gods and the divine world but saw the world of the gods as far removed and uninvolved in human affairs—the gods existed, but they were unconcerned with us. We can live happily and carefree on our own without worrying about them, with confidence in "true reason" as our guide, nature as the source of our life from which we come and to which we return. "Nothing exists but atoms and the void"; we are accidents of nature; we are free from the oppressive demands and threats of the gods. We are on our own, and this is good news.

Others found the way of salvation from oppressive religion in the popular Stoicism of the first-century Roman world. Founded by Zeno around 300 BCE and profoundly expressed in the *Meditations* of Marcus Aurelius in the second century CE, the Stoic view of life was widely accepted in the first century (cf. Acts 17:18). There are no gods to be either feared or worshiped. The stories of the gods really represent the rule of divine Reason, which permeates the universe. Whatever happens is in accord with this all-pervading Reason. Since human beings participate in this divine Reason, to be authentically human is to accept what comes, guided by impersonal divine Reason, to go with the flow, roll with the punches, in the calm confidence that "nothing happens without a reason" and "all is for the best." The good news is that we are free to mind our own business, keep our cool, and live our own lives untroubled by erratic and demanding gods. One could experience a sincere conversion not only in the mystery cults but also through the freedom promised by Epicureans and Stoics.

In first-century Thessalonica, there were thus several ways of getting along, of being "spiritual but not religious," of coming to terms with the spiritual powers that dominate lives. Few folk in Thessalonica were unhappy with the religion they had before Paul came to town. We should not imagine them as despairing worshipers of lifeless idols waiting for someone to come along and tell them about the real God. For Julia and her sisters and brothers in the little congregation that met in the neighbor's home down the street, it was a radical move, a true conversion, to turn from this world of fickle powers that controlled their lives, to regard them as powerless, nonexistent nonrealities—"dead idols" is perhaps an appropriate label after all. This conversion was not to the practical atheism of the Epicureans or the sophisticated atheism of the Stoics, both of which rejected the popular view that there were personal gods with whom we have to contend. For Julia and her congregation, conversion was a turn to the world as it really was, a world not populated by a plurality of competing powers, a world in which "success" no longer meant learning how to move skillfully among these powers to achieve one's own goals, without awareness of or regard for the final goal toward which the road we are on is leading. The real world in which Julia and we live is the world of the living God, the one true God who has revealed his own character and purpose by sending his Son to us. Julia and her fellow believers had been converted. We twenty-first-century believers may think of ourselves as untouched by Paul's language of turning from dead idols; our lives are pretty much under our own control, not bothered by having to deal with little tin gods. However, if we dare to ask whether our lifeworld is dominated by fickle, arbitrary, conflicting powers that promise life and happiness—*American Idol* was not named on a whim—or whether we live in a world over which the one living God is sovereign despite all appearances ("idol" means "image," "appearance"), this means we are asking whether we have been converted.

The opening words of Augustine's *Confessions*:

> Great art Thou, O Lord and greatly to be praised; great is Thy power, and Thy wisdom infinite. And Thee would man praise; man, but a particle of Thy creation; man that bears about him his mortality, the witness of his sin, the witness that "Thou resistest the proud": yet would man praise Thee; he, but a particle of Thy creation. Thou awakenest us to delight in Thy praise; for Thou madest us for Thyself, and our heart is restless until it repose in Thee.

> Augustine, *Confessions*, trans. Edward Bouverie Pusey, in *Augustine*, Great Books of the Western World (Chicago: Encyclopedia Britannica, 1952), 1

In coming to know the living God, Julia thus comes to know herself as she really is. It is not a matter of psychology, as though the gospel merely gives her an egocentric understanding of her own inner self. To be converted to *this* God means I myself am not as I have always understood myself, autonomous and self-centered. I do not find the meaning of my life by taking my own pulse or probing my own psyche. As Augustine prayed, "You have made us for Yourself, and our hearts are restless till they find rest in You." To be made in God's image is not to have some divine component down inside us but to find our true being as a beloved creature of God, participating in God's purpose for the whole creation, looking back in gratitude for God's gift of life, looking forward to a future we cannot imagine, a fulfillment that lies beyond all our ambitions and achievements in this world, to "love God and enjoy him forever." Julia's conversion and ours are a conversion away from ourselves and our self-centeredness, yet we cannot turn from our this-worldly idols to the living God without receiving a new understanding of ourselves, for we cannot know our own true humanity apart from a new awareness of who God is.[3]

Paul's proclamation in Thessalonica had not been a lecture on the folly of idolatry and the reasonableness of believing in one "supreme being." Paul had not come to town with a persuasive theory about divinity but with the good news of God's act in Christ—God sent his Son into the world, we humans killed him in the best interests of religion and society, but God raised him from the dead as the leading edge of God's new world in the making. The God in whom Julia and her fellow converts had come to believe is the one God who is not one power among others within the world and history, but the One who is the Only One with whom we have to do, the Creator and Lord of history, who is inseparable from the story of his mighty acts in history from beginning to end. This God has a story, the ultimate story, the grand story, of which he is producer, director, and principal actor. As is the case with all persons, to know this God is to know his story, and to know that the meaning of my own life is part of this story. Thus, when Paul came to town with the message that God had raised the crucified Jesus of Nazareth from the dead, this was not just some story of someone who had survived death and had been taken to the heavenly world, not just a weird event on a spring Sunday in 30 CE Jerusalem. The Hellenistic world was familiar with many such stories about their gods and divine beings. Jesus is the *Christ*; it is *Christ* that God raised from the dead. This good news of God (1 Thess 2:2, 8, 9) is identical with the good news of Christ (3:2). While "God" vocabulary was familiar to the Thessalonians, "Christ" was peculiar to

Judaism and the Jewish Scriptures: the anointed savior figure whom the God of Israel, the Creator of all things and one Lord of the universe, would send at the end of history to bring an end to the world's troubles and establish God's kingdom of peace and justice. To be converted to the living God is to see the world and oneself as the creation of this God, to see one's own little story incorporated into God's big story, to see one's own little stretch of the road as part of God's grand design for universal history that ends in the city of God. *This* is "comfort."

The New Between-the-Times World of Eschatological Existence

Living in Two Ages

Paul's theology, the understanding of the world and life bound up with the gospel he communicates and nurtures in the new congregation, operates within the Jewish framework of the two ages. The fundamental difference between the traditional Jewish view Paul had previously held that looked forward to the coming of the Messiah and the view of Paul the Jewish Christian is this: the Messiah who is to come is the Messiah who has already come—the messianic king has already appeared in history, but the fullness of the messianic kingdom, the kingdom of God for which Jews and Christians pray, is still to come. The present life of the believer is between-the-times existence, but this does not mean that Christian believers live in the empty space between the old that is past and the new that is still to come:

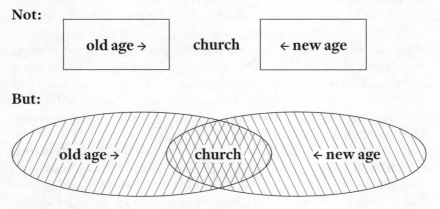

Figure 1. Between-the-Times Existence

The already/not yet of Christian existence means that the reality of the new age is *already* dawning but the old age has *not yet* disappeared (cf. 1 Cor 10:11). Christians live in the conflicting force fields of overlapping ages. The fundamental Christian confession that Jesus is the Christ is not merely a statement of something special about Jesus; to confess that the Christ has come but that the old age continues carries with it a new view of the world, including of ourselves.

Apocalyptic Worldview

Paul did not come to Thessalonica explaining a new worldview. The new vision of the world came with the gospel he preached. Nor did he arrive in town instructing people in the "teaching of Jesus." Paul's letters have virtually nothing to say about the "life and teaching of Jesus." This also seems to be the case with his initial preaching and instruction to his new churches. The view developed in nineteenth-century liberal theology on the basis of Enlightenment idealism (e.g., Harnack's *Essence of Christianity*) periodically reemerges both in popular theology and in some academic circles: Jesus was the teacher of love, inclusiveness, and social justice, but Paul and his cohorts transformed this simple message into a dogmatic and exclusive religion about Jesus. Other canonical documents, especially the Synoptic Gospels, present much more of Jesus's teaching and the example of his life, but in studying Paul it is important to understand that Paul's minimal reference to Jesus's life and teachings is not simply a minus but has its own grasp of the good news of God's act in Christ.

Even if all the material in the four Gospels had been available to Paul, their presentation of the life and teaching of the pre-Easter Jesus would have been no help on the major issue of Paul's mission, the inclusion of gentiles in the people of God. In Luke's Gospel, as in the others, the divine mission that opens God's kingdom to all peoples emerges only after the resurrection, as Jesus's prophecy of what will happen under the guidance of the Holy Spirit (Luke 24:44–49). Contrary to the popular view, there is nothing in the Gospels that indicates the pre-Easter Jesus was open and accepting of gentiles. The Synoptic Gospels never present Jesus entering a gentile home, eating with gentiles, or welcoming them into his group of disciples. Even the Fourth Gospel, which compresses the life of the pre-Easter Jesus and the post-Easter ministry of the Spirit into a single story more overtly than the Synoptics, never presents Jesus eating with gentiles. His encounter with the Samaritan woman (John 4:1–26)—hardly a gentile—clearly intends to reflect the post-Easter mission of the church and the inclusiveness of the church in the author's own time ("the hour is coming, and is now here" = "the coming hour is now," 4:23), but even here there is no eating with Samaritans, entering a Samaritan home, or calling Samaritans into the community of disciples. Jesus speaks as a Jew who contrasts "we worship what we know" with "you worship what you do not know" and declares that "salvation is from the Jews" (4:22). In the Synoptics, gentiles appear in Jesus's teaching as negative examples to be avoided (Matt 5:47; 6:7; 10:18; 18:17; Luke 22:25). Sometime after the resurrection and the beginning of the church, Luke presents Peter taking the controversial step of preaching the gospel to gentiles, but this is not a recovery of the inclusive ministry of the pre-Easter Jesus (Acts 10–11). Peter declares that he has never eaten with gentiles, has never eaten nonkosher food—which, of course, means that in all his time with Jesus he had never learned that he should associate with gentiles. "You yourselves know that it is unlawful for a Jew to associate with or to visit a Gentile; but God has shown me that I should not call anyone profane or unclean" (Acts 10:14, 28). It was not the memory of Jesus's teaching and his pre-Easter example, but God, after Easter, who had shown him and the church this. No one in Acts ever appeals to the teaching or example of Jesus as a warrant for the mission to the gentiles; it is Peter's heavenly vision and the guidance of the Holy Spirit in the life of the church that lead the followers of Jesus to accept everyone into the community of faith. Matthew is even more explicit, portraying the pre-Easter Jesus limiting his mission to "the lost sheep of the house of Israel," forbidding his disciples to preach to gentiles or Samaritans. The command to go to all nations is first issued by the risen Christ and proclaimed as a result of the Christ event (Matt 10:5–6; 28:16–20). The post-Easter mission of the church was inspired by the risen Christ active in the life of the church, not the pattern represented by continuation of the mission of the pre-Easter Jesus to the Jewish people.

Paul's gospel was the gospel of Jesus Christ, that is, the good news of what God had done and is doing in the Christ event. It is Paul, not Jesus, who proclaims God's acceptance of all people, and Paul does this not on the basis of something Jesus had done or said but on God's act in Jesus Christ. When Paul proclaimed the Christ event as the decisive, definitive act of God, this was done on the basis of the resurrection, and was done within the framework of apocalyptic thought, and carried with it the whole worldview of apocalypticism.[4] It was by understanding the meaning of this event within the apocalyptic framework that the early church was enabled to proclaim that this event of the life, death, and resurrection of Jesus as a whole is good news—not merely good ideas or good advice ("you are a child of the universe . . . you have a right to be here. . . . Strive to be happy"). Something had *happened*. Better: *God* had done something that, if it really happened, made all the difference.

This means that 1 Thessalonians, like all Paul's letters and the New Testament as a whole, is understandable only within this apocalyptic framework in which resurrection is central and essential, the worldview that forms the background and context of the various expressions of the Christian faith, so that eschatology and apocalyptic cannot be relegated to the margins or a final chapter of systematic theology but are woven into the fabric of the whole. This does *not* mean that (post)modern readers must adopt an apocalyptic view of the world as their own—impossible for most of us in any case—but that if we want to hear and understand our Bible in its terms, we must understand something of its apocalyptic worldview.

This also means that understanding Paul's gospel within his own apocalyptic framework means it is grossly inadequate to suppose that Paul wrote to the new church in Thessalonica mainly to deal with their misunderstanding of the chronology of eschatological events. If this were so, and the preacher or teacher were not interested in apocalypticism, the brief "apocalyptic section" (4:13–18) on the "rapture" can be allowed to fall into benign neglect, and the rest of the letter can be searched for "preaching values" easier to digest and which our congregation or class will find more relevant. This narrow-gauge reading would seriously misjudge the character of the letter as a whole, historically and theologically, as though most of Paul's text were mere padding for the real purpose of the letter. Paul indicates that he would like to be present personally and fill in their theological gaps, broadening and deepening their faith. Instead, he sends this letter as a substitute for his own presence, regarding the letter as a whole (not just 4:13–18!) as important for strengthening their faith (3:10). Even so, the letter does this not so much by explicit teaching of particular doctrinal items of the faith as by *projecting a world* the text assumes to be the real world. Paul does not argue for this worldview but simply presupposes it. For the most part, Paul did not communicate his theology by discursive argument. The transforming power of the letter is often communicated more or less unconsciously, as Paul implants his symbolic universe in the reader's mind and soul more by what he presupposes as the framework for all his thought than by specific instruction.[5] The narrative structure of his theology is indicated twice in 1 Thessalonians, at the beginning and at the end, with the triad faith → love →

hope (1:3; 5:8), in which *faith* points primarily to past events, *love* to present experience, and *hope* to the reality of God's salvation consummated in the future. This three-act temporal drama of salvation is fundamental to Paul's theology, recurring often, specifically in his final letter (e.g., Rom 5:1–10, and comments below). We always experience our lives as that short stretch of the road between remembered past and hoped-for future. Paul's theology gives meaning to the present by framing it between the memory of God's saving acts in the past and the hope of God's ultimate future.[6]

PAST—The one true God, the Creator of all things,
> has chosen Israel as the covenant people for the sake of the whole world,
> has acted / is acting / will act in Jesus Christ,
> the truly human / truly divine one,
> for the salvation of the world,
> has sent missionaries to all people,
> through whom by his own word spoken through human words
he has called the church into being.

PRESENT—This church is the community of faith and love nourished by God's own word,
> called to witness in word, life, and deed
> to the meaning of God's saving act in Christ
> in the power of the Holy Spirit,
> including its own suffering,

FUTURE—until God's final establishment of justice
> at the consummation of history,
> to occur soon.

Paul insists that the meaning of our lives is determined by the mighty acts of God that involve past, present, and future—ours and the world's. Here Paul looks back to a real past in which God raised Jesus from the dead and called the Thessalonians into the church, looks forward to the consummation and judgment of history when God's Son comes from heaven, and sees the present as a time of "waiting" (1 Thess 1:9–10)—the letter will instruct us not to misunderstand "waiting" as passive dawdling but to see it as active hope. These three dimensions of Paul's gospel are expressed in the triadic formula with which he frames the letter. His opening words speak of the believers' past/present/future as "your work of *faith* and labor of *love* and steadfastness of *hope* in our Lord Jesus Christ" (1:3), and his closing words include "since we belong to the day, let us be sober, and put on the breast-plate of *faith* and *love*, and for a helmet the *hope* of salvation" (5:8). For Paul, faith-love-hope is not a bumper-sticker list of themes or inspirational ideas but a summary of the new symbolic narrative world, past-present-future.

Faith-Love-Hope, Past-Present-Future

Bible readers are familiar with the climax of the "Love Chapter" (1 Cor 13) and its order of "faith, hope, love." The focus of that powerful chapter is on love as the greatest gift of the Holy Spirit. To get this order, important in the context of Paul's instructing the Corinthians, he has modified his own original order, occurring in 1 Thessalonians 1:3, then reproduced in 5:8, and again in Colossians 1:4, where the elements represent the structure of Christian faith and life as a whole. The tendency in Christian tradition has been to regard them as "virtues," or "ideals" to be striven for, but for Paul they represented the outline of God's acts in history and the believer's life from beginning to end.

The most striking challenge to the way Julia had been accustomed to thinking about herself and the world was not the good news she had come to believe about the living God and his act in Jesus Christ. This transforming good news brought with it a new vision of the world in which she lived and her place in it, the new meaning of the road she was already on, where this road came from, where it was going, the meaning of her little life on the big road. If this gospel Paul preached and she had come to believe is true, the whole world and the meaning of her life within it would be different.

Chapter 2

1 Thessalonians:
Theological Facets for Converted Beginners

First Thessalonians is Paul's earliest extant writing, and thus the earliest Christian text we have. This does not mean it represents "primitive" Christian or Pauline theology, later to be outgrown by more mature reflection. When Paul writes to the new congregation in Thessalonica that was only a few months old, groups of Christian believers had existed in the eastern Mediterranean for twenty years, believers who had already engaged in re-thinking the meaning of their traditional biblical and Jewish faith after the Messiah had come, congregations that had already struggled with radical new moves in the light of their resurrection faith, such as the incorporation of gentiles into the ongoing people of God. Paul himself had already been a Christian missionary for fifteen years or so, already had a wealth of experience involving conflicts and rethinking the meaning of the faith, had been formulating and reformulating his theology for some time (see Acts 1–15 for a later perspective on these developments, Gal 1:2–2:21 for Paul's own retrospective view). On the other hand, the period that be-gan with Paul's withdrawal from the missionary program at Antioch, his own Aegean mission marked by founding the gentile churches in Philippi, Thessalonica, and Corinth, represented such a decisive turn in his mission that he could refer to it as the beginning of the gospel (cf. Phil 4:15). These events just prior to the writing of 1 Thessalonians constituted a decisive new turn in his missionary career. Although Paul remained intent on staying in communion with the earliest Jerusalem church and its leaders, when he wrote to the new congregation in Thessalonica he no longer considered himself under the supervision of the church in Jerusalem or Antioch, but was intensely engaged in thinking through his own approach to the es-sence of the gospel and the nature of the church (cf. "my gospel," Rom 2:16; 16:25; 2 Tim 2:8).[1]

AUTHOR: Paul

DATE: circa 50 CE

ADDRESSEES: Church in Thessalonica, composed mostly or entirely of gentile Christians.

PROVENANCE: Corinth.

LITERARY SOURCES: The book includes earlier Christian traditions, interpreted through the author's apostolic experience. No specific source documents are identifiable.

For evidence for the above conclusions here presupposed, and alternative views, see bibliography at the end of this volume.

Though Paul and his colleagues were engaged in major reinterpretations of the meaning of the faith, he was neither the inventor of Christianity nor its "second founder." Although Paul had surely written letters prior to 1 Thessalonians, it is at the beginning of this period that he initiates a new creative mode of communicating with the fledgling congregations and nurturing them in their understanding of their new life together—the apostolic letter. While 1 Thessalonians is like a sermon or lesson in that it is not a general essay but addresses a specific point in the life of a particular congregation, it is not a casual writing but speaks from the depths of the preacher's heart and the breadth of the Christian faith.

There are no polemics in 1 Thessalonians, nor was the letter written to deal with crucial problems. The destiny of some members of the church who have died before the parousia is addressed in the brief section 4:13–18, but this was not a "crisis" that precipitated the letter nor its main subject matter. Nor were there disruptive "idlers" who had to be dealt with. In this earliest text in our New Testament, we get to hear Paul the pastor speak to the congregation with whom he would like to be present, expounding the core realities of the church, without the sharpness, overemphasis, and one-sidedness of later polemical situations. When the letter is read in this way, it is remarkable how much it has to say, how deeply, indirectly, and unself-consciously the church's faith, love, and hope are set forth.

"I Already Know What a Church Is, Right?"
The Being and Essential Nature of the Church

The gospel proclaimed by Paul brings with it a new understanding of the world and the believer's place within it. The church, the community of faith, love, and hope, is a community of memory and hope that knows it lives between the times. Like the initial readers of 1 Thessalonians, we, too, begin our Christian journey not at the beginning of a story that starts with us but by being incorporated into a grand narrative long since under way. We come on the stage in act 4 of the universal drama (1. Creation, 2. Covenant, 3. Christ, 4. Church, 5. Consummation). We know we have a role to play, though our part is not scripted line by line. We must take responsibility for improvising and ad-libbing. We want to do it responsibly, responding in a trustworthy manner to the gospel with which we have been entrusted (1 Thess 2:4). We take our stance as members of the church, seeking along with our brothers and sisters to engage Paul's letter, in quest of a deeper, richer understanding of what it means to say, "I belong to the church." That is, we will delve more deeply into this New Testament text for what it wants to say to us about the church—its *ecclesiology*. This does not mean that Paul came to Thessalonica promoting a new group he wanted people to join. His gospel was the good news of what God had done in Christ. But Paul's call to decision implied an ecclesiology, as did Jesus's. Paul's letter to the new converts focuses on the meaning of belonging to the church, implicitly and explicitly. In contemporary mainline churches, this is what we need to hear, even if we do not typically ask these kinds of questions. Paul addresses our concerns about God and the meaning of our lives—mostly indirectly, in his presuppositions and assumptions that challenge our own—by speaking to us as members of the church. It is the church that confronts people today, not the Bible or the "historical Jesus." As we drive by church buildings or rub elbows with church people in our daily activities, everyone we meet is inescapably confronted with a community called "church," whether they be insiders or outsiders, members or nonmembers, and if the latter, whether they are sympathetic, indifferent, or hostile observers. To rightly understand this community is the gateway into understanding biblical theology and Christian faith.

We thus want to read carefully through 1 Thessalonians, pausing now and then to ask afresh about theology and ethics, that is, about the being and essential reality of the church—what the church *is*—and ask what kind of life church members are called to live, individually and corporately.

1 Thessalonians 1:1—We Already Belong to the Church

The first words of the earliest extant Christian writing address its audience as those who belong to the *ekklēsia*, the church. When we hear these words in the twenty-first century, we cannot help but bring a preunderstanding of "church" with our hearing. We may have a mixture of good and bad images, but we will already know something about what a "church" is from our cultural conditioning and personal religious history. No matter what this preunderstanding is, we can be sure that it is not the same as that triggered by the first readers of this text.

The new converts in Thessalonica had heard the word *ekklēsia* their whole lives, but it had nothing to do with God, Jesus Christ, or the Holy Spirit. The word meant *called out* and was applied to the assembly of a Hellenistic city, the local congress of free citizens called out from the population to participate in the legislative body that decided issues of local political and social importance. This was a legally constituted group, not a voluntary, casual gathering of those who happened to be interested (cf. Acts 19:39). The members of the new congregation in Thessalonica knew what the city *ekklēsia* was, but few, if any, of them would have been members of it. Yet the letter addresses the whole congregation, men and women, free and slave, as *ekklēsia*.

Paul, too, knew this common cultural meaning of *ekklēsia*, and his usage has overtones of this political context, but his understanding was not primarily shaped by his culture but by his Bible. The LXX typically uses *ekklēsia* as the designation for the people of Israel, the congregation called out of Egypt, led through the wilderness, settled by God in the promised land, with an identity and mission distinct from the nations (*ethnē* = "nations," "gentiles," the same word in Greek). Paul's exact phrase "church of God" is found in his Bible for the people of Israel (*ekklēsia theou*) (Neh 13:1; cf. 1 Cor 1:2; 10:32; 11:22; 15:9; 2 Cor 1:1; Gal 1:13). Unlike the Hellenistic assemblies, the people of God are the *ekklēsia* independently of their actual gathering, not only when they are assembled "in church," but as the reality that determines their identity and life every day.

Unless they were already acquainted with this meaning of *ekklēsia* from Jewish tradition or Scripture, the new congregation in Thessalonica would not have previously heard the word used with this meaning and would have had to learn to understand themselves as members of the church with this biblical and Jewish meaning. Paul's letter to them does not explain this—it is not "teaching a doctrine of the church"—but simply presupposes it. This must mean that his initial preaching, and the instruction by church teachers in the meantime, had given them a new picture of the world as created by the one God who had chosen and called a particular people as his means of blessing for all people (Gen 12:1–3). The new congregation in Thessalonica was composed mostly or entirely of gentiles, but they likely were acquainted with Jewish people and their synagogues. Now they are addressed as themselves belonging to this chosen people, renewed and expanded by the fulfillment of the Jewish hope of the Messiah. They had come to share this faith on the basis of the preaching and teaching of Paul and his associates (all of them Jews who had become Christians—without ceasing to be Jews). These teachers included gentile members of the congregation who had been instructed and appointed as bearers of this new faith. The letter was to clarify and deepen their new identity as members of the ongoing people of God. Their baptism had initiated them into a new community and given them a new history, just as becoming a citizen of the USA requires a grasp of history, incorporating my personal story into the ongoing story of the nation to which I now belong. Immigrants who become citizens have previously been aware of the USA and had a variety of images of this country. Becoming insiders, adopting and being adopted, requires information and adjustments on one's understanding of the meaning of citizenship (Phil 3:20; Eph 2:11–22).

As was the case with the new converts in Thessalonica, such study, preaching, and teaching want to open our eyes to who we really are, who we already are. A quick perusal of 1 Thessalonians reveals that what is true of the word *ekklēsia* is also true of a whole new insider vocabulary. We have been inserted into a history that is new to us, the history of Israel the people of God. To churches comprised mostly or entirely of gentile believers, Paul can say, almost incidentally, "You know that when you were pagans . . ." (*ethnē*, "gentiles," 1 Cor 12:2). He can speak of the early Israelites, those who came out of Egypt and were saved by God at the Red Sea, as "*our* ancestors" (1 Cor 10:1). He can declare that Abraham is the ancestor of "all who believe"; whether Jew or gentile, all Christian believers are joined with all Jewish believers as descendants of Abraham (Rom 4:1; Gal 3:7). The responsibilities of our new identity include learning some new words—giving new content to old words—that reflect who we are, including "saints," "Christ," "elect," "salvation," "resurrection," "parousia," "Son of God," "Holy Spirit." We have heard the words before; study of the Bible fills in the authentic meaning of these words that define our identity.

1 Thessalonians 1:1—the Church Already Participates in the Reality of God

The church of the Thessalonians is "in God the Father and the Lord Jesus Christ." These strange words had apparently become familiar to them. Paul does not explain them, but they had never heard "church"/*ekklēsia* used in this mysterious way prior to Paul's preaching and their induction into the church. To belong to this community is to have one's life, one's being, somehow located or anchored in the transcendent world of God. As Paul will remind the new congregation in Philippi, founded just prior to his church-founding visit to Thessalonica, the names of church members are written not only on earthly membership rolls but also in the heavenly "book of life" (Phil 4:3; cf. Rev 3:5; 13:8; 17:8; 20:12, 15; 21:27). This breathtaking claim is far different from the conventional cultural understanding of the church that many to whom we preach may have inherited, and which may even have conditioned the preacher's own perception. Paul wants the Thessalonians and us to see that the church is not merely a voluntary assembly of like-minded people but a community brought into being by the Holy Spirit, a community that somehow participates in the transcendent world of God. This is part of the apocalyptic framework of the Christian gospel.

1 Thessalonians 1:4a—the Church of the Thessalonians Is Addressed in the Intimate, Loving Language of the Family

Paul writes 1 Thessalonians from Corinth, where he is engaged in founding another new church. But he wants to be back with the new converts in Thessalonica. He is not interested in baptizing as many as possible, then moving on to the next town to do the same. He loves the new little congregation in Thessalonica. They love Paul. And the new Thessalonian converts love each other. Love is not a command to be obeyed nor an ideal toward which to strive but the reality they presently experience, the basic character of the new community to which they belong (1 Thess 1:3; 3:6, 12; 4:9, 10; 5:8, 13).

This astounding new actuality is not to be taken for granted. People who were previously strangers find themselves bound to each other and the universal church as "brothers and sisters" (1:4; 2:1, 9, 14, 17; 3:2, 7; 4:1, 6, 10, 13; 5:1, 4, 12, 14, 25, 26, 27), by One who is their Father (1:1, 3; 3:13). They need no instructions from Paul, for they are taught by God (4:9) to love their brothers and sisters in the congregation. There was no precedent in the ancient world for using *philadelphia* (familial love) in a metaphorical, but real, sense for a believing community. Their greeting was the "holy kiss" (5:26), more than a ritual, more than a cultural convention, inadequately rendered by such paraphrases as "Give a handshake all around" (J. B. Phillips) or "Give the Lord's followers a warm greeting" (CEV). So far as we know, there was no analogy in ancient society, Jewish or gentile, to the sacred kiss as practiced in the Pauline churches, which occurs here for the first time in Christian literature. More than a handshake, the sacred kiss was a sign of group identity, a physical expression of accepting and being accepted, of loving and being loved as members of a real family. As a holy kiss, it not only is contrasted with erotic kisses but also identifies church members as belonging to the *holy* community (see below on 1:5). The relation of the new converts to Paul and other missionaries is not merely institutional or official but familial. They are bound to Paul as nursing mother (2:7) and as father (2:1), and to their sister congregations throughout the world ("every place," 1:8), for example, Achaia and Macedonia (1:8; 4:10) and Judea (2:14). Paul assures them that at the grand consummation of the ages shortly to occur, the crowning glory of Paul's own life will not be the apostolic office he has held or a theological text he has written but they themselves, his brothers and sisters in the church (2 Cor 3:2–3). The eschatological hope is being together not only with the Lord but with all the Lord's people, those still alive and those returning with the Lord (1 Thess 2:19–20; 3:13). The communion of saints was not a doctrine but an experienced part of their new world. The repeated "beloved" (not only by Paul and fellow believers but by God; 1:4; 2:8; cf. 4:9)[2] refers not merely to warm feelings but also to the concrete act of God in calling them to belong to his own people and their mission to the world on God's behalf.

1 Thessalonians 1:4b—the Church Is the Elect Community, Chosen by God

"For we know, brothers and sisters beloved by God, that he has chosen you." These words are part of Paul's opening thanksgiving for the Thessalonians, not a matter of instruction but something "we know"—the "we" is inclusive, embracing a knowledge already shared by Paul and the new converts in Thessalonica, a foundational element of their self-understanding on which he and they can build, not new information from the letter to be assimilated. The congregation's new faith commitment had already brought difficulty and suffering (1:6), and they may well have been asking themselves and each other, "How did we get ourselves into this?" Paul's response is very difficult for us modern Western mainliners to hear: "You didn't. It was God's act. God chose you; you didn't choose God." Of course, they had made their own decisions to become members of the new community. But in retrospect, and in the biblical theological perspective they were learning to understand as representing the reality of the world and their own lives, they knew they hadn't *applied* and been accepted from a pool of applicants. They had been minding their own business when Paul and his associates showed up, still bruised from their previous missionary engagement in Philippi; they had heard his preaching, had *been* spoken to, had *been* chosen, had *been* added to the people of God. They not only had "turned to God" (1:9); they had *been* turned. There was a church in Thessalonica not because of what they had done but because of what God had done. They called out to God only after God called them in (1:4; 2:12).

This theme of election, already present and presupposed in our earliest New Testament document, is not incidental or marginal but inherent in biblical apocalyptic. This note is sounded repeatedly not only in Paul's letters but across the spectrum of New Testament theology. In the previous volume we discussed the Johannine Jesus's declaration to his disciples, "You did not choose me but I chose you" (John 15:16). Here we only note that the theme of election first emerges as basic to understanding the corporate nature of the Christian life, the meaning of belonging to the church. Paul does not begin with a doctrine of justification by faith, the salvation of individuals, who then, as a second and optional step, come together to form a church. In our society, the groups to which we typically belong tend to see themselves as composed of self-sufficient, private individuals who voluntarily join organizations that do some good in the community and meet the needs of their own members. We tend to disengage from them when they no longer serve our purposes. We are conditioned by our time and place to see the church to which we belong as such a voluntary association of idealistic individuals, perhaps distinguished from similar secular groups by its religious orientation. Paul's theology comes at the meaning of church membership from the opposite direction, *beginning* with church as people-of-God, which already exists before Paul comes to Thessalonica and before the Thessalonians had ever heard of Christ. Thus, topics that are often seen as central foci of Pauline theology, such as ethics and justification by faith, are not thought of individualistically but as components of Paul's ecclesiology. For example, what is at stake for Paul in the doctrine of justification is not the issue of individualistic salvation, how a sinner can find acceptance before a righteous God, but the location of non-Torah-observant gentile Christians in historical continuity with Abraham and the people of God elected with him. *This*, which Paul will have occasion to explicate in later letters, is already present in his earliest letter. Even before his conversion, Paul's concern was not the Torah as such. Practice of Torah meant faithful adherence to Israel's identity markers, including Sabbath observance, circumcision, and food laws; these were intended to maintain the distinctiveness and sanctity of Israel. Paul's concern with Torah was the identity and mission of *Israel* to the world, not legalism, not simply the normative claim of the Torah, not individualistic spirituality or perfection.[3]

This language of call and election accords with the depiction of Israel in the Jewish Scriptures that the Thessalonians are now learning to hear as also their own Scriptures. Israel came into being as the liberating act and call of God. The slaves in Egypt did not go looking for God. God sent Moses to them. The new converts in Thessalonica have been called into this ongoing covenant community, as have we. Paul does not "teach" this in 1 Thessalonians but simply assumes it, speaking of believers in Christ as those-included-in-Israel (not "replacing Israel"!), having the status, attributes, characteristics, blessing, responsibilities, and purpose of God's people Israel. A few years later, when God's election of gentiles for inclusion in the people of God had become *the* hot-button issue, Paul will carefully expand and elaborate this theology on the basis of God's promise in the Scriptures, but we see in the assumptions on which 1 Thessalonians works that from the beginning Paul understood the inclusive church to be the result of grafting gentiles, the "branches of a wild olive tree," into the Abrahamic root (see below on Rom 9–11).[4] When Paul preaches, God acts and adds people, Jews and gentiles, to the church, the ongoing people of God in history. This is not a matter of converting some individuals, who then, as a second and optional step, form themselves into a church. The biblical understanding of election is not a matter of God's choosing particular individuals at all. Election is a corporate issue; it claims that God has chosen a people within history as the instrument and first installment on God's salvation of the world, and that God continues to call people into this elect, holy community.

All such New Testament language is the confessional language of the believing insider, not the objectifying language of the spectator. The outsider assumes a transcendent perch from which to evaluate the purported acts of God, critically analyzes the coherence of such language, draws out its implications, weighs it in the logical balances and finds it wanting. Confessional language is the retrospective confession of faith, "God has chosen us," which functions authentically on another plane than the language of logical inference, "therefore, God has rejected them." Such language makes a confessional statement of grateful praise to God about "us," not a doctrinal statement of analytic logic about "them." All such language is faith's effort to give God praise and thanksgiving, confessing that salvation, in this world and beyond, is grounded in who God is and what God has done, not in who we are and what we have done or not done. Paul's closing words in this encouraging letter are not "You have made a good choice, now stick with it, be faithful, and try harder" but "The one who calls you is faithful, and he will do this" (1 Thess 5:24).

1 Thessalonians 1:5–6—the Church Is Called into Being by the Power of the Spirit

As Paul elaborates in later letters (Gal 5:22; Rom 5:5), the love that empowers the church is not mere human niceness but is itself the gift of God, God's own love poured into the believer's heart by the Holy Spirit. There is a new church in Thessalonica because the Spirit of God was at work in both preachers and those who responded to their preaching. Paul does not here spell out the nature of these demonstrations of the power of the Spirit that accompanied the initial proclamation of the Christian message and the conversion of the new Thessalonian Christians. These extraordinary events may have included healings and other exceptional phenomena as described by Paul in later letters (1 Cor 12:27–30; Rom 12:6–9). They certainly included the new power of love given by the Spirit, considered the supreme spiritual gift in both 1 Corinthians 13:1–3, 13, and Romans 13:8–10, and the gift of powerful speech in which human speech became God's own word (see below on 1 Thess 2:13). The Spirit was not given to a privileged few but to the church as such, which has both the capacity and the responsibility to discern authentic from harmful claims that the Spirit is at work (1 Thess 5:19–22).

The Thessalonians lived in a culture in which people already believed in various spiritual beings and powers. "Spirit" is part of the vocabulary of the faith that both they and we need to reinterpret in the light of biblical revelation. In both the Hebrew and Greek of Paul's Bible and ours, the word for "spirit" is the same word as "breath" (*ruach*; *pneuma*). Think Genesis 2, where God breathes his own breath into the earthly clay that was to become Adam, and he becomes a living human being. Think Ezekiel 37, where the dead bones of exiled Israel come to life when the breath/Spirit of Ezekiel's preaching brings them back to life—a scene in which the words of the preacher's breath become the life-giving breath of God. Think Psalm 104:29–30, where the breathy Spirit of God enlivens all creation. Think Edwin Hatch's hymn "Breathe on Me, Breath of God." Think Walter Chalmers Smith's hymn "Immortal, Invisible, God Only Wise," with its lines

> To all, life thou givest, to both great and small,
> In all life thou livest, the true life of all.

Think of the churches to which we belong, in which we preach and teach. Once they did not exist, then something happened, and now there are churches. What happened? We may think of founding evangelists and ministers; local and denominational church-planning committees; pioneer laypersons determined that there be a new church here; loving, dedicated Sunday school teachers who kept the doors open; splits within denominations or congregations that generated new congregations; personal jealousies and ambitions; urban renewal; white flight to the suburbs; factory openings or closings that generated or eliminated jobs that caused people to move; and much more on the human scene, the earthly clay of which churches are composed. Paul would remind the Thessalonians and us that in and through all this, in spectacular and in hardly noticed ways, the Spirit of God is at work that calls the people of God into being and gives them life. The imagery of the "body of Christ," which Paul amplifies later in 1 Corinthians and Romans, does not occur in 1 Thessalonians, but the reality is there: the breath that generates and continues to give life to the community of faith is the Spirit of God, God's own breath.

1 Thessalonians 1:6—the Spirit of God, the Holy Spirit, Generates a Holy Community

The language of holiness and sanctification is more dense in 1 Thessalonians than in any other New Testament document.[5] Paul did not bring this language to Thessalonica; the Hellenistic world in which Paul and the Thessalonians lived already knew spirits aplenty, just as it knew the concept and vocabulary of holiness, but to speak of *a* or *the* "holy spirit" would have been utterly new and strange. The typical Greek or Roman spoke easily and often of "spirits," for this world was filled with spirits, good, bad, and indifferent. Likewise, the vocabulary of holiness was common coin in the Hellenistic world, applied to the realm of temples and sacrifices, priests and sacred objects and rituals, but it was not combined with "spirit," and religious associations of laypeople did not refer to themselves as "holy ones" (*hagioi*, "saints"). In first-century Thessalonica, it was odd and a bit disconcerting to speak of a "holy spirit" and to refer to an assembly of religious people as "holy ones." It was only in the biblical and Jewish tradition that spirit language was inherent in God language, a dimension of the transcendent world of God the Creator. Only in the biblical-Jewish tradition did believers speak of the *Holy* Spirit (e.g., Ps 51:11; Isa 63:10–11; Dan 4:8–9; Wis 1:5; 9:17; Sus 45; 2 Esd 14:22), often identified as the *Spirit of the* LORD [*Yahweh*] (e.g., Judg 3:10; 6:34; 11:29; 13:25; 14:6; 1 Sam 10:6; 16:13; 23:2; Isa 1:2; 1 Esd 2:8) and/or the *Spirit of prophecy* (Num 1:25–29; 1 Sam 10:6, 10; 19:20, 23; Neh 9:30; Isa 61:1; Ezek 1:5; Joel 2:28; Mic 3:8; Zech 7:12). Even more striking: Israel not only spoke of the one true God as the Holy One but also spoke of themselves as a holy people who shared in God's own holiness (e.g., Deut 7:6; 14:2, 21; 26:19; 33:3; Ps 31:23; Isa 62:12; 63:18; Dan 7:18, 27; 12:7; Wis 10:15, 17; 2 Macc 15:24; 3 Macc 2:6). Such language did not refer, of course, to moral or spiritual excellence (though it did not exclude these!) but to being distinctive, set apart for a sacred purpose. As God the Creator is distinctive from the creation, so God's people are called to be a different, distinct community, not blending in with the creation or culture but set apart as witnesses to the one holy God.

Even though all or virtually all the members of the new congregation in Thessalonica were ethnic gentiles, as the holy community now included in the biblical people of God, they are now *contrasted* with gentiles. Though not ethnic Jews, they now belong to Israel, the covenant people of God. They are no longer numbered among those who worship idols but have turned to worship the one true and living God (1 Thess 1:9). They no longer live lives of "lustful passion, like the Gentiles who do not know God" (4:5), and do not belong to the night and the coming wrath, "as others do," but to the day (5:4–8). They do "not grieve as others do who have no hope" (4:13) but look forward in confidence to the coming salvation and kingdom of God (2:12). This contrast between insiders and outsiders, the awareness that they are not merely a group of individuals, each with his or her own private religion, is not smugness nor superiority but their sense of belonging to a distinctive community, the biblical people of God. This is the meaning of holiness, the meaning of belonging to the church.

It is unfortunate that the vocabulary of holiness has too often been heard in mainline churches in a negative, off-putting way ("holier than thou," "a holy Joe"). There is a legitimate us/them mentality that properly belongs to Christian identity in the present between-the-times life of the people of God, a distinction that must be preserved as part of the church's mission, but it is not the last word and will be ultimately dissolved (see below on Rom 5; Eph 1). In the Bible and in our own time, being holy is not our achievement, of which we can be proud. The holiness of the people of God is both gift and challenge. Israel *is* holy, is made so by God's election and call that constitute them as the people of God. Israel hears God addressing them in the Scripture, "You are a people holy to the LORD your God; the LORD your God has chosen you out of all the peoples on earth to be his people, his treasured possession" (Deut 7:6, and often). Israel is also challenged to live out their essential being in actual practice. "For I am the LORD your God; sanctify yourselves therefore, and be holy, for I am holy" (Lev 11:44). This dialectic of indicative/imperative is already present in the biblical understanding of Israel. The new converts in Thessalonica are learning to understand themselves as belonging to this holy community and to live out their new being in everyday life. We will pursue this ethical aspect of church membership further in the discussion of Pauline ethics below.

Paul has no occasion in 1 Thessalonians to emphasize his apostolic role and the apostolicity of the church. Paul mentions his apostleship and related authority only once, and incidentally, but not without communicating that apostolic authority belongs to the essential nature of the church (1 Thess 2:7). The new converts knew that their conversion and their understanding of belonging to the church had come through the apostolic ministry of Paul and his associates, that they had no independent access to the foundational truth about their new faith and the church to which they belonged, that they had not arrived at their new self-understanding on their own, could not have done so, and were not authorized to shape their new church according to their own common sense and best judgment. They were an apostolic church and could be nothing else. The meaning of this is unproblematic in 50 CE Thessalonica, but issues will later arise in Paul's churches that will call for clarification.

1 Thessalonians 1:7—the Church Is One and Catholic

The new church in Thessalonica celebrates its new identity as a congregation in which each member is loved and accepted. But when they were baptized, they became members not only of the house-church congregation in their hometown; they were incorporated into a network of congregations that already spanned the eastern Mediterranean, with a mission to establish such congregations in the whole world. From the letter itself, we learn incidentally that the church to which they belong has congregations in Judea (2:14) and Macedonia and Achaia (1:7–8), and contacts in Athens and Corinth (3:1), where Paul is carrying on a church-founding mission as he writes to the Thessalonians (cf. Acts 17:10–18:1). They have never seen most of the members of the church to which they belong, a large and multicultural company with whom they are already united, in a unity to be visibly manifest at the parousia (1 Thess 2:19–20; 3:13; 4:14–17).

We mentioned the legitimate and necessary us/them mentality that is inherent in belonging to the people of God who are called to live out a particular mission within God's salvific plan for the world. It might be helpful for those to whom we preach, as well as for ourselves, to ask how far church members extend this "we." Some do not extend it even to other members of their own congregation or parish; instead, they think and speak of events in their local congregation as what "they" are doing. Others extend it to their congregation and other congregations of their denomination, but other denominations in the same town are "they." When on vacation, and driving by church buildings of our own denomination, do we say "we" or "they"? Are churches of other denominations in other towns "we" or "they"? When we travel in other countries, are the churches we see "we" or "they"? Paul does not lecture the Thessalonians on the reality that God has added them to the one, holy, catholic, apostolic church, but his letter addresses them as members of this communion of saints that is destined finally to include all God's people, all humanity and the cosmos itself, a conviction that Paul and his students will elaborate in later writings (see on Rom 5:12–21; Eph 1:10).

1 Thessalonians 2:7—the Church Is Apostolic, an Ordered Community with Leadership Constituted and Empowered by God

Mainline Protestantism, especially in democratic and individualistic North America, has been especially nervous about such claims. Paul does not insist on his own authority but suggests that he is an apostle authorized by God (2:7). He does not hesitate to issue apostolic commands (e.g., 4:2, *parangelias*; 5:27, *enorkizō*), which are more than suggestions. Likewise, Paul appointed or supervised the selection of chosen leaders for the congregations, who now "have charge of you in the Lord and admonish you," leaders they are to respect and with whom they are to cooperate (5:12–13). The congregation as a whole is charged to instruct the "disorderly" (5:14), those who disregard the church's authorized leaders and individualistically go their own way without regard to the order of the apostolic church. ("Disorderly" [*ataktoi*] has often been mistranslated as "idlers," as though the word refers to people who have quit their jobs due to their superheated eschatological enthusiasm. Note the context!) Respect for the established order of the church is on the pattern of the biblical and historic people of God to which they now belong, a dimension of membership in the apostolic church. Though subject to abuse and being hijacked by individualistic ambition, this focus on church structure and authorized ministers is a matter of the church's life and mission. Such concerns will be elaborated in later letters, as the church struggles with the formation of appropriate leadership structures for changing times (see especially the theology of ministry in Ephesians, Acts, the Pastorals, and John 21), but concern for an ordered church is not a sign of the church's decline into "early catholicism." The necessity and value of authorized leadership emerge in our earliest Christian text.

1 Thessalonians 2:13—the Church Is Called into Being by the Word of God

Whether or not preacher or congregation is conscious of it, Paul's thanksgiving for the Thessalonians could be the prayer of every preacher: "And we also thank God continually because, when you received the word of God, which you heard from us, you accepted it not as a human word, but as it actually is, the word of God, which is indeed at work in you who believe" (NIV). In my initial study of the theology of Revelation, I reflected on the generative power of the Word of God and its relation to the human words of the preacher. Here I invite you to imagine two scenes, one from my own experience, the other from the life of a pastor in another country and another time.

Several years ago I was invited to present a lecture to a group of ordained ministers and lay leaders on the spectrum of understandings of ministry and eldership found in the New Testament. The sizable group listened with moderate interest and engagement as I lectured on the function of presbyters/elders in the early church, but only came to life when an ordained minister responded to something I had said about the minister's responsibility to proclaim the gospel in such a way that the congregation is brought within hearing distance of the word of God that comes through the Scripture. With passion and a bit of hostility, he said, "I don't talk about 'preaching the word of God,' and don't know what anyone means, or can mean, by that phrase." This response, vocalized or not, is not unusual among some mainline preachers and congregational leaders, who tend to leave such language to evangelicals and fundamentalists. I responded, none too well, along the lines that "word of God," like all our language for God, is metaphorical in the same sense that "love of God" is metaphorical, and that as we do not hesitate to speak of God's love, we should not shrink from speaking of God's word. We never claim to have God's love as an objective, packageable reality that we can deliver at will, but only do our own deeds of love in God's name with the prayer that in and through our deeds of love God's own love will be made real (1:3!). So also, the preacher must never claim to have this word of God in an objectifying sense, as though "others may have their human theology, but I preach the word of God." It is perhaps for this reason that some mainline preachers tend to avoid this terminology and some mainline churchgoers resist it. Both need to be biblical theologians at this point, not merely responding in terms of our cultural conditioning. To be sure, the word of God is not on tap, at the preacher's disposal, which he or she can dispense at will. We preachers can only do our best to proclaim the biblical faith as best we can in our own words, making it our intention to bring the congregation within hearing distance of the word of God that comes through the fusion of text and sermon, leaving the rest in God's hands.

The other scene is from 1924, in a lecture hall of the Phillips University in Marburg, Germany. A Swiss pastor had been invited to address this distinguished theological faculty (Rudolf Bultmann was in the audience) on his theology of preaching. Theological education had been dominated by the idealistic liberalism of the nineteenth century and wanted to engage and learn from the revolutionary "theology of the Word of God" advocated by Karl Barth and his associates. Eduard Thurneysen, friend and colleague of Barth when Barth had been pastor of a neighbor congregation, spoke on "Scripture and revelation." Thurneysen declared to his receptive audience,

> It is only by God's own speaking that the truth about God can be spoken and understood. . . . If there is to be authentic talk about God, God himself must speak. . . . God is the alpha and omega, the First and the Last, the One behind whom we cannot inquire. The truth of God is not a truth that can be grounded by appeal to other truths, but God himself is the ground of all truth. . . . This is my experience as a pastor, but this is the way it is wherever the Bible is taken seriously.[6]

Thurneysen cites Barth that "self-evident" truths can be used only as analogies, not as the basis for faith. Such commonsense assertions operate entirely within the this-worldly framework of human reality and thinking, where they have their validity. But they can tell us nothing of God. God must speak, or we will forever have only our own best constructions of who or what God is, that is, idols, the graven images of our own imaginations. But the good news of the incarnation is that, in and through human, fleshly words (John 1:14), the one true God has spoken, and this Word is what calls the church into being and sustains it in its mission. The church has turned from idols to serve the living and true God, the God who speaks (1 Thess 1:9–10; see further on Rom 10:14–15 below). This was not merely Paul's and the Thessalonians' subjective opinion ("for me it is the word of God, though it may not be for you") but objective, ontological reality. This is the same kind of simultaneous paradox as in New Testament Christology. The truly human Jesus of Nazareth is the truly divine Son of God (cf., e.g., Mark 15:39, where the same adverb is used as in 1 Thess 2:13, *alēthōs*, "truly, in reality"). The apostles' preaching manifested not only the horizontal human dimension but also and simultaneously the transcendent divine dimension. The believers in Thessalonica had heard the Christian message not only as the *report* of an event in the past that had its source in God, communicating what had happened in the Christ event of the past, but also as *address* in the present, as God spoke to them, generating faith and transforming their lives.

How, then, should we live? This shared faith generates the ethic and life of the church, to which we now turn.

The Loved/Loving Community— Experienced and Lived Out in the Present

There were decent, responsible, ethical people in Thessalonica before Paul and his associates arrived proclaiming the Christian faith, just as there are lots of good folk in our towns who are not members of the church. Most of the people to whom Paul preached were already both religious and ethical. Just as he did not come preaching a new religion, so he did not arrive in town teaching a new ethics. What he did do was to proclaim the saving act of God that generated a new community with a different way of life. The way they would have seen it, Paul announced a radically new combination of religion and ethics. Their previous ethics were based on their philosophical views of the world and life, whether these represented serious thought or only the adoption of pop philosophy, commitments to family and friends, community traditions and standards, patriotic loyalty to their town and country. Religious faith and ethical conduct previously had little to do with each other.

For Paul (and the New Testament generally), Christian faith calls for a new life, and conversely, ethical decisions represent and are based on decisions of faith. Working through 1 Thessalonians, our close reading reveals that the extended theological thanksgiving of the first three chapters takes a sharp, more "practical" turn at 4:1. Paul typically first proclaims the meaning of the faith (chaps. 1–3), which then becomes the basis for the call to the Christian life and the content of Christian ethics (chaps. 4–5). In the actual composition of his letters, the two poles are inseparable, interactive, interwoven, and interdependent. They are not like the two halves of a basketball court but like the poles of a magnet.

God's act	human response
God the Savior	the saved community's life
the Christ event	the believer's life "in Christ"
euangelion (gospel)	*paraenesis* (exhortation)
grace (*charis*)	gratitude-faith
charis-as-God's-grace	*charis*-as-human-gratitude
theology	ethics
indicative	imperative
promise	challenge
narrative	exhortation
kerygma	*didachē*
"is"	"ought"
"What?"	"So what?"

The theological "what" of Christian faith must become the ethical "so what" of Christian life. Otherwise, all attempts to provide instruction on how to live become mere moralism, good advice, well-meaning efforts at guru wisdom, or—heaven forbid!—one person's trying to impose his or her values on someone else, rather than the joyful good news of the gospel.

The Basis and Norm of the Christian Life Is God's Act in Jesus Christ

Jesus continues to be present as the risen Christ in the congregation through the power of the Holy Spirit. Paul sets forth the basis, norm, character, and content of the Christian life—which is the authentically human life—in the dense section 4:1–12, which begins, "Finally, brothers and sisters, we ask and urge you in the Lord Jesus that, as you learned from us how you ought to live and to please God (as, in fact, you are doing), you should do so more and more. For you know what instructions we gave you through the Lord Jesus." Along with the preaching of the Christian message, they have received "instructions" on "how you ought to live." We immediately note that these instructions are "in the Lord Jesus Christ" and "through the Lord Jesus"; that is, they are Christian ethics based on life "in Christ," communicated *through* the risen Lord of the church's faith. Though the ethic Paul teaches is at its core the same as that of Jesus (the love commandment and its implications, see below), Paul does not claim that the ethical instructions he gives are based on the teachings of Jesus. He does not come to town urging people to live by the ideals and principles of Jesus the great teacher—to which the appropriate response would be "Why Jesus? Why not Plato, Zeno, or John the Baptist?" There is nothing in 1 Thessalonians about the Sermon on the Mount, the radical demands of discipleship made by Jesus on Galilean hillsides or Jerusalem synagogues; there are no parables of the kingdom, no ethical lessons from the example of Jesus. This is true not only of all Paul's letters but of all the New Testament except the Synoptic Gospels.

When Paul speaks of the Christian life as based on the model of Christ who served others, he has in mind the cosmic Christ who laid aside his divinity and transcendent power to participate fully in our human weakness, whose life of obedient suffering was vindicated by God (Phil 2:5–9), not the earthly Jesus who laid aside his garments to wash the disciples' feet (John 13:1–17). Likewise, when Paul points to Christ as an example of unselfish giving, he points not to the pre-Easter Jesus who gave to the poor and needy but to the cosmic Christ: "For you know the generous act of our Lord Jesus Christ, that though he was rich, yet for your sakes he became poor, so that by his poverty you might become rich" (2 Cor 8:9). This, of course, does not refer to a time when Jesus of Nazareth was wealthy but then abandoned his riches in order to help the poor—as Francis of Assisi would later do, in Jesus's name—but to the incarnation of the preexistent transcendent Son of God who left the heavenly splendor to enter the poverty of human existence. Paul's ethic does not function by citing the teaching and example of the 30 CE Jesus, once given in Galilee and Judea, now handed on and "applied" in the churches, but by instructions given in the post-Easter church "in" and "through" the risen Lord Jesus who continues to speak his own word that calls to faith and discipleship—not "sayings of Jesus" but "the word of the Lord" (1 Thess 4:15).

This mode of Christian preaching and teaching makes many of us modern mainliners nervous. When we get serious about ethical issues, whether it be how strictly truthful to be on our 1040 forms, how we should view abortion and same-sex marriage, how we should respond to the presence of undocumented foreigners in our country, whether living together should best be accompanied by a marriage license, or how to vote and how to spend our money, Paul's approach seems alien to our commonsense individualism by which we "let our conscience be our guide." If we back away from it but still want some sort of conformity to the Bible, we regularly choose the Gospel reading for our sermon rather than the letters. We may find ourselves asking, "What would Jesus do?" or wanting some help from the "life and teaching of Jesus" that we can "apply" to our own situation. We like the "real Jesus," not the "cosmic Christ." We understandably suppose it is not only easier but more authentic to preach from what Jesus himself says and does in the Gospels than from what the letters say about him. Those who hear us preach and teach, and perhaps we ourselves, tend to like clear rules and coherent principles, such as we supposedly find in Jesus's teaching. We may, however, be seduced by the supposed ease with which texts from the Gospels may become sermons, for the Gospels, too, presuppose the cosmic story. All the Gospels identify the Jesus who teaches and preaches in the pre-Easter narrative of the gospel story and is identified with the risen Lord of the church's faith. The Jesus of the Sermon on the Mount (Matt 5–7) is the Jesus who says at the end of the story, "All authority in heaven and on earth has been given to me. Go therefore and make disciples of all nations, baptizing them in the name of the Father and of the Son and of the Holy Spirit, and teaching them to obey everything that I have commanded you. And remember, I am with you always, to the end of the age" (Matt 28:18–20).

The Gospels only appear to be easier; they, too, proclaim not only the teaching *of* Jesus but also the gospel *about* Jesus, and offer instruction in the ethics of the risen Christ, but it is easier to read our own values and concerns into a story from the Gospels than into a Pauline or other epistolary text. If we work at hearing the biblical theology and word of God mediated by the letters, with the goal of letting our congregations hear the biblical message, we will find ourselves—to our own delight and that of our congregations—becoming more authentic preachers and teachers of the Gospels as well. None of this means that Paul should be contrasted with Jesus—we mean the Jesus of the New Testament, not the Jesus behind the New Testament we may construct for ourselves. To even pose ethical questions in the mode of whether we want to be "followers of Jesus" or "members of the church" is a false choice. "One cannot overemphasize the central point: for Paul, Jesus is good news for us Gentiles *not* because of anything Jesus had said or done during his lifetime, but because the event as a whole was the decisive act of *God*."[7]

Before proceeding to the content and character of a life devoted to following Jesus, we look back over the earliest Christian document addressing new converts to the Christian faith and ask how much it refers to the "life and teachings of Jesus," and then do the same for all the Pauline letters and other epistolary documents of the New Testament.

The "Life and Teachings of Jesus" in the Epistolary Mode of Confession of the Christian Faith

If we had only the letters of Paul, how much would we know about the deeds and words of the pre-Easter Jesus of Nazareth? Many regular churchgoers, and perhaps some preachers and teachers, may never have asked this question and might be surprised at the answer. When we read through the New Testament, by the time we come to Romans we are already familiar with the gospel stories of what Jesus did and taught. We may even unconsciously forget that the canonical New Testament is not arranged in chronological order, that all Paul's letters were written before the earliest gospel.

When we read through the Pauline letters, including those written in his name by his disciples after his death (here taken to be 2 Thessalonians, Colossians, Ephesians, and the Pastorals), we are struck that they all confess their faith in the narrative form we have noted above, the grand narrative of the mighty acts of God for the salvation of the world, of which the story of Jesus Christ is the climax and center. But in the letters, the story of God's saving act in Jesus does not focus on what Jesus said and did in Galilee, Samaria, the Decapolis, and Judea. The saving act takes place on a cosmic stage. The demonic enemies overcome by the saving act are not the local evil spirits that bedevil individuals in a first-century Roman province but cosmic enemies that permeate the political and economic systems of human societies, as well as our personal relationships and individual psyches. Salvation takes place by the reality of God's act in the man Jesus but is never explicated by particular stories and sayings from his life. It is of supreme importance *that* it really happened, but there are few details of *what* the earthly Jesus said and did or *how* believers should picture the earthly life of Jesus.[8]

This kerygmatic theology about Jesus *does* indeed include data from his earthly life. Paul and the other epistolary authors do not spin out philosophical abstractions about the meaning of the Christ event that float in the world of ideas above the nitty-gritty of history, but they nail it down (literally!) in something that happened in historical reality. Surprisingly to many readers of the Bible, *this data is minimal.* Except for the statements that Jesus was born, that he lived a truly human life in obedience to God, and that he died a shameful death, the events of his earthly career are barely mentioned.

A. M. Hunter, a respected conservative scholar of the last century, eager to identify the maximum amount of Jesus tradition in Paul (including the disputed letters), lists the following as the sum total of Paul's knowledge of the earthly Jesus that can be gleaned from his letters: Jesus was a man (Rom 5:15), a Jew (Rom 9:5), born of a woman and under the law (Gal 4:4), a descendant of Abraham and in the line of David (Gal 3:16; Rom 1:3). He had brothers (1 Cor 9:5), one of whom was called James (Gal 1:19). He ministered among Jews (Rom 15:8). He had a band of twelve disciples (1 Cor 15:5). He was meek and gentle (2 Cor 10:1), obedient to God (2 Cor 5:19), and possessed endurance (2 Thess 3:5) and grace (2 Cor 8:9). He was delivered up (1 Cor 11:23, which Hunter takes to be a reference to the betrayal by Judas—though it more likely refers to the act of God in delivering over Jesus to human hands, as in Isa 53:6, 12, and often in the Synoptic Gospels). He celebrated a last supper with his disciples. He was crucified and buried.[9] Even on a generous interpretation of the evidence, this is not an impressive list.

> "Paul tells us next to nothing about the life and ministry of Jesus. Had we possessed only Paul's letters, it would be impossible to say much about Jesus of Nazareth."
>
> —James D. G. Dunn, *The Theology of Paul the Apostle* (Grand Rapids: Eerdmans, 1998), 184

No letter quotes a saying of Jesus or relates any extraordinary event about him.[10] Paul refers four times to a "command" or "word" of the Lord (1 Thess 4:15–17; 1 Cor 7:10, 25; 9:14). The lengthiest, 1 Thessalonians 4:15–17, is not found in any of the Gospels and is unlike anything they attribute to the pre-Easter Jesus. In none of the other three "sayings of the Lord" that Paul refers to does he make it clear that he understands the saying to be from the pre-Easter historical Jesus. This Lord is of course identified as the same person who lived and died in history, but Paul thinks first of the risen Lord, not of the earthly life of Jesus. He probably understands all four sayings to be commands of the risen Lord Jesus, even if they contain elements of pre-

Easter tradition. There is only one saying similar to sayings in the Gospels, the instruction about divorce in 1 Corinthians 7:10. It is different from the Gospels' versions of the saying in both form and content (cf. Mark 10:11; Matt 5:32; 19:9; Luke 16:18), and adds Paul's own interpretation within the saying itself. In citing this "command of the Lord," Paul distinguishes it from his own teaching. Yet Paul can also refer to his own instruction as "command of the Lord" (1 Cor 14:37; cf. 7:25). The line between what "the *Lord*" *says* (not what "*Jesus*" *said*) and what Paul says is thin, for he is an apostle who claims that "Christ is speaking in me" (2 Cor 13:3). Even if all four sayings are regarded as from the pre-Easter earthly Jesus, or intended by Paul to be understood as such, this is still a very small number. Paul's citation of Jesus's words at the Last Supper (1 Cor 11:23–26) are in a different category, taken from the liturgy of the church, not from a list of incidents in the "life and teachings of Jesus" Paul presumably taught his converts. Here, too, the words Paul received "from the Lord" represent a Pauline way of speaking about the presence of the risen Christ in church tradition.[11] They are fused with Paul's own comments in which the first-person speech of the Lord blends seamlessly with Paul's own commentary referring to the Lord in the third person (vv. 23, 24, 26).

The issue is not whether Paul and the other epistolary authors "could" have known the tradition from and about Jesus. Most scholars regard it as very unlikely that Paul ever met or heard Jesus in person.[12] Nonetheless, and even though he was converted after the death of Jesus, there is no doubt that Paul had opportunity to learn stories about Jesus and sayings from him. He spent fifteen days with Peter (Gal 1:18), during which time he also met and talked with James the Lord's brother (Gal 1:19; 2:9), and spent some years as a missionary of the Antioch church, which cultivated the tradition from and about Jesus. Paul *could* have learned much about the details of Jesus's life and teaching, and no doubt knew more than is reflected in his letters. This, however, is not the point. The issue is to what extent Paul considered such knowledge to be important to his understanding of the Christian faith. While there is virtually unanimous agreement that the letters contain few details about the life and teaching of the pre-Easter Jesus, the issue is not their possible quantity but "what place the Jesus of history had in relation to the heart and center of his preaching."[13]

It is argued by some scholars such as Dunn that the letters have virtually nothing to say about the pre-Easter Jesus because they were all written to churches of people who were already Christian, who had been taught the details of Jesus's life and teaching as part of the missionary preaching that converted them and didn't need to be told them in a letter.[14] Sometimes this argument is coupled with the suggestion that the letter genre would have been "inappropriate" for such talk about Jesus, which fits into the *gospel* genre, as though Paul might have said to himself something like, "As I write this letter, I would tell some stories and cite some sayings from Jesus here, but that would be more appropriate for a gospel, and I'm writing an epistle."[15] To say the least, this is anachronistic—there were no gospels, and no one had thought of writing a gospel when Paul wrote his letters. In any case, to argue that Paul knew and valued the traditions of the pre-Easter Jesus but did not need to cite them in his letters because he had already taught them to the churches and they could be presupposed fails to convince. Paul could and did presuppose knowledge of the Jewish Scriptures (even among his gentile mission churches!), but he repeatedly cites them nonetheless. In the letter to the church in Rome, which Paul had not founded and had never visited, a letter whose purposes includes summarizing his own mission preaching (of which the Roman church was suspicious), Paul never refers to the "teaching of Jesus" and never refers to the earthly life of Jesus the Teacher. In his earlier letter to the Corinthians, a church he had founded and previously visited, he does not call on the readers to follow the "teachings of Jesus" but "my ways in Christ" (1 Cor 4:17).[16] This is not Pauline egotism but ecclesiology, incorporation "in Christ" (see below).

Even on such central points as confessing God to be the "Father of our Lord Jesus Christ" (eight times in the undisputed letters, nine more times in the deutero-Pauline corpus) and the use of "Abba" as the intimate, familial address to God in prayer, Paul does not cite the teaching or example of Jesus as presented in the Gospels (e.g., Luke 11:2–4; Mark 14:36) but cites the guidance of the Holy Spirit in post-Easter Christian worship (Rom 8:14; Gal 4:6).

> "The Pauline churches are not supposed to memorize and actualize Jesus' sayings but to practice being crucified with him."
>
> —Jürgen Becker, *Paul: Apostle to the Gentiles*
> (Louisville: Westminster John Knox, 1993), 120

Many churchgoers, and some who preach to them, are not entirely aware that in the New Testament it is Paul, not the pre-Easter Jesus, who emphasizes the ethic of inclusiveness. The Bible does not present a "universal" Jesus who was then obscured by a "narrow" Paul. On major items of

Christian faith that are important to Paul, such as the inclusion of gentiles in the one church of God, Keck writes:

> Even if Paul had known the entire body of Jesus traditions that later ended up in the four canonical Gospels, he would have discovered that, except for Jesus's positive comment about the Roman officer who asked Jesus to heal his son (Matt 8:10), Jesus had said not one good word about Gentiles, but rather expressed his disdain for them by using them only as negative examples of what to avoid. Paul would also have seen that there is not much point in telling his Gentile audience that Jesus was a wise, insightful teacher who lived what he taught, healed the sick, criticized pretensions and the misuse of religion (e.g., Mark 7:9–13) and invited people to follow his way, for such figures were found in the Greco-Roman world already.[17]

If Paul had presented Jesus in these terms, he would have needed to compare him with other wise teachers of the Hellenistic world who advocated equality and tolerance, and to have shown that the teaching of Jesus was somehow better. "But even if some hearers would have welcomed the good news that a teacher had come who was even greater than Socrates, that information would not have been the good news as Paul understood it. . . . What made the Jesus who died on a despicable cross good news was the framework, the context—or as some might say, the Great Story—in which Paul saw the Jesus event as a whole; namely, Jewish apocalyptic thought, for this enabled him to understand the meaning of Jesus's resurrection."[18]

For Paul and the early church, Jesus is remembered as a person who really lived and died in the (recent!) past and is still known in the life of the Christian community as the present and living Lord of the church, more colloquially: the Jesus "back there" and the Christ "up there." John Knox points out that Paul simply had a different starting point for his way of thinking about the good news of what God did in the Christ event than some ancient and many modern Christians.

> Paul's thought about Christ the person always moves from the "Christ who lives" to the "Jesus who died," always from the one known to the one remembered. It is the present living reality which comes first to his mind when he speaks of Christ. . . . The wonder of the resurrection to Paul consisted in the fact that this one whom he now knew as Lord had actually suffered death upon the cross. They speak of "Jesus whom

God raised up," Paul speaks of "Christ and him crucified." . . . At first sight this last phrase seems to leave out the Resurrection entirely. But it seems to do so only because we suppose Paul's thought was moving, as ours customarily does, in a forward direction . . . but when Paul wrote the phrase, he was thinking *first* of all of the risen, exalted Christ, and his thought moved *backward* to the cross.[19]

None of this, of course, is to be taken as playing Pauline theology against the kind(s) of theology we find in the Gospels, as though one were better than the other. The church would be immeasurably poorer if we had only the cosmic, incarnational Christology of the letters, without the pictures of Jesus in the Gospels and his words and deeds presented there. Both Gospels and letters are priceless treasures for the church and for humanity. Here we want to become more aware that each genre of New Testament confession has its own validity, which is not enhanced by confusing it with the other, and to explore more deeply the Pauline approach to Christian faith and life.

It is post-Easter, ecclesial, Pauline theology, in fact, in which some of the Christian ethical perspectives and commitments sometimes attributed to Jesus first come to expression. Case in point: There is nothing in the Gospels like Galatians 3:28: "There is no longer Jew or Greek, there is no longer slave or free, there is no longer male and female; for all of you are one in Christ Jesus." There is nothing in the Gospels that suggests that when Jesus called twelve disciples as the core of the renewed Israel, the people of God that would become the inclusive church, he included women, slaves, or Africans (also, no white Europeans). It was in the post-Easter church, with new insight and power guided by the Holy Spirit (the Spirit of *Christ*, Rom 8:9), that this vision of the renewed people of God became reality.

As we now return to our discussion of the Pauline perspective on Christian life and ethics—centered in the love command—we might remind ourselves that Paul does not support the centrality of *agapē* by citing the teaching of Jesus of the Gospels but points to the Jewish Scripture (Mark 12:28–31 = Deut 6:4–5; Lev 19:18) and to the post-Easter experience of the love of God poured out in believing hearts by the Holy Spirit (Rom 5:5).

The Content and Character of the Christian Life Is Holy Love

In his earliest extant letter, as in his last and most profound, Paul sums up the content and character of the believer's new life in the one word "love."

In this he is no different from Jesus (Mark 12:28–34; Matt 22:35–40; Luke 10:25–28; John 13:34; 15:17; 17:26). It is difficult for people, whether outsiders or insiders to church life, to experience the powerful strangeness of the New Testament's talk of love. Outsiders are inclined to fill in the content of "love" with romantic or warm and fuzzy images from the culture. People who have been around the church a lot have heard the word "love" so often (like "grace" and "peace") that its shocking strangeness, its alterity, its difference-from-conventional, its *holiness* that threatens our comfort zone have faded. Its threatening wildness has been domesticated.

The well-intentioned effort sometimes made to recover the power of the Bible's language of love by explaining that "the New Testament has a special word for love, *agapē*," has become traditional, incorrect though it is. The typical explanation claims that whereas English has only one word for "love," Greek has three distinct words: *eros, philia*, and *agapē*. Love represented by *eros* is selfish love, erotic love, all "get"; *philia* is the give-and-take love of friends and colleagues; *agapē* is unselfish concern for others, all "give." It is true enough that the ancient Greeks, like modern Americans and others, knew there were different kinds of love. It is not true that each of these was linked to a particular word. It was no more possible in Greek than in English to make clear that one was referring to a specific kind of love by using a specific word. *Eros/philia/agapē* cannot be represented by "lust"/"like"/"love," or even by "self-centered"/"give-and-take"/"unselfish giving." The various Greek words were mostly interchangeable, with overlapping semantic fields, as a few minutes' examination of a Greek lexicon or concordance will make clear. *Agapē*, for instance, is used interchangeably with other Greek words for love in 1 Thessalonians 4:9 and often elsewhere (e.g., Wis 8:2; John 5:20; 16:27; 21:15–17). *Agapē* is frequently found in the Song of Solomon for sexual love, and in the New Testament for the greedy love of money (2 Pet 2:15) and for loving the world rather than God (2 Tim 4:10). Christian love as active, unselfish care for others is indeed a distinctive kind of love, but the distinction is not a matter of vocabulary. Thus, when Paul spoke of Christian love as the most valuable gift of the Spirit, he had to explain the nature and content of such love, just as modern preachers must do (1 Cor 13!). Here, we may make only four important observations.

Christian Love Has a New Center and Source

Love does not begin in the believer's heart and proceed outward to others. Love begins with God, and the love in which believers find themselves embraced comes from God, through God's act in Christ, mediated to them individually by their belonging to the community in which God's love flows through church members to each other and beyond, to everyone (1 Thess 3:12). They know they are loved by their new brothers and sisters in the church, and they know that this is not merely a matter of having found a group of nice people with whom they can associate, but in and through this community God's own love is made known to and through them. They are called to love others because they themselves are already loved by God; "beloved" means not only loved by Paul and other church members but loved by God (1:4; 2:8; cf. 4:9). They, as individuals and a community of faith, are not mere recipients but vehicles and channels of this love. Their works are "labor[s] of love" (1:3) that embody God's love. To be sure, people loved each other in Thessalonica before Paul and his missionary colleagues came to town. There were loving relationships between husbands and wives, parents and children, friends and neighbors; there was love of city and country. But in the Christian gospel, love received a new center and source. It would have seemed strange in Thessalonica to speak of the gods loving people and religious people sharing such love. Parents in Thessalonica loved their children, but they did not teach them to sing "Ze-us loves me, this I know, for the *Iliad* tells me so."

Christian Love Not Only Has a New Center; It Has a New Circumference

Practically everyone likes the idea that living a decent life involves transcending one's innate selfishness and caring for others. "Love your neighbor" is easy enough to accept in a limited sense, but the question is always, "Who is my neighbor?" (Luke 10:25–29). In realistic terms, how far should such love extend? In 1 Thessalonians, Paul's first response is that love extends to the whole church, the new community of faith, love, and hope to which I now belong, "love of the brothers and sisters" in the new family of God, "taught by God to love one another" (1 Thess 4:9), a love that includes the newcomer Paul and his colleagues who proclaimed the gospel to them (3:6), and their local leaders who continue to nourish them in the faith (5:13). All these had previously been strangers who might have passed each other on the street without a second glance but who now are bound not only to God but also to each other in the love of God. This insider love should not be disdained as though it were exclusive and sectarian. Making a decision to confess the crucified and risen man of Nazareth as Lord, being baptized and participating in a group suspected and disdained as antisocial and unpatriotic, needed mutual love and support, emotionally and economically. In the church, the new converts, previously strangers to each other, had found a new family in which they were loved not for what they had done or hadn't done but because of what God in Christ has done for all. This is the foundation and power of the new ethic that is openheartedly serious without being tight-lipped and grim.

The ethic of Paul and early Christianity preserved the radicality of Jesus's eschatological ethic, the ethic of the kingdom of God, which was not a general human ethic that could be realized by the individual, me-and-Jesus. Such a way of living one's life presupposed belonging to the community of those who had responded to Jesus's call to discipleship, in Paul's time and ours, the Christian community. Thus 1 Thessalonians makes belonging to the church the primary reality of being a follower of Jesus. The life it calls for makes sense only for insiders, just as Jesus's ethic makes sense only for those who are his disciples in the sense that they belong to the community of those who believe his message of the present and coming kingdom of God. In both cases, this is an ethic based on a commitment to God's act in Jesus. Paul and early Christianity had translated this ethic into a post-Easter conceptuality; the basis is not following Jesus's call in Galilee but being baptized into the church. Jesus's proclamation of the kingdom of God morphs into Christology and ecclesiology. Thus in 1 Thessalonians and in the New Testament letters generally, kingdom of God vocabulary recedes (only 2:12 in 1 Thessalonians) and talk about Christ and the church soars. Far from being a decline from Jesus's message and mission, this is its continuing post-Easter realization—what God began in the incursion into the world in the life of Jesus continues in the life of the church in which God/Christ/Spirit continue(s) to be powerfully at work. In both Jesus and Paul, the ethical life of the believer is grounded in God's eschatological renewal already under way. There is no general, individualistic, commonsense ethic in either Jesus or Paul, but the calling of a community in and through which God's own love is made explosively real. This love thus extends to the whole church, local, denominational, and ecumenical. The new converts in Thessalonica are learning that they love and are loved by brothers and sisters in the wider Christian community whom they have never seen, "throughout Macedonia" and in Judea where their church actually began (2:14; 4:10), and in Philippi, where a new church like themselves had sent gifts to support Paul while he was carrying out the church-founding mission in their own city (Phil 4:15).

Nor does such love stop at the edge of the church membership roll—the love of God flows through the individual believer and the church into the whole world, for the Lord "make[s] you increase and abound in love for one another and *for all*" (1 Thess 3:12).

Christian Love Is a Matter of the Will and Action, Something Believers Can Choose to Do or Not

Doing right is a matter of the will of God, a matter of commands and obedience (4:1–3; 5:18). Love may or may not have accompanying feelings. Feelings cannot be commanded, but love is a command. Love remains "general" in 1 Thessalonians. This is not because love is essentially vague, as though it were a broad feeling of good will toward everyone. Quite the contrary: love is essentially particular, focused and specific. One cannot love people in general in some vague way that does not involve specific actions—"I love humanity; it's people I can't stand." Paul speaks generally because he is not dealing with particular problems in Thessalonica. In later letters, the particular meaning of love will become clear as Paul gives instructions on what love means in concrete situations (Rom 5:5; 12:9; 13:8; 14:15; 1 Cor 13:1–14:1; 16:14; 2 Cor 5:14; 8:24; Gal 5:6, 13, 22; Phil 2:1; Philem 5, 7). The particulars of love cannot be prescribed by a list made in advance. One doesn't know what love requires until the situation arises, but members of the community of faith embraced in the love of God respond creatively to every new need.

This is why Paul doesn't cite the "life and teaching of Jesus," or appeal to particular sayings of Jesus to settle disputed points. Analogous to the proverbial "Give a man a fish, and you feed him for a day; teach him how to fish, and you feed him for a lifetime," Paul does not dole out sayings of Jesus to give ethical instruction on particular points. But neither does he teach "the great principles of Jesus" that may be "applied" in new situations. As Matthew will later teach members of his church to be "Jesus theologians" who can respond faithfully and appropriately to situations the historical Jesus never envisaged,[20] so Paul's theology helps people to be "Christ theologians," to think through what it means to live in the new age, embraced by a loving community, guided by the Holy Spirit working through its Scripture, traditions, and new experiences to see ever more clearly its mission in its own time and place. Both Paul and Matthew, each in his own way, make Jesus's biblical double command of love for God and neighbor the foundation for an authentic life.

Christian love is holy love. Paul's "summary of Christian ethics" in 4:1–12 weaves together love and holiness. Not only love, but holiness, is understood in a radically new way (see above on 1 Thess 1:6). Surprisingly, not only to the Thessalonians but also to us, the holiness of the new community is not expressed in such practices as rigid adherence to a religious calendar of holy days, times, and places, or in strict adherence to dietary laws, but in how we handle our sexual appetites (4:3–8) and how we do our daily "secular" work (4:9–12).

"For this is the will of God, your sanctification: that you abstain from fornication [all types of sexual sins] . . ." (4:3). This instruction is not given because Paul is hung up on sexuality and considers abstinence from sex a mark of the holy life. Paul the Jew has no ethic of pagan "spirituality" in which spirit is good and flesh is evil. Sexuality is the good gift of God, which means it is not at our own disposal. The idea that my sexual conduct is not merely my own business but is vitally involved with my religious faith was a strange idea to most of Paul's hearers but central to the Jewish faith of Paul (and Jesus). This is so for three reasons: (1) In the biblical and Jewish tradition, what is "right" is not a matter of merely following my own ideals, conscience, acceptance of community standards, or reason versus passion, but the revealed will of God. (2) Sex always involves other people; it is a matter of my-relation-to-others, not merely my-own-business. Love, caring-for-others, includes this most intimate and personal dimension of my own life. My sex life involves not only myself but also my partner and generates a chain reaction in the lives of others as well. (3) In the Bible and Paul's Jewish tradition, sexual immorality was directly related to unfaithfulness to God. The relation between God and Israel is pictured as the relation of husband and wife. God is faithful. Israel's unfaithfulness to the marriage covenant is idolatry. Idolatry is a rejection of God the loving husband. Though Paul does not here get specific, as he will in the particular situations addressed in later letters, he does set out the framework in which all Christian ethical decisions are to be made.

Not just religious actions but doing one's day job responsibly is also a mark of the holy people of God. As part of Paul's instruction on being the community of holy love, Paul says, "Aspire to live quietly, to mind your own affairs, and to work with your hands, as we directed you" (4:11). This is not because a supposed "eschatological excitement" has caused some church members to quit work and wait for the soon coming of the Lord (see below on 4:13–18), but "so that you may behave properly toward outsiders and be dependent on no one" (4:12). Holiness means the community is marked off from the world and the called-out church is distinct from society at large, the people of God in contrast to "gentiles" (see above on 1:6). Outsiders were understandably prone to dislike and misunderstand this new group that seemed to be out of step and misfits in normal society. Church members were not to encourage this perception but to live normal, workaday, respectable lives that did not create false stumbling blocks to the church's mission. Doing a good job at work and supporting my family become a matter of authentic Christian witness, a mark of the holy people of God, an important factor in how I make ethical decisions. People are watching, and what they think influences the success of God's mission among them. Love is holy love; holiness is loving holiness.

The Believing/Faithful Community—Founded on Past Events

We have been reflecting on the nature and mission of the church as presented in 1 Thessalonians, the community whose present life is characterized by "labor of love" (1:3). For Paul, such love is inseparable from faith, is in fact the product of faith, is God's gift to believers (1:3; 3:6; 5:8; cf. Gal 5:6, "faith working through love"). "Believer" is one of Paul's favorite words to describe the new life that distinguished church members from others, insiders from outsiders (1 Thess 1:7; 2:10, 13; cf. Rom 13:1; 1 Cor 6:5, 6; 7:12; 14:22; 2 Cor 6:15; Gal 2:4).[21] As love is oriented to the present, the faith of the new converts looks back to events that had actually happened, events that constituted the basis and content of their faith. These past events included their own conversion, and this is where Paul's letter to them begins. When Paul says to them, "Your faith in God has gone forth everywhere" (1 Thess 1:8 ESV), he is referring to something that had happened to them, a part of their own experience, a crucial event in their lives and his. They had not always been believers. Something had happened to and in them, an act of God that Paul considers part of the good news itself, integral to the faith that is shared by all the churches. The gospel "comes to" them as an event in their own experience (1:5). Included in their faith that is now proclaimed to others is the "founding visit" (*eisodos*, 1:9; 2:1). They had been converted. No one in the church to which this earliest document in the New Testament is addressed had grown up in the church or in a Christian home or culture. This would change by the end of the New Testament period (cf. 2 Tim 1:5), but in 50 CE *every* church member in Thessalonica had made a radical, public decision that separated that person from his or her previous life, often including family, friends, neighbors, business associates, and sometimes a job. The conversions of those people also united them with each other.

If we ask where this faith comes from, we look not only to our own past experience but also beyond, to acts of God in the historical past prior to our own hearing of the gospel. The new believers in Thessalonica do not look inward, as though they had come to be Christian believers by probing their own spiritual depths, nor upward to personal revelations from the heavenly world, nor outward to spiritual leaders who had taught them how to be properly religious. As Paul will later elaborate, there is no need to look to the heavens, to bring Christ down, nor to the depths, to bring Christ to the surface. "The word is near you," and it is the word that generates faith (Rom 10:6–17). This word was not about "what you should do" but about "what God has done." Paul did not preach "You should be converted, as I was," but he preached about something that had happened, prior to their conversion and his. Their faith came into being when their own life story was intersected by another, larger story, brought to them by Paul and his fellow missionaries.

Sometimes interpreters of the New Testament have assumed a firm distinction between evangelism and nurture, between the original missionary message that announces the gospel and calls unbelievers to faith and the postbaptismal instruction that nurtures them in the faith. Especially in the wake of C. H. Dodd, missionary preaching has been called *kerygma* and inner-church instruction designated *didachē*.[22] This is a useful distinction but far from absolute. Paul's missionary proclamation must have included didactic elements, for to communicate his message he would have found it necessary to explain basic ideas—proclaiming that the Christ had come, had been killed, but God had raised him from the dead involved responding to obvious questions ("What's a 'Christ'?" "What's a 'resurrection'?"). The event of being converted involved not only *kerygma* but also *didachē*, a "form of teaching" (Rom 6:17). Likewise, the church's postbaptismal instruction could not assume that communicating the gospel was a once-for-all event that happened in the process of the believer's conversion, as though the kerygmatic dimensions of Christian faith could be left behind as no longer needed by those who were already members of the church. In Paul's last and most profound didactic letter, he declares to the insiders of the Roman congregations that he wants to come in order to proclaim the gospel to them (Rom 1:15). We insiders never outgrow our need to hear the original gospel proclaimed; it remains always new, it continues to generate faith, in outsiders and insiders alike. In our secularized society, the line that separates believers from unbelievers runs through the congregation and through each church member. The need for conversion from unbeliever to believer is present every time we preach, so that preaching to insiders needs the kerygmatic dimension as well as the didactic and pastoral. Pastors who are not also evangelists are still living in the Constantinian world of Christendom. The faith cannot be assumed to be culturally transmitted; insiders cannot help but have one foot still on the outside. Mainline preachers and teachers may shy away from thinking of themselves as evangelists, but it is inherent in the call to ministry, which is always ministry of the gospel.

Nonetheless, it is true that all New Testament documents are written to insiders in the Christian community and thus do not have as their goal continually rehearsing the foundational elements of the Christian proclamation those insiders came to believe when they were converted. *No* New Testament text is addressed to outsiders to convert them; *every* New Testament text is directed to the converted to deepen and clarify the faith they already have. The original readers of these texts, however, were intentionally reminded of their conversion, the great turning point in their lives in which they heard the church's evangelistic message while they were still unbelievers. We have learned from studying Revelation from this point of view that second-generation insiders of "dead" churches are called to *remember* the powerful events that gave them new life (Rev 2:5; 3:3). Paul the evangelist, Paul the pastor, considers it crucial to repeatedly remind the new converts that they already know this life-giving message. The congregations in which we preach and teach also need this, but they may not realize it, do not ask for it, and cannot do it on their own. They recognize it when they hear it. They are hungry but have no appetite and do not know how to ask for the bread that satisfies their hunger. This is why the church has ministers and teachers.

What did Paul *preach* when he came into a town where there were no churches and no one had ever heard of the Christian faith? This question is terribly relevant for the church around the world, perhaps especially so in countries with a long Christian tradition that have become secularized, thinking of the Christian faith in terms of cultural Christianity, whether from right, left, or center. If we read carefully through 1 Thessalonians, asking what we can learn about the content of the initial, faith-generating proclamation of the gospel, we find it is brief and clear. Paul's evangelistic message was not an idea, religious theory, or list of principles, just as it did not begin with an argument that the Thessalonians were sinners who needed saving or shallow people who needed to be more spiritual. His message was a story, a story that blends God's act and their own response, the God who acted in

Jesus and in their own personal history and who continues his saving acts until the end:

> The time of fulfillment has come, and the one, true, living God has acted in his Son, Jesus Christ, for their salvation (1:9–10).

> The decisive act was the death of the Lord Jesus Christ "for us" (4:14; 5:9–10).

> God raised Jesus from the dead (1:10; 4:14).

> The gospel came to them as the word of God in words both proclaimed by Paul and received by them in the power of the Holy Spirit (1:5; 2:13).

> They were called by the word of God into God's chosen people, who had existed as part of world history before them and continues in the world as God's act (1:4; 2:12).

> The saving event will be completed when God's Son comes from heaven in the near future (1:10; 5:8–9).

This condensed outline does not represent the structure of Paul's missionary sermons, as though he began with "First, we must learn that polytheism is wrong, for there is only one true God. Once we are convinced of that, we will go on to the second point . . ." The gospel began with the announcement of what God had done. God had raised Jesus from the dead. This, of course, does not mean that we should picture Paul standing on street corners or in his tent-making shop repeating a one-sentence sermon, "Christ is risen," nor that our sermons, church-school lessons, or discussions in Bible study groups should do this. The proclamation of the resurrection carried with it the whole new world, from God the Creator through the formation of a covenant people, climaxed in sending the Messiah, whose death and resurrection inaugurated the new age. The new symbolic universe inseparable from this message turned the conventional world upside down, and the real world appeared, right side up (cf. Acts 17:6, of Paul's preaching in Thessalonica). This was breathtakingly new to them, as it is to us. Appropriating this new message took some explaining, some intense and complex theological hermeneutics. However, in this first emergence of the death and resurrection of Christ as the core of the Christian gospel, there is no *theory* of *how* Jesus's death "for us" (cf. 1 Cor 15:3–5) is the saving act of God, no explanation of why we need dying for, just as there is no explanation of how the resurrection should be conceptualized. The gospel declares the reality of these events but does not explain theories about how they fit into our thought patterns and understandings of the world. The meaning of the saving event would call for a lot of teaching and new understanding, not adding on increments of a new religion but revisioning the world and life as we had supposed it to be in terms of the way the world truly is, the renewed world now inaugurated by God's saving act in Christ. They continued to learn the content and contours of this new world, as do we.

The conversion of the Thessalonians was an abrupt about-face from their previous understanding of the world and life. But appropriation of the meaning of the life-changing gospel cannot be done in a moment. Paul continued to teach them while he was present, and by the time he had left a few weeks or months later, he had trained some teachers to continue his instruction. He had also provided creedal/catechetical summaries of the faith, as anchor points for their continuing theological development. His letter to them seems to contain allusions and quotations from this traditional material that would evoke the traditions he had taught them (1:9–10; 5:9b–10). As Paul writes this letter, he is founding the church in Corinth. He will later have occasion in writing to the Corinthians to explicitly quote the creedal summary of the gospel he had taught them. This creedal summary must have been in his mind as he wrote 1 Thessalonians, which has the same structure and content. Paul had presumably taught the new converts in Thessalonica:

Christ died	he was raised
for our sins	on the third day
according to the Scriptures	according to the Scriptures
and that he was buried	and that he appeared to Cephas,
	then to the Twelve

This gospel can be summarized in a paragraph; a lifetime of living and reflection cannot exhaust it. It begins with the announcement that God has raised Jesus from the dead and called us to be God's people, inseparable aspects of the one message: what God has done, is doing, and will do in history; what God has done, is doing, and will do in and through us. When the Christian faith is stated so basically, some insiders may suppose this is too elementary; they may suppose they have heard it all before and say, "Of course we believe in the death and resurrection of Jesus." But some things cannot be said with an "of course" in front of them. Whoever says, "Since we're in the church, of course we believe in God, of course we believe in the resurrection of Jesus," has never heard the question. In the face of a tragic world in which babies die of hunger, a world with no obvious meaning except what we—whistling in the dark—make for ourselves, to say "*of course* we believe God raised Jesus from the dead" is never to have faced the seriousness of the question. Some who say, "Here we go again," have never been, and it is the task of the church's preachers and teachers to help them hear the basics of the saving gospel. This does not mean, of course, that every sermon needs explicit reference to the cross and resurrection—which is already present in the church's liturgy, hymns, and Eucharist. It does mean that preachers should be aware of this substructure of New Testament theology, that it should form the presupposition of every sermon, with implicit and explicit references heard and overheard often in the preaching and teaching of the church. Listeners will become aware that this is the tip of a theological iceberg. As new occasions arise in later letters, Paul and his followers will have ample opportunity to broaden, deepen, and focus this basic gospel on new situations.

The Hoping/Expectant Community— Empowered by the Reality of the Future

"Think we're gonna win Friday night?"

"*Well, we're not giving up hope.*" (Translation: "No, but we'll be there to support the team.")

"They say we might get a raise next year."

"*It's possible. Wouldn't rule it out. At least we can hope.*" (Translation: "Probably not. Sure would be nice, though.")

"Pastor, am I going to get well, get out of this place, and go home to my family?"

"*We all hope so. You know the doctors are doing all they can.*" (Translation: "No, but we are trying to say it in a positive way.")

> In the New Testament, hope is not "maybe" or even "probably." Hope is reality, the not-yet that already shapes the now.

"Hope" is often used in our culture in the sense of "wish for, with or without a possibility of realization," sometimes simply synonymously with "wishful thinking." As with love and faith, so with hope: it is a word we hear often in our culture, but preachers and teachers of the biblical faith cannot allow the culture to fill in the meaning of "hope." Neither faith, nor love, nor hope is a matter of probabilities, not even of favorable odds. Christian faith does not make statements such as "The chances are about eight to five that God exists, and it is quite probable that God so loved the world that he gave his only Son for us." Christian love does not say to God, others, or self, "I'm fairly sure that I love you." Nor is Christian hope a dressing up of improbabilities with a cheerful face and positive thoughts. Just as Christian faith looks back in the sure conviction that God has acted in past events that transform the present, so Christian hope looks forward in joyful confidence to future realities that already transfigure the present. The biblical understanding of hope is displayed in the faces of children two days before Christmas, when the anticipated future is as real as it gets. The meaning of Christian hope is felt in the third trimester heartbeats of the couple who have longed for a baby. In the New Testament, hope is not "maybe" or even "probably." Hope is reality, the not-yet that already shapes the now.

In Paul's letter to the Thessalonians, hope is not a concluding eschatological note, but, as in the New Testament in general, it is an essential part of the triadic chord faith/love/hope that frames the discourse and is woven into the melody throughout (1:3; 5:8). New converts are "to wait for his Son from heaven" (1:10), equipped not only with the "breastplate of faith and love" but also having "for a helmet the hope of salvation" (5:8). Conversion means they now have something to look forward to, something not of their own making, a reality that gives them *hypomonē* (1:3; endurance, steadfastness, hanging-in-there). Some new members are tempted to drop out and return to their conventional life. Retention of new members, however, is not only a matter of membership-development techniques but also is the expression of the common faith, love, and hope. Waiting for his Son from heaven is at the furthest pole from passivity; it is filled with "labor of love" (1:3).

This "waiting" is not just for things to get better. The waiting is personal; it is for someone, for the Son of God from heaven (1:9). At the end of the road, whether of universal this-worldly history or of our own personal life, we do not meet the Force, the Unmoved Mover, the Supreme Being, the Oblong Blur, Nirvana, the Great Ocean of Being. In the only way our finite minds can express the reality, we find ourselves speaking in biblical imagery: we meet a person. Nor is the glory of the coming kingdom pictured in terms of pearly gates and golden streets. At the end of the road is the infinite fulfillment of relationships that have become dear to us in this life. At the parousia, the relationships formed within the Christian community manifest the eschatological glory. This anticipates what Paul will say later to the Corinthians, that when prophecies pass away and tongues cease, love endures into the new age (1 Cor 13:8–13).

> Christ's death, O God, we proclaim.
> Christ's resurrection we declare.
> Christ's coming we await.
> Glory be to you, O God.
>
> From the order for the Eucharist in the variety of editions of the Book of Common Prayer and the "Model for Christian Celebration" suggested for denominations participating in the Consultation on Church Union in the COCU Liturgy of 1968, edited by Douglas Dornhecker and Keith Watkins. 2010 edition, now published online: https://keithwatkinshistorian.files.wordpress.com/2010/10/the-cocu-liturgy-of-1968.pdf

This letter contains nothing explicit about "going to heaven." In 1 Thessalonians, *we* do not go to him; *he* comes from heaven to us. Salvation is not only to live but to "live with him," a reality that begins even now (1 Thess 5:10). When Paul wrote 1 Thessalonians, he and his first readers expected to live until the parousia. Even then, Paul had every confidence that if he or they died before the parousia, believers were "with him" (the Lord Jesus) in the meantime and would come "with him" to rejoin the whole family of God (3:13; see below on 4:13–14). Eschatological salvation consists not only of being in the immediate presence of God but also of being together with God's redeemed people; *this*, Paul insists, is eschatological joy and glory (2:19–20). This is a profound understanding of what it means to say, "I belong to the church," "I believe in the communion of saints." This is why we walk through the cemetery on the way to the sanctuary, why we celebrate All Saints' Day. Imagine your best moments of church life, the sharing and celebration of the love and service of God with one's sisters and brothers in the church, and multiply it by infinity. For Paul, this is the meaning of living by hope. Such insights emerge only incidentally—Paul is not teaching eschatological doctrine about "what happens when we die" but simply presupposes that at the end of our road stands the God revealed in Jesus, and that salvation is being with God and all God's people. Paul makes it clear, here and elsewhere, that being eschatologically reunited with God and all God's people is deeply personal. It is *not* like a drop of water finally being absorbed in the ocean. Through the centuries, the church has regularly affirmed in its liturgy, "he shall come again, with glory." "His death, we show forth, his resurrection we proclaim, his coming we await."

Eschatology Gets Particular, Focused, Concrete:
1 Thessalonians 4:13–18

Paul, like New Testament authors in general, has a firm eschatological hope of the ultimate victory of God, already begun, prefigured, and guaranteed in the resurrection of Jesus. God's eschatological act in raising up Jesus is the basis of the confident Christian hope of eternal life. Paul expresses this hope in various images he does not try to harmonize into a single, comprehensive, consistent system. Eschatology provides the framework and permeates the content of all he says. As a pastoral theologian, from time to time Paul focuses his eschatology in response to a particular need in the life of the church. This is what happens in 1 Thessalonians 4:13–18, the most famous text in this brief letter.

This text has sometimes been regarded as the main purpose of the letter, as though the "eschatological excitement" of the new converts who expected the parousia any day had thrown them into confusion when some of their members died, so that Paul writes 1 Thessalonians to correct their eschatology, with the rest of the letter constituting mere filler. In this view, they were upset that their departed loved ones would miss out on the eschatological glory, and some of them had quit their regular jobs and had become busybody "idlers" as they awaited the imminent coming of the Lord. "Idlers," however, is a misunderstanding and mistranslation. Paul's instruction to "live quietly, mind your own business, and earn your own living" (4:1 CEB) is not directed to those who had quit work because of their "eschatological enthusiasm" but is integral to his general instruction to the new converts to live a respectable life that does not generate suspicion among outsiders. "Idlers" (5:14 NRSV) is better translated "disorderly" (CEB) or "undisciplined" (NJB)[23] and is not directed to people who have quit their jobs but to those resisting the leadership of the orderly church Paul had established (note context).

We have seen that 1 Thessalonians is much more than instruction on the last point of an outline of Christian theology; it represents the breadth and depth of Paul's theology to be elaborated in later letters. One element of the faith of the new converts in Thessalonica had apparently occasioned some pain and perplexity. Some members had died, and because the Lord had not yet come, their families, including their new church family, not only suffered the grief that accompanies the loss of a loved one but also wondered whether their departed members would be included in the grand eschatological celebration soon to come. It is this pastoral situation, some actual deaths among his beloved church members in Thessalonica, that calls forth the response of 4:13–18, not Paul's interest in communicating a "speculative" eschatological program. Like preachers today, Paul responds not by "teaching eschatology" as though there were a single, comprehensive set of eschatological doctrines all Christians should know, but by drawing upon his store of traditional resources for a helpful word from God for this particular situation. Like preachers today, he has such a word from the Lord. This word is not attributed to the pre-Easter Jesus but to the risen Lord spoken through a Christian prophet. Five features of Paul's response are important for us.

1. Paul speaks of two groups, Christian believers and the "others . . . who have no hope" (4:13). We need not find such language smug and off-putting. Paul is absolutely not saying that there is no hope *for* those outside the Christian community, but that they do not, and cannot, live *by* the Christian hope. He is talking about two kinds of grief. Christian believers grieve for their departed loved ones; the Christian pastoral response is not "don't grieve" but "we do not grieve as those who live without hope." Nor is the meaning of hope here restricted to "going to heaven"; my own understanding of Paul's meaning can be summarized as "knowing that one's life is incorporated into the plan of God for his people and the world, which leads to ultimate salvation" (see on *paraklēsis* below). Christians mourn their dead, but their mourning is tempered by a firm hope unbelievers cannot know.

2. The new converts in Thessalonica are deeply bothered by a particular question: "Have those believers who died missed out on the eschatological glory to come at the parousia?" Paul's pastoral answer is confident and clear: "No, they have not." This is the whole point of this passage. It responds to the deep concern of the grieving congregation and families in Thessalonica with a clear and heartening word: we and they, alive and dead, will celebrate together in the grand family reunion to come.

3. This word is not Paul's own. He has a word of the Lord to share that addresses this particular hurt. Like the prophetic word of the risen Jesus in Revelation, this word is not a generality—"Don't worry, it's all going to be just fine"—but consists of a specific, revealed apocalyptic drama. Like

Revelation, its content is not to be taken literally, but its symbolism points to something real. The particulars of this scenario:

> Jesus returns from heaven.
> Those who have died "in Christ" are raised.

The surviving remnant of the people of God (usually translated "we who are left"), that is, those who are still living at the parousia of the Lord, experience a grand reunion with their resurrected loved ones, go out with them to meet the returning Lord in the sky, and escort him back to the earth, "and so we will be with the Lord forever."

4. This imagery is modeled on the reception given to a returning ruler by the residents of a Hellenistic city, who go out to meet him and escort him into the city, and is reminiscent of the triumphal entry of Jesus into Jerusalem pictured in the Gospels, with shouts of "Blessed is the king who comes in the name of the Lord!" (Luke 19:38). Here, the believers go to meet the Lord Jesus, who has returned to establish God's kingdom, and escort him back to earth.

5. Like Revelation and apocalypticism in general, Paul has more than one picture of the ultimate events. In 1 Thessalonians 4:13–18, his prophetic word pictures the Christian hope as being reunited with departed loved ones in the resurrection at the soon coming of the kingdom of God. At the parousia, God will bring together dead believers and the surviving remnant in a grand reunion. Earlier in the letter, Paul had pictured the returning Lord bringing the dead saints with him (3:13). In his next letter, Paul will encourage the Philippians in ways that picture both departing to be with Christ immediately after death (Phil 1:23) and the Lord coming from heaven and raising the dead (Phil 3:8–11, 20–21). His instructions to the Corinthians insist on the reality of a future resurrection of believers (1 Cor 15) but also picture death as departing to the heavenly world to be with Christ (2 Cor 5:1–10). Throughout history, some interpreters have gone beyond Paul and combined these images into one schematic program that involves separation of soul and body, the souls going immediately to heaven or to some "intermediate state," later reunited with their bodies at the final resurrection. Such efforts to construct a consistent eschatological scenario in which all the pieces fit go beyond Paul and the New Testament in general, which never develops such a systematic view. *Each* picture expresses, in its own way, the Christian hope of eternal life in the presence of God. Even N. T. Wright, whose solid studies of the resurrection faith of Judaism and early Christian-

ity go much further than Paul himself in this regard, still insists, precisely in connection with this text, on maintaining "the paradox and tension inherent in belonging to the risen Messiah on the one hand and being bodily dead, and not yet raised, on the other."[24]

"Therefore encourage one another with these words" (1 Thess 4:18). This most detailed apocalyptic text in 1 Thessalonians is nonetheless not given as a matter of eschatological doctrine for the curious but is summed up as *paraklēsis* in 4:18, often translated "comfort" or "encouragement" (cf. 2:3, 12; 3:2, 7; 4:1; 5:1, 14).[25] This significant word cluster that reverberates throughout Paul's letters (58 times in the undisputed letters, 143 times in the New Testament) surrounds and permeates the didactic section of 1 Thessalonians (4:1, 10, 18; 5:1, 14). Paul can even sum up his message and his appeal in this one word (2:12; 3:7; "appeal" in 2:3 is *paraklēsis*). This biblical use of the word is important for Paul throughout his writings. In the framework of Paul's own symbolic universe, he represents himself as standing in the line of the biblical prophets, especially Jeremiah. The translators of the LXX used the *parakaleō* vocabulary to render *nacham*, the term that came to be used for God's eschatological comfort/consolation of Israel, becoming a synonym for eschatological salvation, the fulfillment of God's plan for history, the coming of the kingdom of God (e.g., Isa 40:1 KJV, familiar to many as the opening words of Handel's *Messiah*: "Comfort ye, comfort ye my people"). In some later Jewish thought, the comforter (*Menaḥem* is from the same word) even became the name of the Messiah. Jesus probably, and early Christianity certainly, drew from this stream of tradition in which the language of "comfort" and "consolation" expresses eschatological salvation. Those who mourn, who lament the unjust state of the world and long for the coming kingdom of God, are promised that they will be *comforted* (Matt 5:4; the future passive represents the fulfillment of God's promise of eschatological salvation). The coming of the Messiah fulfills Israel's hope for the "*consolation* of Israel" (Luke 2:25). The eschatological gift of the Holy Spirit, and even the Messiah himself, is called the *paraklētos* (Paraclete): comforter, encourager, advocate (John 14:16, 26; 15:26; 16:7; 1 John 2:1). All this, of course, makes clear that, when heard with the associations of modern English words, translating the terms as "comfort," "consolation," or "encouragement" is not only inadequate but also misleading. There are no connotations of soothing subjectivity in "comfort," no associations with token "prizes for losers" in "consolation," and "encouragement" has nothing to do with pep talks, motivational speakers, or cheerleading (contra, e.g., *The Message*'s paraphrase of *parakalesai* in 1 Thessalonians 3:2 as "cheering you on"). *Paraklēsis* is not feel-good sentimentality but an invitation to courageous living based on the faithfulness of God, being aware of one's place in God's plan for the world and history. The words are resonant with the final realization of God's promise of a new creation of justice and peace. For Paul, preaching as such, both evangelistic and pastoral, is not religious motivational speaking, cheerleading, threatening, or scolding, but *paraklēsis*.

Paraklēsis is the claim that God's promises are now being fulfilled, an announcement that brings with it a reorientation of life from night to day. Eschatology is not mere interesting or incredible speculation about the end times but bears with it a call to ethical responsibility. The world to come is already dawning, and believers are day people (5:1–11; cf. 5:8) who live by a "daybreak ethos . . . leaning into the future," out of step with the present world that takes its signals from "normal" common sense based on experience of the past.[26] What is at stake in this eschatological gospel is not time-tables for the last days but whether we see ourselves as belonging to the continuing darkness or are already oriented to the new day. Then, "whether we are awake or asleep we . . . live with him" and "encourage (*parakaleō*) one another and build up each other" with these words (5:10–11). In the New Testament, hope is not "maybe" or even "probably." Hope is reality, the not-yet that already shapes the now.

Although we have only scratched the surface, these soundings may encourage further and deeper explorations. We have seen that this brief letter already presents common structures and numerous themes that resonate through all Paul's letters. While nothing like a complete statement of Paul's theology, 1 Thessalonians is clearly neither "primitive" nor merely directed to straightening out the confused eschatology of the Thessalonians. We might find ourselves saying, "I didn't know there was so much in 1 Thessalonians." Having enhanced our skills, sharpened our eyes, and developed a healthier appetite, we can now approach other biblical texts with enhanced anticipation. This earliest extant New Testament document opens the door to our study of Paul's last and greatest letter. The gap between 1 Thessalonians and Romans is not as great as we may think.

Chapter 3

Romans: Template for Pauline Theology

In the chronology here presupposed, Romans was probably the last letter Paul wrote (1 Thessalonians, Philippians, Philemon, 1–2 Corinthians, Galatians, Romans). As Paul writes Romans, he is looking back on his missionary career and its theological struggles, pondering the statements of the faith and the instructions contained in his letters, just as some readers of this book may be looking back on a program of studies in which they have already worked through Paul's letters in historical order. Romans gives us a comprehensive view of Paul's theology as a whole, as it developed near the end of his career in response to the particular crisis generated by the flourishing of the gentile mission, in dialogue with Christians of various views and backgrounds who had been believers for decades.

There is a sense in which it is Paul's testament, a statement of the legacy he wanted to leave behind to the church in the capital city of the world, in case he didn't make it there himself (Rom 15:30–33). Although Romans is by no means a systematic theology, it is Paul's longest, most reflective response to the question, "How, then, should we understand the gospel, the Christian faith?" Some treatments of Paul's theology thus begin with Romans, as a template for grasping his theology as a whole.[1] Romans is a letter with an extensive didactic discourse sandwiched between the letter opening (1:1–17) and conclusion (15:14–16:27). The following rough outline allows us to grasp the structure of Paul's thought as a whole:[2]

Sin: Universal Human Need of Salvation	1:18–3:20
Grace: God's Saving Act	3:21–4:25
Liberation: The Meaning of Salvation	5:1–8:39
History: God's Eschatological Plan	9:1–11:36
Ethics: The Saved Life in Action	12:1–15:13

Starting with sin is not an evangelistic strategy. Neither Jesus nor Paul approach us by first trying to convince us of the seriousness of sin, as though we must first see our need and cry out for help, so that the good news of salvation can then be announced. The reality of the matter is, we can't see our plight until we are grasped by the solution; we don't know we are lost until we have *been* found. The structure of Romans is not the outline of an evangelistic sermon; it is not the way either Jesus or Paul preached. Romans, like every line of the New Testament, was written to people already converted, to clarify and deepen their faith, not to convince outsiders they should become Christians.

AUTHOR: Paul

DATE: circa 57 CE

ADDRESSEES: House churches in Rome, with Jewish roots and traditions, predominately gentile Christians as Paul writes.

PROVENANCE: Corinth.

LITERARY SOURCES: Paul draws heavily on the Jewish Scriptures and on earlier Christian traditions, interpreted through the author's apostolic experience. Except for the Old Testament, no specific source documents are identifiable.

For evidence for the above conclusions here presupposed, and alternative views, see bibliography at the end of this volume.

Sin: Universal Human Need of Salvation (Romans 1:18–3:20)

The Omnipresent Reality of the Power of Sin

The structure of Paul's theology begins with his lengthiest and deepest analysis of the human predicament. The first part of 1:18–3:20 depicts the pagan world as enslaved to sin (1:18–32). But those who condemn such sins are not justified in God's courtroom merely because they condemn such sins as wrong. This includes Jews who have the law (2:1–24). It is a great blessing to be numbered among the chosen people of God, but this status does not save anyone from the law's condemnation of sin, as the Jewish Scripture itself repeatedly declares (3:1–20). All are guilty, and all are under the *same* judgment (3:21). Paul's pronouncements about sin are not confined to this opening section, as though the negative stuff can be gotten out of the way before we go on to the more positive proclamations of grace and the Christian life. The meaning of salvation always includes an awareness of what we are saved from. Insight into the threatening power of sin is interwoven into Paul's long section on the glorious freedom of the Christian life. Romans 4 declares the blessedness of the person whose sins are covered, not counted against him or her by the Lord. Romans 5 discloses that individual sins are embedded in the story of the whole human race. Romans 6 presents Christian freedom as liberation from sin's enslaving power. The freedom from the law celebrated in Romans 7 presents God's good law as having been commandeered and misused by the power of evil. Romans 8 exults in the believer's already/not-yet freedom as deliverance from death and the cosmic power of sin. As Leander Keck has emphasized, Paul reserves his most radically penetrating pronouncement about sin for the final section on Christian life and ethics, "whatever does not proceed from faith is sin" (14:23).[3]

Where Does Paul Get This?

In his first words in the body of the letter, Paul claims that the nature of sin and its judgment by God are "revealed from heaven" (1:18). It is the sending of the Son as God's revelation that discloses the human problem—the question is first seen in the light of the answer (Gal 3:23–24). We don't become aware of our situation just by looking around or within. We learn of the world's sinfulness, and our own sinful participation in a rebellious world, through God's revelation in the Christ event—which includes Jesus's life, death, and resurrection, the coming of the Spirit, and the foundation of the church.[4] This revelation is not merely information but action; *apokalyptetai* ("is being revealed") means not only "make known" but also "make effective," "put-into-action."

> I was sitting on our back porch late one afternoon, enjoying the sunset and deeply engrossed in a good novel. After an hour or so, as my eyes had adjusted to the fading daylight, Karen switched on the porch light and called out, "What are you doing, sitting out there in the dark?"
>
> You already know what I said:
>
> "I didn't know it was dark until you turned on the light."

The Human Problem in Terms of Law

Paul here casts his argument in a legal framework, in which everyone and everything stand before God in the courtroom, subject to the wrath of God, that is, the condemnation demanded by justice. Even when speaking of a human court, Paul calls the execution of a judicial sentence "wrath" (Rom 13:4). In Paul's world, this was indeed often violent (crucifixion!). Paul's language of God's wrath pictures the justice of God the Judge (3:5–6, 15, 19; 4:15). The language of the wrath of God thus portrays neither an emotional, vindictive outburst nor the cool, impersonal working of an automatic moral law, as though this is just the way the universe works. Paul pictures the whole world, all creatures, as under the judgment of God. The sin problem can be reduced neither to an evolutionary stage we will outgrow nor to a static, necessary element in human existence, something about human beings as such, "just the way we are."

For Paul, sin is the willful violation of the covenant law of God. For Israel, this meant the claims of God's covenant revealed in the Scripture. This Scripture is the law for Israel, the people of God. It does not distinguish between religious law and secular law. This law was given to Israel, not to the world in general. It never criticizes Greeks and Romans for not keeping the Sabbath or the food laws. Their law is written in nature and in the hearts of all people. But Paul writes for insiders of the people of God, to whom the law has been given, people who "know the law" (7:1). Thus when Paul speaks of the law (*nomos*), he mainly thinks of the Torah given to Israel. The Jewish Scripture is the substructure of all Paul's thought. The revelation in this Law/Torah is not only, or even primarily, God's commands but God's saving, liberating acts. The rules and directions are enclosed in a narrative of the saving acts of God. This story, which forms the framework of Paul's thought and his argument, includes the covenant law as an integral part, but the saving act of God is primary, the basis for commandments that define the expected human response. For Paul and every Jew, the Torah is not a burden but the gift of God for which the believer gives thanks (7:12, 16; cf. Pss 1; 19; 119; etc.). Nonetheless, when the relation of sinful human beings to God is construed in legal terms, all are condemned. Before the law, one is either guilty or innocent. There is no difference (Rom 3:22–23): all are pronounced guilty (11:32).

The Human Problem Is Not Only a Matter of "Law"

The next section of Romans (3:21–4:25), expounding the saving act of God, begins with *chōris nomou*, "apart from the law." Paul realizes that there is more than one way to think and speak about the human problem and its divine solution. For example, he often thinks in terms of reconciliation, the overcoming of estrangement, as the meaning of salvation—human beings are alienated from themselves, from others, from the world (including the whole cosmos), and from God, so that salvation is *reconciliation*, not merely the removal of the threat of punishment required by the law (5:10–11; 11:15; see more fully on 2 Cor 5; etc.). Or sin can be thought of as slavery—voluntary, inevitable, and universal—in which I am both victim and willful participant, so that salvation is deliverance, freedom. Even though law is a valuable and strong metaphor for conceiving the relation of sinful humanity to the God of justice (see below on Rom 7), such a theology has fundamental weaknesses.

1. Law operates, and must operate, in terms of lists of right and wrong *actions*, but the sin problem is a matter of both act and being. The lawbreaker can't be convicted in court for *being* evil but only for *doing* evil. Yet sin is not only on the surface of my life, expressed in actions; it lies at the core of my being. In biblical and Pauline theology, sin and condemnation are not just a matter of what I do but of who I am. Sin is radically defined in Romans as unfaithfulness (14:23)—not a list of individual acts but a comprehensive stance, an all-permeating condition, a state of distrust, resentment, and rebellion against God of which I am barely aware, and from which I could not extricate myself even if I tried. Since I don't know I am enslaved, I don't even try to be free.

Thus the Pauline (and biblical) understanding of the human problem is not that a good mind or soul is trapped in a bad body but that the whole person has been corrupted by the power of sin. This means that what is called for is repentance, the renewal of the mind (12:1), not just the escape of mind and soul from the material body, as often in Greek thinking.[5] The power of sin not only generates individual wrong decisions and actions; it corrupts my world, my lifeworld. If the world in which I live, the world constituted by my thought and language, is corrupt, then I am corrupt. As Serene Jones states, "Language, like our bodies, is not something we can step in and out of. . . . Language provides the imaginative material out of which experience itself emerges."[6] It is thus not surprising to us that in gathering up Scripture texts that declare the depth and universality of human sin, Paul focuses on the linguistic aspect (throat, tongue, lips, mouth, Rom 3:10–17, and especially such biblical texts as Isa 6:5).

> "No man is an Island, entire of itself; every man is a piece of the Continent, a part of the main; if a clod be washed away by the sea, Europe is the less, as well as if a promontory were, as well as if a manor of thy friends or of thine own were; any man's death diminishes me, because I am involved in Mankind; And therefore never send to know for whom the bell tolls; It tolls for thee."
>
> —John Donne, Meditation XVII

2. Sin is not only the particular acts of the solitary individual. Individual sins are rooted in the corporate and cosmic ground of human existence. Sin certainly involves individual decision and responsibility. Neither Paul nor his Bible wants to minimize or avoid human responsibility. The law inescapably points this out. Standing before the law, no individual can claim to be without guilt. But my problem is not only, or mainly, that I as an individual have transgressed the law. My sin is not only, or mainly, my individual evil, but my inevitable involvement in corporate human sin and guilt. My life is inextricably interwoven with the whole human race and all of human history—past, present, and future. Decisions and actions I make now are inevitably influenced by decisions and actions of my ancestors and contemporaries. My present decisions and actions (about the environment, for instance) will affect countless people in the future. I do not and cannot make such decisions alone. They are embedded in the warp and woof of the social fabric into which my life is inevitably woven. To claim that I am a sovereign individual is contrary to genetics, history, psychology, sociology—and the Bible. In biblical theology, to claim that the sovereign individual alone is responsible is contrary to what it means to be a human being. After the Fall/rebellion of Genesis 3, "No child is any longer born into a situation of innocence."[7]

Guilty as charged.

Truman Capote's 1966 novel *In Cold Blood* is in two parts. The first part narrates the details of the random murder of the four members of the Herbert Clutter family in their own home in a small rural community in western Kansas in the early morning hours of November 15, 1959. The killers, Perry Edward Smith and Richard Eugene "Dick" Hickock, had recently been paroled from the Kansas State Penitentiary. They were caught, tried, and executed.

The second part narrates the details of their execution. A spectator to the hanging, repulsed not only by the crime but by the punishment, asked, "Who is the hangman?"

The response: "We the people . . ."

Law is oriented to individual sin and punishment, but by its very nature, law is ineffective in dealing with the corporate dimension of humanity. The court cannot put a corporation, state, or nation in jail. Individuals in a corporation, state, or nation can be convicted and punished, but this does not deal with the problem.

Humanity itself is enmeshed in something bigger and more powerful than we are. Sin is a power, not a list of wrong things. I can't decide whether something is sinful or not by asking, "Is it on the list?" I cannot avoid being a sinner by not doing things on a list, no matter how long the list. "Sin is all-pervasive, insinuating itself into all human relationships, corrupting and using the good, not just the bad,"[8] and extending beyond humanity to the world itself.

3. A third weakness of the law metaphor in portraying the human problem is that it cannot do justice to the personal element in the biblical view of sin. All sin is personal; sin is not just violation of a rule but is a personal rejection of the Creator by the creature. In a court of law, there is no "sin" in the religious sense; there is a violation of city, state, or national law. The judge does not make the law or enforce it, and the violation is not against the judge personally. In the biblical paradigm, all sin is against God, having not only horizontal effects on other people but also vertical relations with God the Creator.

In Jesus's story of the prodigal son, the young man's actions certainly had painful effects in the life of his family. His big brother, and especially his father, suffered the results of his self-centeredness. When he sees the error of his ways and returns home, his confession is, "Father, I have sinned against heaven and before you; I am no longer worthy to be called your son."

This is the only reference to God ("heaven") in the parable. The young man recognizes that his sin against his family is a sin against God. This is in step with the penitential psalms, as summed up in Psalm 51:3–4:

> For I know my transgressions,
>> and my sin is ever before me.
> Against you, you alone, have I sinned,
>> and done what is evil in your sight,
> so that you are justified in your sentence
>> and blameless when you pass judgment.

This is the meaning of Romans 14:23, "Whatever does not proceed from faith is sin." All sin is personal, against someone, but a failure to trust God.

Thus this whole section is not about "sin" as a topic. As is the case with biblical theology as a whole, the subject is God. This is seen in the Bible's vocabulary for sin. The subject is complex and nuanced. The primary Hebrew words that come into the LXX, and thus into Paul's writings, as *hamartia*, "sin," are the following:

Chata, used mainly in the sense of "missing the mark," "going astray," and such (Prov 19:2; Judg 20:16). This can be understood somewhat idealistically—"trying hard but not quite making it"; "nobody's perfect, nobody hits the bull's-eye every time." One's intention is right, but execution is not perfect. The sheep goes astray, the archer misses the mark. But in the Bible, even such words are not seen as failure to reach an ideal but as disobedience of the command of the personal God.

Pesha, used mainly in the sense of rebellion. The image is of a father, king, or other rightful authority. The children or subjects reject this authority and rebel (e.g., Isa 1:2; 1 Kings 12:19). This is Paul's primary understanding of sin, in Romans and elsewhere. Whether one realizes it or not, intends it or not, sin is active opposition to God, refusing to have God the Creator as God (Rom 1:25). Sin is not merely that we may try to be acceptable to God and don't quite make it (as the "rich young ruler" may have supposed, Luke 18:18–23), but that we claim that we, with a healthy ego and sense of self-worth, are acceptable as we are ("I'm OK, you're OK," in the slogan of a faded pop psychology). We don't claim to be perfect, but we don't regard this as such a big deal. Nor do we typically understand our failures and foibles as active opposition to the rule of God in our lives and in the world. Even traditional theology, at least from Augustine on, has regarded the human plight as the "fall" from paradisiacal perfection rather than a rebellion against our Creator. Biblical theology never refers to the human sinful situation as a "fall," which is a somewhat benign concept. When I fall, I can get up, dust myself off, and continue on my way, perhaps having learned something from my mistake. If I can't get up, salvation is having someone help me up, dust me off, and send me on my way. No big deal. But what if I am a rebel, am fighting for the wrong side, and don't even realize it?

God is the Creator. We are creatures. The appropriate human stance, native to a truly human being, is to honor God as God and give thanks (Rom 1:21). To be truly human is to wake up every morning with "thank you" on our mind and lips, to live each day in grateful praise as God's obedient creatures. This is the context in which the Bible's talk of "fools" is to be understood (Rom 1:22). In the biblical vocabulary, to be a fool is not a matter of IQ or education. The rich man whom God calls "fool" (Luke

12:20) does not lack intelligence or education. He is smart and knows how to make money—a lot of it. Self-centered arrogance, not ignorance or dull-wittedness, is the mark of a fool. He is a fool because he lives in God's world as though God did not exist; he literally does not know what world he is in, as though our desires and our plans are the ultimate meaning of our lives. The fool who says in his heart, "There is no God," is not the theoretical atheist but someone who makes himself the center of the universe and the measure of all things (Pss 14:1–3; 53:1–3). For Paul, those who claimed to be wise but became fools in their thinking include Plato, Aristotle, and the great thinkers of humanity, along with all other human beings. Sin is rejecting the Creator and perverting the creation, which then becomes simply an object, a neutral mass of material to be manipulated according to our own will.

This is why Paul can choose homosexual practice as a key illustration of the nature of sin, elaborating it more than any other on the list in Romans 1:24–32. In the view of Paul and his Jewish tradition and context, God created all people as heterosexuals. Some people perversely refused to accept God as their Creator and rejected the role God had created for them. For Paul, it is not the homosexual act per se that is the essence of sin but the rejection of God as Creator. Paul illustrates the nature of sin with something first-century Judaism already regarded and condemned as sinful. He gets traction and leverage for his argument by appealing to the common understanding he shares with his readers. He is not "giving biblical teaching about homosexuality" but basing his argument on what he and they already assume. This is analogous to his statement about divorce in 7:1–3, where, in teaching about the role of the law in God's plan, he states that a woman is considered an adulteress if she marries another man while her previous husband is still alive, but when he dies, she is free to remarry. He is not giving "the biblical teaching about divorce" but is using the common understanding as support for his case about the law. Just as in Genesis 3, eating the fruit was not sinful in itself. Wanting to be like God was the primal sin, illustrated by eating the fruit. In Paul's first-century context, same-sex relations represented the perversion of God's creation, refusing to honor God as the Creator. Many people of our own century, including the present author, regard homosexuality as a complex reality in human experience, with genetic, psychological, and cultural factors. The Jewish Scriptures and the Judaism of Paul's day, and Paul himself, regarded all people as *created* with a heterosexual orientation. But some "perverted" this good gift of God into *same-sex* relations. Yet pastors know that gay people with whom they talk say, "This is the way God made me." This is not the place to engage in an extensive discussion of a complex subject, but we can here come to a better understanding of the meaning of this text as Paul intended it. Though we might choose a more appropriate illustration, the essence of sin is rejection of the Creator, wanting to be one's own God.

Thus for Paul, all sin is idolatry, the worship of images and false gods, a sin against the truth, for God is the faithful and true one (Rom 3:3). Paul claims that everyone worships and that worship of something or someone is inherent in human existence. Sin is not the failure to worship but worshiping something or someone less than the Creator. Paul, and the Bible as a whole, views human life as incomplete in itself, unable to provide its own meaning, unable to secure itself and its own happiness. Whatever provides this meaning and orientation of my life, whatever promises to fulfill it, fills the God slot in each human life, that is, is an idol, a graven image. The worship of images, including excessive devotion to one's own self-image, is idolatry, displacing the Creator from his claim to be the one true God. Sin is not transgressing one or more commandments on the list but a rejection of the first commandment, which always includes the second: "I am the LORD your God, who brought you out of the land of Egypt, out of the house of slavery; you shall have no other gods before me. You shall not make for yourself an idol [= an image, even if not metal but 'only' mental]. . . . You shall love your neighbor as yourself" (Exod 20:2–4; Lev 19:18).

Grace: God's Saving Act (Romans 3:21–4:25)

In accord with Israel's confessions of faith declared in his Bible, Paul's theology continues as the recitation of the mighty acts of God. At 3:21 he does not switch from a section on what we do (sin) to a section on what God does (salvation). As the preceding section declares the revelation of *God's* act in revealing and judging human sin, he now proceeds to God's saving act of revealing (making known, putting into effect) *God's* saving grace.

God's saving act is *chōris nomou*, apart from the law, on another basis than law.

We should not understand this as though the Jewish law has now been superseded, replaced, or nullified, as though God once dealt with humanity on the basis of the Jewish law but now, since the Messiah has come, this law no longer applies. We should not understand "the" law—there is no article in the Greek text—to refer only to the Torah, the law of Moses, but to law as such.[9]

We should not understand this as though the law has been reduced to one commandment, the law of love, or the requirement of faith. Both Jesus and Paul considered the double commandment of love for God and love for neighbor to be the summary of the law (Mark 12:28–31; Rom 13:8–10), but this does not mean that whereas God once required obedience to a long list of commandments in order to be accepted, there is now only one requirement. Nor has God reduced law to one commandment, "believe in Jesus." Faith/faithfulness is not in the same category as commandments, as though the difference between law and faith is a matter of the length of the list.

And we should certainly not understand this to mean that in order to accept sinful humanity, God had to find a way that satisfies the requirement of the law, so he found someone else who would take the law's punishment. Such a view thinks in terms of the law as a separate power or principle, superior even to God, who must satisfy its requirements to show (to whom?) that he is a just God who cannot ignore the law's just requirement that every violation be punished. This would be the ultimate legalism: God himself must go by the law and find someone to punish before he can be "just," and then be gracious to the rest of us.

Although Paul could speak of his understanding of the faith as "my gospel" (2:16; 16:25), he did not understand his theology to be his own creation. He always considered his explication of the faith to be based on the Scripture in continuity with earlier Christian tradition and creedal statements (e.g., 1:2–4; 4:23–24; 15:4; 1 Cor 15:3–5). Here, Paul's exposition of the saving act of God incorporates a brief, dense paragraph heavily dependent on church tradition (Rom 3:25–26), confirmed and illustrated by citing the biblical examples of Abraham and David. A brief overview of the key terms of Paul's multilayered vocabulary of salvation may help us come within hearing distance of the biblical message, which is permeated with such language.

Dikaiosynē tou theou—
the Righteousness of God/Justification from God

Paul's initial thematic statement included the "righteousness of God" in the central core of his theology as explicated in this letter (1:16–17; cf. 3:5, 21–22; 4:6; 10:3; cf. 2 Cor 5:21; Phil 3:9). In both Hebrew and Greek, the words for "righteousness" and "justice" are the same, with their corresponding verbs likewise from the same root in each case (Heb. *tsadaq*, *tsedeq/tsedaqah*, *tsaddiq*; Gk. *dikaioō*, *dikaiosynē*, *dikaios*). These sets of words look alike on the page and sound alike to the ear. Unfortunately, in English we do not have such a single set of words from the same root and usually express their Hebrew and Greek counterparts with a combination of the sets "righteous," "righteousness," and "justice," "just," and "justify." This has the unfortunate effect that English readers not steeped in the biblical vocabulary may like words for justice but tend to back away from "righteousness" as a bit quaint or off-putting, rarely occurring in ordinary conversation. We like to "work for justice" but hesitate to use the word "righteous," which often carries the connotation of self-righteousness.[10] A thumbnail sketch may help us recover the breadth and depth of the connotations of Paul's own usage.

The "Righteousness of God" Can Mean a *Quality of God*

Righteousness is inherent in God's eternal character and being. God is essentially the Righteous One, proclaimed by Israel's prophets and sages and celebrated in Israel's songs (Pss 7:9, 11; 11:7; 116:5; 129:4; Prov 21:12; Isa 24:16; 45:21; Zeph 3:5). Righteousness and justice belong to God's essential being, to God as God. God is not righteous by measuring up to some ideal or external standard—which would then be superior to God. There is nothing or no one beyond God to which humans can appeal for justice—this was the galling quandary of Job (cf. Job 9:33). God is free and cannot be called to give an account to any higher authority; otherwise, God would not be God. This understanding of God's righteousness will be important in Paul's declarations about election and predestination in Romans 9–11. God does not will the good because it is right; it is right because the righteous God wills it. One legitimate understanding of the "revelation of God's righteousness" is that God discloses his eternal character as the Righteous One.

The "Righteousness of God" Can Mean *the Act of God*

God acts in the present and the future to make right what is not right. Thus another biblical key word for righteousness/justice is *mishpat*, which is not only the law of right but also the act of the judge who decides, interprets, and acts to vindicate the right. A legitimate understanding of the "revelation of God's righteousness" is that God acts to establish and vindicate the right in opposition to the wrong.

The "Righteousness of God" Can *Mean Status from God for Sinful Human Beings*

God grants forgiveness and acceptance of persons not on the basis of their own attainment or who they are but because of who God is and what God has done, does, and will do. This dimension of God's righteousness can be understood in two ways, which need not be mutually exclusive:

> "Imputed righteousness"—God's righteousness is declared, imputed to sinful beings who are not righteous in themselves. This is not a "legal fiction," treating the accused "as though" they were innocent. It is the act of God's amnesty, the declaration and certification of the Supreme Judge that the accused, though *guilty*, are *forgiven*. So regarded, the righteousness of God is *justification*. A legitimate understanding of the "revelation of God's righteousness" is that God acts to confer the status of righteousness ("not guilty," "acquitted") on the guilty sinner.

> "Imparted righteousness"—Sinful beings are not only declared righteous but are made righteous. God's righteousness is more than a change of status. God's own righteousness is conveyed to them, is active within and among them. So regarded, the righteousness of God is *sanctification*. A legitimate understanding of the "revelation of God's righteousness" is that God acts to make an unrighteous person righteous, conferring God's own righteousness on and within the person.

This effort of analysis is not intended to distinguish separate meanings in a way that choices must be made, nor is it meant to suggest that Paul had a diachronic, step-by-step understanding of God's saving act. While in Romans Paul emphasizes the justifying act of God that confers new status and being on sinful humanity, all these dimensions reverberate in his language of the righteousness of God.

Charis—*Grace/Gratitude*

The word "grace" (*charis*) and its cognates (*charisma*, "free gift"; *charizomai*, "freely give"; *charitoō*, "be gracious to") are used in two distinctive ways. On the one hand, *charis* means the act of freely giving (e.g., Rom 3:24; 4:4; 5:2, 15, 17, 20, 21). On the other hand, the same word is used for the response to grace, that is, gratitude, thanksgiving (note that in English, too, there is a linguistic connection between *grace* and *gra*titude). Grace is not only what God does, *grace* is the *grate*ful (grace-filled) human response evoked by God's grace (e.g., 7:25; 1 Cor 10:30; 15:57; 2 Cor 2:14; cf. "say grace" for the mealtime prayer of thanks). Thus, in some texts there is no distinction between God's gift and the human response—both are expressed by the one word *charis* (e.g., 2 Cor 8:1; 9:14, 15). This is analogous to the word for "faith" (*pistis*, see below), which means both the faithfulness of the trustworthy God and the believer's response of obedience-in-personal-trust.

Cheap Grace?

Heinrich Heine is purported to have said on his deathbed, "Gott wird mir verzeihen, das ist sein Beruf" ("God will forgive me, that's his job").

—Alfred Meißner, "Heinrich Heine. Erinnerungen" (1856), chap. 5

"But whoever understands grace knows that it is always amazing grace."

—Dietrich Bonhoeffer, *The Cost of Discipleship*, trans. Reginald H. Fuller, rev. ed. (New York: Macmillan, 1959), 45–61

The language of grace, absent from the preceding section expressed in the imagery of the law court, appears in Romans 3:24–25 in the dual imagery of slave market and sacrificial altar. "Redemption" (*apolutrōsis*) pictures a slave whose freedom has been purchased. This is a difficult image for us twenty-first-century readers, who tend to think in terms of abolition of the institution of slavery rather than the liberation of individual slaves. The image will be elaborated in 6:1–23. Here, the point is that slaves cannot liberate themselves. They do not earn their freedom by keeping the law or by any other achievements of their own but are delivered from slavery by the gracious act of God.

"Sacrifice of atonement by his blood" is even more difficult for modern readers. The phrase renders *hilastērion*, the term for the lid of the ark of the covenant in the holy of holies of the tabernacle and the temple, thought of as the throne of the invisible presence of God. The sacrificial blood sprinkled there served as the means by which the holy God forgave and accepted his sinful people Israel. The use of sacrificial imagery to communicate the reality of the saving act of God in Christ is too big a subject to expound here. The following five brief points will point us toward Paul's meaning.

First, the shift from forensic to sacrificial imagery involves altar, sacrifice, and priest. Such imagery says something about the understanding of human existence as lived before God—we cannot just arrogantly intrude into God's presence with the expectation that God will welcome us, as though we had a "right" to do so, as though we could presume "of course God forgives, that's his job." We need a priest, a mediator, someone to make it possible for the likes of us to enter the presence of God.

Needy God

The incarnation
is the ultimate act of the love of God,
who in his creation,
especially in his most beloved creature,
human beings created in his own image
has created his significant other
without whom
he does not want to be God.

— Reinhard Feldmeier and Hermann Spieckermann, *Menschwerdung*, Topoi Biblischer Theologie (Tübingen: Mohr Siebeck, 2018), 329

Second, the concept of sacrifice is deeply engraved on the human heart. For millennia, humans have felt the need to offer something valuable to the deity, something we would like to keep for ourselves but gratefully sacrifice to God. This can be done with a whole range of overlapping motives, from most selfish to most self-giving, from crass superstition to a profound, inexplicable, inarticulate need to give something back to the Giver of Life, to be related to the universe not as a great It but in the *I-Thou* relation that changes both me and the One to whom I respond in prayer and praise. One of the more profound insights into the meaning of sacrifice is the meditation of the Jewish philosopher-theologian Martin Buber:

You know always in your heart that you need God more than everything; but do you not know too that God needs you—in the fullness of His eternity needs you? . . .

In instruction and in poems men are at pains to say more, and they say too much—what turgid and presumptuous talk that is about the

"God who becomes"; but we know unshakably in our hearts that there is a becoming in God that is. The world is not divine sport, it is divine destiny. There is a divine meaning in the life of the world, of man, of human persons, of you and of me.

Two great servants pace through the ages, prayer and sacrifice. The man who prays pours himself out in unrestrained dependence, and knows that he has—in an incomprehensible way—an effect upon God, even though he obtains nothing from God; for when he no longer desires anything for himself he sees the flame of his effect burning at its highest.—And the man who makes sacrifice?—I cannot despise him, this upright servant of former times, who believed that God yearned for the scent of his burnt-offering. In a foolish but powerful way he knew that we can and ought to give to God. This is known by him, too, who offers up his little will to God and meets Him in the grand will. "Thy will be done," he says, and says no more; but truth adds for him, "through me whom Thou needest."

What distinguishes sacrifice and prayer from all magic?—Magic desires to obtain its effects without entering into relation, and practices its tricks in the void. But sacrifice and prayer are set "before the face," in the consummation of the holy primary word that means mutual action: they speak the Thou, and then they hear.[11]

Third, although the Bible's sacrificial language and imagery—like the language and imagery of prayer—necessarily involve ideas and practices of the ancient world that modern people may find superstitious, distancing, or even repulsive, our secular world still uses the language of sacrifice in meaningful ways—soldiers or firefighters may sacrifice their lives for others. Some people live a good life every day because someone else died for them.

Fourth, the New Testament's interpretation of the salvific significance of Jesus's death in terms of sacrifice does not picture Jesus offering his blood to God as a bribe or propitiation, to persuade an angry God to be merciful to us sinners. Even the Old Testament sacrificial ritual does not involve Israelite sinners propitiating God by offering a blood sacrifice. For Israel, God is by definition the One-Who-Cannot-Be-Bribed (Deut 10:17; 2 Chron 19:7; Sir 35:17–26). The objective of the sacrificial act is not changing a hostile God to one who is appeased by the sight of blood. In Romans 3:25, God is the one who offers the sacrifice, who sets forth his Son as the one who suffers for others.

Fifth, it is crucial that this be understood as involving two parties (the righteous God and sinful humanity), not three (God, Jesus, sinful humanity).

God does not punish a third party, Jesus, so that sinners could be acceptable to God. Nor does Jesus strike a bargain with God: "If I die for them, will you be satisfied and let them off the hook?" In this regard, the doctrines of the Trinity and the deity of Christ are not optional "speculation." As stated by Reinhold Niebuhr, "The good news of the gospel is that God takes the sinfulness of man into Himself. . . . Christian faith regards the revelation in Christ as final because this ultimate problem is solved by the assurance that God takes man's sin upon Himself and into Himself and that without this divine initiative and this divine sacrifice there could be no reconciliation and no easing of man's uneasy conscience. . . . [This is] the central truth embodied in the doctrine of the Atonement."[12]

God could not just say, "It doesn't matter." It matters. The saving act of God "cost God something."[13] God did not ask someone else to pay the price.

Pistis—*Faith/Faithfulness*

Analogous to the way *charis* means both "grace" and "gratitude," *pistis* means both "faith" and "faithfulness"—again in ways that are different from English usage. Just as English has no verb "to righteous" corresponding to the noun "righteousness," so there is no verb "to faith" corresponding to the noun "faith." In Greek and Hebrew, verb and noun belong to the same word family, are variations of the same root (*pisteuō*, "believe"; *pistis*, "faith/faithfulness"; *pistos*, "believing/faithful"). English must say "faith" or "belief" (noun) and "believe" (verb). In most contexts, the biblical flavor is retained better with "faith" as a noun. Thus, when Paul declares that the righteousness of God is manifest *dia pisteōs Iēsou Christou* (Rom 3:22; cf. 3:26; Gal 2:16, 20; 3:22; Phil 3:9), the reference could be to the believer's faith in Jesus Christ, that is, obedience-in-personal-trust in God's saving act in Christ (so RSV, NRSV, REB, NAB, NJB, NIV, TEV, CEV). Without denying the believer's response, the phrase can also point to the faithfulness of Jesus Christ (so KJV, NIV margin, TNIV margin, CEB, and many commentators).[14] How best to translate the word in each case is an exegetical decision, but in terms of the theology expressed, it is clear that God's saving event embraces the faithfulness of God enacted in the faithfulness of Jesus (as clearly in, e.g., Rom 3:3), to which the human response is trust in God's saving act (as clearly in 4:3–5). Paul declares that salvation can never be a matter of human attainment, whether this be thought of as doing "works of the law" or making a "decision of faith." Salvation comes to sinful humanity by God's faithfulness to the covenant promises in sending the Messiah and the faithfulness of Jesus in giving his life for others, which are finally one and the same thing. It is clear throughout that Paul is not differentiating two human ways of salvation, the way of works and the way of faith, but contrasting all *human* efforts with the act of *God*. Paul never says that anyone is justified by his or her faith, as though one believes in faith rather than works.[15] Paul did not believe in the power of faith but in the power of God, the gracious, trustworthy God whose faithfulness is manifest in Christ. Faith does not justify. It is God who justifies (8:31).

Promised in Scripture . . . Written for Our Sake

Paul begins the letter by quoting a traditional formula that the "gospel of God" was "promised beforehand through his prophets in the holy scriptures" (1:1–2) and concludes this foundational section of his argument by declaring that biblical promises were written not just for the people of God in ancient times but also for our sake (4:23). Paul concludes his whole letter with the same affirmation (15:4), "For whatever was written in former days was written for our instruction, so that by steadfastness and by the encouragement of the scriptures we might have hope." Paul's point is that God has remained the same during the whole sweep of the biblical story. The saving act of God by grace through faith is already illustrated in the case of Abraham, prototype of the people of God who lived before the law was given by Moses, and by David, Israel's greatest king and prototype of salvation to come enacted in Jesus Christ, son of David (1:3; cf. 2 Tim 2:8). In the undisputed letters, Paul refers to David only in Romans (1:3; 4:6; 11:9), which was presumably an important point of contact with the continuing Jewish tradition of the Roman church.

The focus of Paul's attention is Abraham, and how he became righteous, that is, accepted by God, enabled to stand before God as himself the vehicle of God's grace. A short time prior to Paul's writing Romans, Abraham had become an important figure for Christian faith in the Pauline churches in the intense dispute with the false teachers in Galatia. The Scripture testifies that while Abraham was still an uncircumcised gentile, with eyes wide open to the impossible possibility of God's promise, he trusted in God's faithfulness and so not only was justified by God but also became the founder and paradigm of the believing community. Salvation is pictured in terms of ecclesiology, as incorporation into this community of believers, as belonging to the people of God. The issue is focused on the questions of how one gets into this saved community, who is in and who is out. "Who is a Jew?" is a crucial question (11:28–29). Paul's forensic language can be (mis)understood as a matter of individual faith, as the sinful individual stands in God's courtroom. In the next section (Rom 5–8), Paul will explicate the meaning of salvation for those justified by grace through faith. His portrayal of Abraham's trust in God's faithfulness already anticipates the breadth and depth of the believer's inheritance fully manifest in Christ. God's promise is not just of physical descendants or of the land of Canaan, but that the believer will "inherit the *world*" (4:13; cf. 8:17–22). The impossible possibility of salvation for God's sinful, rebellious creation is not merely the work of one who supplements our imperfections but of one who justifies the *ungodly*, not merely one who reshapes our best efforts but the One who creates out of *nothing*, not only the Great Physician who heals our maladies ("while there's life, there's hope") but the One who gives life to the *dead* (4:5, 17, 19, 24). Paul continues in the following section to set forth the meaning of salvation in the powerful imagery of participation in the new creation.

Liberation: The Meaning of Salvation (Romans 5:1–8:39)

The courtroom and sacrificial imagery of the preceding section, focused on justification, recedes into the background, and a new root metaphor emerges as the means of envisioning the reality of God's saving act: *liberation*. For Paul, salvation is liberation from all the enemies of life—not only from the condemnation (wrath) of God's court but also from the enslaving, larger-than-life axis powers of sin, law, and death. This section opens with the declaration that we have been justified by God's faithfulness that generates faith, so that we now have peace with God—shalom, the all-embracing fullness of life God intends for the whole creation (5:1). Just as Paul never uses "sins" in the plural except in quotations or traditional material, so he never uses "forgive" or "forgiveness" as the summary meaning for salvation. For Paul, salvation is not essentially the forgiveness of particular sins but deliverance from the enslaving power of sin (cf. John's identification of Jesus Christ as the Lamb that *takes away* the sin of the *world*). It turns out that my fundamental problem is not only, or mainly, that I violate God's law and need justification/amnesty/forgiveness, but that my essential being is embedded in a rebellious creation; that I, intentionally or not, am hostile to God; and that my hostility is not merely my free decision. My problem is not just that I am a lawbreaker who needs forgiveness, but that I am a slave who needs deliverance and cannot liberate myself, a slave who doesn't realize my own bondage until I have been set free.

Living in Two Ages

This freedom is the result not only of God's justifying pronouncement. Paul's apocalyptic theology pictures the saving event as God's invasion of a rebellious cosmos, establishing a beachhead in lost territory, the incursion of the promised age to come into the present age. Paul's gospel of salvation operates within the Jewish framework of the two ages. The present evil age will be succeeded by the coming age of salvation. In the Jewish context of Paul's thought, this transition from the present to the coming age could be thought of in two basic patterns. In a helpful oversimplification, the first pattern can be called *prophetic eschatology*, in which God raises up a deliverer within history to bring in the promised kingdom of justice and peace. This is the pattern envisioned in the prophetic texts we read in Advent, such as Isaiah 9:2–7 and 11:1–9.

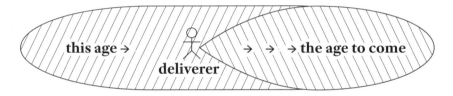

Figure 2. Prophetic Eschatology

In the apocalyptic view, developed in the later period of Israel's history, Israel's seers saw deliverance coming from beyond history, the incursion of God's kingdom into the present from the transcendent world that would transform the existing world into the kingdom of God.

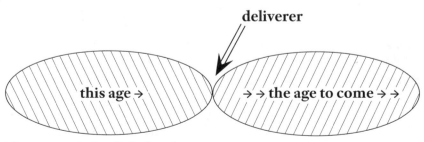

Figure 3. Apocalyptic Eschatology

Paul and other New Testament theologians adopt elements of both patterns, but they primarily interpret the hope of Israel within the apocalyptic framework. The fundamental difference from the traditional Jewish view that looked forward to the coming of the savior figure—whether God, the divinely empowered messianic king, or the Son of Man from heaven—is that for Christians, the Messiah has already appeared in history but the fullness of the messianic kingdom, the kingdom of God for which Jews and Christians pray, is still to come. The present life of the believer is between-the-times existence, life in the overlapping force fields of the old and new ages. Christians know they live in the decisive time "on whom the ends of the ages have come" (1 Cor 10:11).

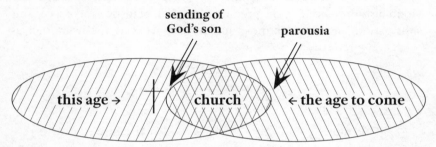

Figure 4. The Two Ages

This Age	The Age to Come	
Creation	New Creation	5:2; 8:19–39
First Adam	Second Adam	5:12–21
Rebellion	Reconciliation	5:1, 11, 19; 8:6–7; 11:15
Cross	Resurrection	6:1–11
Sin/Law/Death	Righteousness/Grace/ Life/Hope	3:9, 23; 5:12, 17, 19; 6:3, 13 / 5:5, 20–21; 6:14; 7:1–8; 8:4, 8–9 / 5:2; 8:20
Condemnation/ Wrath	Justification	1:18; 2:5, 8; 4:15; 5:1, 15–18
Slavery	Freedom	6:12–23; 8:2, 14–17, 21, 32

Such thinking is expressed in terms of Paul's apocalyptic worldview. This worldview, of course, was not Paul's invention. Soon after Easter, pre-Pauline Christian prophets and teachers had interpreted God's saving act in Christ within this conceptual framework of apocalyptic Judaism. Paul presents his understanding of the reality of the world and history as seen through the lenses of Jewish apocalyptic. Neither Paul nor the early Christian prophets and teachers, of course, said to themselves anything like, "I'm now going to adopt Jewish apocalyptic thought as the conceptual framework for interpreting Christian faith"—they assumed the thought world of their Bible and tradition as representing the world as it truly is. Not only their message but also the presuppositions on which it is based and the framework within which it is expressed presents a challenge to modern readers, just as it pulls the rug out from under our own assumptions we didn't even know we had. Struggle, setbacks, and suffering still lay ahead, but the end was sure and already in sight—it already made the world and life different. The fundamental Christian confession that Jesus is the Christ is not merely a statement of something special about Jesus. To confess that the Christ has come but that the old age continues carries with it a new view of the world. Some profound aspects of the meaning of salvation emerge.

D-Day and V-Day

D-Day was June 6, 1944, when Allied troops landed on the beaches of Normandy. That day spelled the doom of enslaving Nazi power. Although the struggle still lay ahead, there was a real sense in which the outcome was already decided, and the world and life were already different but still looked forward to the ultimate victory over the Nazi regime.

V-Day for Europe came on May 8, 1945, the day of the unconditional surrender of Nazi forces. In postwar theology, when this history was still lived experience, this already/not-yet reality became a vivid metaphor for God's saving act in history. The D-Day of the Christ event had already happened and guaranteed the V-Day of the ultimate victory sure to come. Struggle, setbacks, and suffering still lay ahead, but the end was sure, already in sight and already made the world and life different. This New Testament theology of living between-the-times was explicated by numerous theologians and preachers, most memorably in Oscar Cullmann, *Christ and Time: The Primitive Christian Conception of Time and History*, rev. ed. (Philadelphia: Westminster, 1964).

Salvation in Three Tenses (Romans 5:1–11)

"Paul, are *you* saved?" Paul uses the language of salvation, copiously and without inhibitions. Yet, Paul never speaks of "getting saved," not even when referring to his own conversion/call, his encounter with the risen Christ that turned his life around. If we press the question, in yes-or-no terms, "Paul, are you saved?," insisting on a one-word response, Paul would not hesitate to say "Yes." But Paul's own way of talking about salvation is in terms of the story of God's saving acts—it's not about me, but about the saving acts of God the Creator, the God who acted and acts in history for the salvation of the world and who will bring the story to a worthy conclusion. I am saved, but salvation is not my individual possession, because my little life is incorporated in this big story, the cosmic drama of apocalyptic salvation.[16] This requires talking about salvation as the reality of a past event, an ongoing process in the present, and a confident hope in the final, future saving act of God. This pattern recurs three times in the opening paragraph of this section of Romans on the meaning of salvation:

> We have been justified by God's faithfulness that generated faith in us.
> We have peace with God as we now stand in God's grace.
> We boast in hope of sharing the glory of God. (5:1–2)

> At the right time Christ died for the ungodly.
> We are justified by his blood.
> We will be saved by him from the wrath of God. (5:6–9)

> While we were enemies, we were reconciled to God
>   by the death of his Son.
> We have now received reconciliation.
> We will be saved by his life. (5:10–11)

Mainline churches can learn from Paul to recover the Bible's language of salvation. "Peace with God"—the biblical picture of shalom, total well-being, life as God created it to be—is Paul's bumper-sticker summary of salvation (5:1). This is infinitely more than subjective "peace of mind," though the calming of my internal frets, worries, and insecurities is a blessed by-product of God's peace. It is also more than merely the absence of war, the cessation of hostilities. Our own Christian antimilitarism, right though it is, ought not to deter us from appropriating the martial overtones of Paul's biblical understanding of shalom. Just as the gospel, *euangelion*, is good news from the battlefield—the war is over, God has defeated the enemy and liberated occupied territory—so "peace with God" is the result of God's victory over all enslaving powers.

The good news also includes the revelation that we were on the wrong side during the war, unknowing collaborators with God's enemies, enslaved by them and working for them without even realizing it, perhaps only vaguely aware of the conflict. God's war of liberation created a new situation. The enemy powers that had enslaved us have been forever defeated, and we who were formerly enemies have been reconciled (5:10). This is a different image from that of the courtroom. Sinners charged with violating God's law can be grateful to the judge for granting amnesty but may be totally unaware that a war has been going on, that they have willingly but unwittingly participated in the world's rebellion against God. Paul's morphing from the courtroom metaphor to the military image makes it personal—sinners have been hostile to God (8:7), but they only learn this when they hear the good news that the hostilities are over, that they have been reconciled to God. It's not that God has been reconciled to us. God was never our enemy; God endured our hostility; God acted in love to reconcile us to himself.

New Me or Renewed Creation?

Unfortunately, Paul's "new creation" language has been co-opted and misrepresented by virulent individualism. Thus the RSV still followed the KJV, "If anyone is in Christ, he is a new creation." More correct is the NRSV, "If anyone is in Christ, there is a new creation," and the NIV, "If anyone is in Christ, the new creation has come" (similarly NJB, CEB; cf. Gal 6:15). But even these improvements fail to do justice to Paul's theology that the new creation has come in God's act in Christ, is there prior to and apart from us, and is not dependent on "the way we see it." When we see it, we do not make it happen, but we see the reality of God's new world already under way.

Salvation Is Corporate (Romans 5:12–21)

Salvation is personal but not merely individual. We have been part of a rebellious humanity and are saved by God's incorporating us into the new humanity, God's re-creation of humanity in the image of his Son (8:29). We have seen that for Paul, and for the Bible in general, sin not only is my individual transgressions of God's law but is also corporate, involving the groups to which I inevitably belong—family, community, state, nation, and ultimately the human race. We have seen that for Paul, and for the Bible in general, sin is not simply a "fall" that happens to me, an event in which I am only a passive victim. My involvement in the human situation means active participation in the rebellion of humanity against the Creator, a rebellion that devastates not only human and animal life but the cosmos itself. In such a scenario, salvation cannot be merely the forgiveness of my individual sins and the transfer of my individual soul into the realm of the blessed. Salvation, too, is corporate, a matter of incorporation into the new humanity God is creating in Jesus Christ, participation in the new creation that has already begun.

Paul pictures the believer's salvation as life within, and in solidarity with, both the first Adam, the humanity of the old age, and the last Adam—eschatological Adam, the eschatologically renewed humanity of the new age that is already dawning. Just as "all die in Adam, so all will be made alive in Christ" (1 Cor 15:22). The individual is not an independent being, able to exist in sovereign freedom on his or her own, but a cell in a body, organically related to the whole. As the life of every human is woven into the fabric of humanity as a whole—biologically, socially, culturally, we are all "in Adam"—so the life of every human being is integrally related to the new humanity revealed "in Christ."

Just as our estrangement and rebellion from God are not only our individual problem but are grounded in our unintentional but inescapable solidarity with rebellious humanity "in Adam," so our salvation is not only our personal, individual reconciliation to God but also our incorporation and participation into the new reality, our being "in Christ."[17] Paul's distinctive "in Christ" or some variation thereof ("in the Lord," "in Jesus," "in the beloved," "in him," "in whom") is found in the New Testament 171 times, only in Paul and in the literature influenced by him. At baptism believers are incorporated into the new humanity constituted by Jesus Christ (Gal 3:27–28); they are no longer, or not only, "in Adam" but are now "in Christ." Paul uses the phrase to point to an experienced and transcendent reality inseparably linked to the person of the crucified and risen Jesus, a reality that resists conceptual and linguistic clarity. Paul thus uses several overlapping and equivalent expressions. He and all Christians are in Christ (Rom 16:9, and often), and Christ is in them (8:10). To be "in Christ" is to be "in the Spirit" (Phil 2:1), which is the same as "the Spirit in you" (Rom 8:9–10). Beyond this life, the believer will share the full and constant communion with Christ (Phil 1:23, "to depart and be with Christ"), but this reality is not merely future and transcendent; it penetrates the world and life of the believer in the present, who is crucified, dead, and buried with Christ (Rom 6:4–8; Gal 2:19), and whose life is already determined by the power of the resurrection (Rom 6:8–11; Phil 3:10). While Paul's eschatological reservation made him hesitant to say clearly that believers are already "risen with him," it is clear that for Paul the event of Jesus's death and resurrection was not something that happened only to Jesus, nor to individual believers, but it is the crucial event of all human history, a literally world-changing event. For those "in Christ," the story of Jesus has been made their own story.

To be "in Christ" is to be located in a new sphere of being. The believer does not simply admire Christ or follow him but is united with him. At baptism (Gal 3:27–28) outsiders become insiders, nonmembers of the body of Christ are incorporated into a transcendent body of believers (cf. on 1 Thess 1:1 above), the Christian community animated by the Spirit/breath of Christ that is still very much a this-worldly reality. Thus Paul's "in Christ" language is parallel to his "new creation" language (2 Cor 5:17; Gal 6:15). The resurrection of Jesus is the vanguard of God's new creation. This new reality is already present, already impinging on the present world. It is this world made new in which believers already live, though the old world is still very much present with them.

Origin of Evil?

Neither Paul, the Genesis story he interprets, nor any other canonical author offers a speculative discussion of how a 100 percent good creation could still contain the seeds of evil, the potential that could lure Adam away from enjoying his blessed creaturely status as one made in God's image, placed in God's good world to love and serve God. Later authors (e.g., Augustine, Milton, modern dispensationalists) will elaborate elements from the myths of the pre-Adamic rebellion of the angels from the pseudepigraphical Jewish literature, combined with the imagery of Isaiah 14 and Ezekiel 28 into a grand myth, but the New Testament authors do not do this.

Adam and Christ thus represent two domains of human existence, two views of the essential meaning of being human. But the believer's present participation in the dawning age to come, the move from Adam to Christ, is not a move from the "bad Adam" to the "good Adam." The first Adam, and the world to which he belonged, is also God's good creation. "God created humankind [= Adam] in his image . . . male and female he created them. . . . God saw everything that he had made, and indeed, it was very good" (Gen 1:27, 31). But the first Adam (= the human collective, male and female), exercising his God-given free will, turned away from God. Unwilling to be God's grateful creature, Adam/humanity yielded to the temptation to distrust God, wanting to be like God, to be his own God. To be sure, we recognize our own human tendency to avoid responsibility in Adam's attempt in the Genesis story to shift blame from his own decision to Eve (or to God, who created her to be with him [Gen 3:12]), and in Eve's effort to make the serpent responsible. This understandable human response, however, is not a superficial "The devil made me do it." More profoundly, the Genesis story points to the relational dimension of human sin. Neither Adam nor Eve originated sin at their own initiative. There is nothing in the Genesis story that suggests they said to themselves something like, "Let's rebel against our Creator." Their fateful act was a response to something already present in the givenness of their world, pictured as a talking snake who planted the seed of distrust—"God knows that when you eat of it your eyes will be opened, and you will be like God," and anyway, "You will not *die*" (Gen 3:4–5). Pondering the snake's theological thesis, Adam and Eve made the wrong decision. It turns out they did want to be like God—Adam's act was not merely violating a rule, "No eating from this tree." The depth of the story cannot be so trivialized. The essential character and power of sin are not breaking a rule but rejecting God as one's Creator, wanting to be in charge, suspicion that God has ulterior motives in trying to keep us subject to some external authority, the creature's placing self at the orienting center of the universe. Adam and Eve may have talked of "finding themselves," of "focusing" and "looking within" to "find their own center." But Adam was created as an essentially eccentric creature whose center was outside himself, a doxological creature, made to praise God. "Autonomous" existence is not our true nature as God's creatures; salvation is not reclaiming a lost autonomy but restoring our authentic selves as slaves/children of God our Creator/Father (see on Rom 6:12–23 below). We may well remember that the son who left home with his father's money and got his own apartment in another state, supposing that he was now free to live his own life, *came to himself* when he decided to return to father and family (Luke 15:17). Note the first-person pronouns in Ernest Henley's "Invictus," admired by many as nonwhining acceptance of one's own responsibility and claim to autonomy. Neither Jesus nor Paul would consider such a stance as authentically *human.*

"Adam," of course, is the Hebrew word for "humanity." Adam's sin is the act of the human race, in Genesis writ small, a serious story with pathos and even a little humor, a story in which we can recognize ourselves. "One man's trespass led to condemnation for all, . . . by the one man's disobedience the many were made sinners. . . . Law came in, with the result that the trespass multiplied; but where sin increased, grace abounded all the more" (Rom 5:18–20). The sin of the first human pair released a power into the world, an enslaving power that already had them in its grip and would grip all their

Invictus

> Out of the night that covers me,
> Black as the Pit from pole to pole,
> I thank whatever gods may be
> For my unconquerable soul.
> In the fell clutch of circumstance
> I have not winced nor cried aloud.
> Under the bludgeonings of chance
> My head is bloody, but unbowed.
> Beyond this place of wrath and tears
> Looms but the Horror of the shade,
> And yet the menace of the years
> Finds, and shall find, me unafraid.
> It matters not how strait the gate,
> How charged with punishments the scroll,
> I am the master of my fate:
> I am the captain of my soul.
>
> —William Ernest Henley, 1849–1903

Quoted by Tim McVeigh, just before his execution on June 11, 2001, for the terrorist attack on the Murrah Federal Building in Oklahoma City, April 19, 1995, that killed 168 people, including nineteen children. McVeigh wrote out the poem by hand and had copies passed to those witnessing his execution.

descendants. Their sin was not biologically transmitted, but henceforth no human being would be born into an innocent world. From Adam on, by the time each individual became self-aware, they were already enmeshed in the web of human sin. Adam was God's beloved creature, placed in God's good world to enjoy it and care for it (Gen 2:9, 15), but the Creator's intent for humanity and the world was frustrated.

This is the story of the present world. The story has a climax (not a sequel or replacement), for Adam "is a type (*typos*) of the one who was to come" (Rom 5:14). Adam was not the prototype of Christ but the other way around. The *typos* is not the metal character used in letterpress printing that leaves its impression on the page, but the imprint made by the seal, the footprint left behind by the foot—not the nail but the print it makes when driven into human flesh (John 20:25). "Image of God" is used of Adam in the Old Testament, but the New Testament never states that human beings are made in God's image. "Image of God" language is used in the New Testament exclusively of Jesus Christ (2 Cor 4:4; Col 1:15; cf. Heb 1:3). The "first" Adam is not primary but secondary; not originating but derivative; not the model for thinking about the meaning of Jesus Christ but an example, flawed as it turned out, of what God created humanity to be.

> Our unity with Adam is less essential and less significant than our true unity with Christ. . . . For Christ who seems to come second, really comes first, and Adam who seems to come first really comes second. . . . Our relationship to Adam depends for its reality on our relationship to Christ. And that means, in practice, that to find the true and essential nature of man we have to look not to Adam the fallen man, but to Christ in whom what is fallen has been cancelled and what was original has been restored. . . . Adam is only true man in so far as he reflects and points to the original humanity of Christ. . . . Jesus Christ is the secret truth about the essential nature of man, and even sinful man is essentially related to Him. That is what we have learned from Rom. 5:12–21.
>
> But vv. 1–11 only speak of Jesus Christ and those who believe in Him. If we read the first part of the chapter by itself, we might quite easily come to the conclusion that for Paul Christ's manhood is significant only for those who are united to Him in faith. . . . But in vv. 12–21 Paul does not limit his context to Christ's relationship to believers but gives fundamentally the same account of His relationship to all men.[18]

As the "second" Adam, Jesus was not God's improved version of the "first" Adam, but what God had in mind for humanity from the beginning. Adam was suspicious and self-centered—"it's all about me." Jesus is trusting, obedient, loving, the one truly human being who has ever lived, the man for others who doesn't even have to articulate his perspective on life—"it's not about me." Jesus was not "superhuman" or more than human; all the rest of us are less than the full measure of true humanity for which we were created. None of this means, or can mean, that Christ is the "ideal" for us flawed human beings. The one truly human life is not a nebulous ideal but has actually appeared in history, an event that happened in space-time history, the appearance of one human being on this planet in whom God's purpose for all humans was realized, the down payment, leading edge, and guarantee of the new creation already under way.[19] Christ did not become human so that we could become divine, but so that we could become truly human, the persons God created us to be.

Salvation Means Being Dead (Romans 6:1–11)

Whenever I have presented this grand vision of New Testament theology (it is not only Paul's) of the universal reconciliation of all human beings to their Creator, one response is always predictable. If salvation is for everyone, unconditional and entirely a matter of God's grace, why not "continue in sin in order that grace may abound" (6:1)? This response is sincere and logical, made in the name of fairness, justice, and ethical responsibility. Paul will have more to say on this subject himself, but he knows that before it can be heard, he will have to respond to what he has already said—that all human beings are already justified through God's act in the one human being Jesus Christ (5:12–21).

> He had been out of seminary about ten years, had been a good student and now had become a well-liked pastor with a "successful" ministry—a congregation growing in numbers with a healthy and balanced budget, a home in the suburbs, two cars, and a boat. He sat in my office and explained why he wanted to come back to seminary and do some more study, not only to get a DMin but also to get a renewed grasp on the Christian faith, to find a new depth in what it means to be a preacher. "My preaching has become variations on 'It's better to be nice than not to be nice.'" Glimpses of the strange new world within the Bible had broken through to him, increasingly real, exhilarating, and disturbing glimpses. He wanted to be a more authentic preacher of the gospel, the good news that the one eternal God has done something that changed and changes the world.
>
> I'm glad to report that he, and numerous other "successful" ministers, have become so.

The objection does have a certain kind of logical validity, but it is the logic of the old Adam, which hears the proclamation of the triumph of God's grace that overrules all human sin and guilt and concludes, "Why, then, does it matter what I do?" It seems that Paul could have said, as he does elsewhere, that God is the Judge who holds all accountable (2:16; 3:6; 14:10; 2 Cor 5:10), a conviction he holds as axiomatic without ever harmonizing it with his conviction of the triumph of grace. But Paul responds with the logic of the new Adam, the logic of the transformed mind (Rom 12:2): you belong to the new Adam, you have been baptized into his body, you have been *fused* with Christ, cocrucified with him (6:6). We have been baptized. (This is all the confessional language of the insider, not the spectator language of the outsider.) We are joined with him in his death, dead with him. The one who has died is free from sin (6:7).

Paul is talking about an ontological reality, not a matter of our perspective or psychology but an event just as real as Christ's own death and ours. We may consider Paul's theology hopelessly mythological or even fantastic on this point, and if we want to preach or teach his message we will certainly have to struggle hermeneutically and homiletically with how to communicate this reality to our hearers. But we must work at bringing ourselves within hearing distance of what this text wants to say before we can grasp and be grasped by it. Paul is talking about something he believes really happened to us when we were baptized—our baptism joined us to Christ (6:3–6). The *symphytos* of 6:5 pictures the baptized believer as organically grown together with Christ, fused into the body of Christ. *How* this transcendent reality can be conceptualized in the space-time categories of human thought is not "explained"; *that* this reality is the meaning of Christian existence is not doubted. Christian life cannot be merely adding on another layer of niceness to our old life. Our baptism joined us to Christ (5:12–21!). Christ died. We are dead; the crucifixion not only happened *for* us but also happened *to* us. This is who we *are*. Yet we must repeatedly remind ourselves of this reality and reorient ourselves to our new being. Since, Paul insists, the gospel confronts us with the claim that the baptized believer in Christ has been incorporated into the body of Christ, the *crucified* body, we are dead and cannot blithely live the old life as though nothing had happened to us. This would be zombie existence, frantically trying to "enjoy ourselves," *living* in the old world even though we are in fact *dead* to it.

The imperative of 6:11, "consider yourselves dead to sin," is not a mental trick we play on ourselves but is based on the indicatives of verses 3–8: we "have been baptized . . . into his death. . . . We have been buried with him, . . . united with him in a death like his. . . . Our old self was crucified with him. . . . Whoever has died is freed from sin. . . . We have died with Christ." "Consider yourselves dead" is more than psychology, more even than "self-understanding." It is a matter of seeing the reality of our new situation. Here is a homely illustration, couched in the social and political reality of Paul's time: A good and powerful king is deposed and must go into exile with his family. A new regime takes over. After some delay, the rightful king returns and reconquers the rebellious territory. He is gracious to the former rebels and restores them to full citizenship. His daughter, the young princess who returns with him, is now restored to her true position as heir to the throne and is given all the responsibilities that go with her restoration to her true status. This is the ontological, objective reality.

Yet she must choose to be the princess she is, and not continue to live as though the old situation of exile, comfortable and carefree as it was, were still real. Paul's "consider yourselves" means coming to terms with the real world, the world of God's new creation already under way, not living in a phony world that continues business as usual, as though there were no Creator, no Christ event that really happened. Living in the real world is a matter of repentance, of the "renewing of your minds" (12:2), of seeing the world and life as they are, the world in which the Messiah has already come and the resurrection has already begun. Paul's readers, then and now, are called to remember that they do not enter this new world with a blank slate, to figure out on their own what it means, but that they have "become obedient from the heart to the pattern of teaching to which you were entrusted" (6:17 NAB). This pattern of teaching—the basics of Christian faith and theology—was already there in the community of faith before them. It is not only entrusted to them but they are entrusted to it, the life-shaping, perspective-forming view of the reality of the world communicated by the church's Scripture and tradition.

Salvation: From One Slavery to Another? (Romans 6:12–23)

For the Greek and Hellenistic world in the tradition of Greek democracy, the essence of being human is to be free and autonomous. To be a slave is a perversion of one's true being. Slave existence is subhuman; the whole vocabulary of slavery was demeaning and scornful. Greeks did not use such phrases as "slave of the gods" to express their religious faith.

Eastern, non-Greek cultures had kings and emperors as their masters. Those who served the king in high positions were called the king's "slaves," a double-edged title. On the one hand, to serve in a responsible position in the king's administration, to be the king's representative, was a high and coveted honor. But "slave" in this context still had the connotation of being owned by the king and subject to his absolute authority. People did not apply for these jobs but were appointed by the king; they could not leave them if they were dissatisfied or if a better opportunity came up. Jewish use of the vocabulary of slavery in a religious sense was in this tradition. God is the Creator, God is the true King, with absolute power and authority. Humans are created to serve God. To be called "God's slave" (*ebed*, often translated "servant" in English)[20] is not demeaning but an honor. Those trusted with responsibilities in the administration of the one true King could be called

"Slave" or "Servant"?

The primary lexical meaning of both the Hebrew *ebed* and the Greek *doulos* is "slave." Typical is the extensive article "Slavery" in *Anchor Bible Dictionary*, 6:58–73, which helpfully distinguishes slavery in the ancient Near Eastern and the Hellenistic world from more recent forms but nonetheless begins with the comprehensive statement, "Slavery is the institution whereby one person can hold ownership rights over another" (6:58). Slaves owe absolute obedience and are absolutely dependent, have no resources of their own, are at the mercy of their masters. These are the words used throughout the Jewish Scriptures and the teaching of Jesus for slaves of human masters and slaves of God. Some modern translations attempt to soften the negative associations by rendering the words as "servant," as though they meant something like "employee." But in the Bible, the *ebed*/*doulos* cannot resign and go looking for another job but is owned by his or her master; "service is not a matter of choice . . . because he is subject to an alien will, to the will of his owner." We citizens of modern Western democracies have no real parallels in our own experience. Those drafted into the military against their will form a partial—but only partial—analogy. They must offer unquestioning obedience and are totally dependent. They cannot resign or refuse. But they also have legal rights, they are paid for their service, and they rightly think of themselves as temporarily living within a special circumstance and need not give up their mind-set as individually free, though temporarily subject to the authority of others. We have no analogies for the biblical understanding of slavery/servanthood and must learn it from our Bible.

"I am the master of my fate" is the assertion of the rebel; "not my will, but thine be done" is the self-giving prayer of the faithful slave. Getting one's mind around the meaning of "slave," its use and transformation in the New Testament, is a shock, but it is crucial for entering the strange new world of the Bible.

douloi, God's slaves (e.g., Moses [Josh 14:7], Joshua [Josh 24:29], Abraham [Ps 105:42], David [Ps 89:3], and the prophets [2 Kings 17:23], the "servant [= *ebed*, slave] of the LORD" of Isa 42–53, Jesus himself, the one truly human person in all human history who lived out his life in obedience to God). Paul and his fellow workers for the kingdom of God called themselves God's slaves (e.g., Rom 1:1; Gal 1:1; Phil 1:1). We heirs of "Western civilization" have inherited the Greek tradition. Paul, whose life was shaped by Judaism and its Bible, stands in this tradition when he expresses the Christian gospel as the good news that God has acted to free us from the slavery of sin. This means that our old life in Adam, human life as such, was a life of slavery. Paul claims that from Genesis 3 on, the life of every human being has been dominated by enslaving powers from which we cannot free ourselves. To understand Paul (and Jesus and the New Testament generally), we must not recoil too quickly in terms of our natural gut reaction to our conceptions of slavery based on the racist horrors of the American experience prior to 1863 and similar situations throughout human history. We rightly find such slavery repugnant and resist any understanding of human life formulated within this conceptual framework. But once again, this is thinking in terms of the old world, the present age, humanity as the first Adam. Adam was created by God, God's creature owned by God, created to serve God and find the meaning of his life in this service—God's slave. Such a life was a blessed and fulfilled existence, the realization of human potential, the meaning of being human.

With the Great Refusal, the lack of trust in and obedience to the Creator narrated in Genesis 3 and interpreted in Romans 5, the world into which we were born had already become a rebellious world enslaved by powers hostile both to God and to our true selves. Thus, in Paul's view, we were all previously "under" law, with God's law itself victimized by its necessary participation in a world dominated by sin, but now we are "under" grace (Rom 6:14). Neither phrase is to be understood in the benign legal sense of statutes in a book but in a political, military sense of cultural and military control. Both law and grace are powers to which human life can be subjected. To be human is not to be autonomous but to be a slave; to become a Christian believer is to change sides on the battlefield—to be liberated from compulsory service in a rebellious army so that one's life and work can be used as instruments and weapons in the service of our rightful master (6:19). *As in the teaching of Jesus* (Matt 6:24; cf. John 8:34), humans have no choice but to be slaves. The question is not whether to be a slave but to *whom* to be enslaved. Since Adam, humans have rejected God's lordship and wanted to be their own masters. Thus, when the preexistent Christ humbled himself to enter the world as a truly human being, he, too, became a slave (*doulos*, Phil 2:7). Adam's rebellion had sought mastery, what seemed to be an expression of the self-reliant nobility of the human spirit, but in rebelling he got slavery, and that without ever realizing it. Adam did not see this at the time, nor have his descendants. It is not a matter of reflection, not merely self-generated insight. It is revealed from heaven (see on Rom 1:18 above, and cf. 1 Cor 2:10; Gal 3:23). This is the way Paul sees the human situation in retrospect, in the light of the Christ event. The old Adam all around us and still within us makes us resist the idea that human existence is slave existence, for the logic of the old Adam insists that the only alternatives are heteronomous slavery or autonomous independence.

"O God, the author of peace and lover of concord, to know you is eternal life and to serve you is perfect freedom: Defend us, your humble servants, in all assaults of our enemies; that we, surely trusting in your defense, may not fear the power of any adversaries; through the might of Jesus Christ our Lord. Amen."

—Book of Common Prayer, The Daily Office: A Collect for Peace

The renewed mind, in the light of God's revelation in the Christ event, lets us see our true situation: once slaves to sin and a false view of ourselves, now delivered not to an illusory autonomous pseudofreedom but to serve a new master, "in whose service is perfect freedom." Salvation is not deliverance into a realm of do-nothing "freedom" but being set free to be ourselves, to live our authentic being as creatures restored to our place in creation as servants of God. We are set free to serve, but both our freedom and our service are "in Christ," to serve God and others as did the truly human Jesus. Jesus, too, understood the human situation to mean that we creatures have no choice whether or not to be slaves. We cannot serve two masters, and in the present age before the ultimate victory, while the people of God are still the church militant, we who are his followers need constantly to reorient ourselves to our rightful master (Matt 6:24). We have not, on our own, picked a fight with the powers of this age, but we have learned that we have been drafted into a revolutionary army, called to present our arms/weapons as instruments of righteousness (Rom 6:12–19). Previously serving the wrong side, we now present our "weapons" to our new Commander in Chief as an influence that gives mind and muscle to the prayer "Thy will be done on earth as it is in heaven" (cf. Rom 6:12–14; the NRSV footnote "weapons," rather than "instruments," better represents the militant context). Paul will later add that, though our status is creaturely slaves of the divine Lord, we do not carry out our mission with a servile spirit. "For you did not receive a spirit of slavery to fall back into fear, but you have received a spirit of adoption. When we cry, 'Abba! Father!' it is that very Spirit bearing witness with our spirit that we are children of God, and if children, then heirs, heirs of God and joint heirs with Christ" (8:15–17).

Salvation Is Deliverance from the (Good!) Law (Romans 7:1–25)

"Paul and the law" is a complex, many-layered subject that has generated an enormous bibliography and a wide range of "solutions." There is no such thing as a simple, statable, summarizable *topic* "Paul's view of the law." Paul did not carry around a systematic doctrine of the law that could be applied from case to case, but he held a set of core convictions that emerges in a limited variety of ways as he thinks through and responds to various situations in his churches. His most intense, and most extensive, responses are in Galatians and Romans. Thus in Romans 5–8 Paul explicates the meaning of being justified by faith (5:1). In this context, the subject of Romans 7 is not the law but salvation; Paul presents one dimension of the saved life, what it means to be "free from [the] law" (7:3). The following considerations are thus intended to illuminate Paul's explication of the believer's life as a life of freedom, including freedom from the law.

Paul has pictured the meaning of salvation as liberation from wrath (1:18; 5:9) and sin (3:9; 5:21; 6:7, 11–14, 17–22), and will go on to portray the Christian life as freedom from bondage to death (5:14, 17, 21; 6:9, 13; 7:24; 8:2) and the cosmic (8:19–23, 38–39) powers. Does Paul now put "freedom from the law" in the same category? Does he think of the law as one of the oppressive powers from which believers are saved? His earlier letter to the Galatians, probably known to the Roman Christians and fueling their suspicions of him and his version of the faith, had at least come close to this.

No one is justified by the law or by "works of the law" (Gal 2:16; 3:11; reaffirmed in Rom 3:27–28).

If righteousness were through the law, Christ died for nothing (Gal 2:21; cf. Rom 4:14).

Believers did not receive the Spirit through the law but through hearing and believing the gospel (Gal 3:2, 5).

Those who rely on works of the law are under a curse, but "Christ redeemed us from the curse of the law" (Gal 3:10, 13).

The law did not come directly from God but through angels and a mediator (Gal 3:19).

Even in Romans, written in part to allay the misapprehension that Paul had simply rejected the law, he gave his readers reason to suppose his view of the law was a repudiation of his own Jewish heritage and that Christian believers could breathe a sigh of relief that they could simply forget about the law as over and done with.

"The law brings wrath" (Rom 4:15).

When the law came, trespass multiplied (5:20).

"You are not under law but under grace" (6:14).

"You have died to the law" and are free from the law (7:4).

Our sinful passions are "aroused by the law" (7:5).

"We are discharged from the law, dead to that which held us captive" (7:6).

The law brings wrath, increases trespasses, holds us captive. "What then shall we say? That the law is sin?" (7:7). If one insists that Paul give a yes or no, his answer is clear: "No." Not only a simple no but the emphatic *mē genoito*, "absolutely not!" "no way!" "hell, no!" (traditionally "God forbid," a sixteenth-century effort to bring out the intensity of *mē genoito*, which, however, does not contain the word "God"). Just as he had previously maintained that the Christian gospel does not cancel the law but confirms it (3:31 CEB; NRSV, "nullify/uphold"), Paul here insists that the law is not only "holy and just and good" but also "spiritual" (7:12, 14). The freedom of the Christian life includes "free[dom] from the law" (8:2). Yet the champion of Christian freedom seems equally insistent that the law is a spiritual blessing from God that can neither be rejected nor ignored. What's going on here? Neither here nor elsewhere does Paul summarize his "teaching on the law"—he writes letters, not essays on systematic theology. It is not profitable, or even possible, to gather up all Paul's references to the law and arrange them topically in a systematic doctrine of the law. However, though it is often rightly said that Paul is not a systematic theologian, neither does he just rattle off a series of ad hoc, off-the-cuff remarks. Paul is a profound *and coherent* thinker. The law of God is a crucial element in Paul's understanding of God. Just as Paul the Christian cannot think or talk of God without thinking of Christ—though he does not think or write Christology per se—so he cannot think about God apart from God's self-revelation in the Torah. Even though he does not write a consistent, systematic chapter on "the meaning of the law for Christian faith," it is possible to draw from his several letters a series of guidelines, pointers, and perspectives that help us perceive the overall thrust of his theology of the law, which will help prevent gross misunderstanding or oversimplification of his particular statements and bring us into better hearing distance of the word of God that comes through this theology—including his dialectical affirmation of the law.

Definitions

We begin with brief reminders of the definitions and connotations of *nomos* in the New Testament and the Greco-Roman world and *Torah* in Jewish Scripture, religion, and tradition, as Paul would have understood and interpreted them. Greek-speaking Jews did not coin a special word for their law but used the standard Greek word, as had the LXX. *Nomos* can have several meanings in Greek, including not only "law" but also "custom," "rule," "principle," "norm." Yet, when Paul uses the word "law" (*nomos*), he almost always has in mind the law of Israel, the Torah. Thus, even when he begins this section with "I am speaking to those who know the law" (7:1), he is not thinking mainly of their residence in the capital of the empire, fountainhead of the *Lex Romana*, but of the Torah, the law of God. *This* was the issue that concerned his readers. In the law of Israel, there was no distinction between secular and sacred laws, civil and religious laws, the "ritual law" and the "moral law." This law was not general and abstract, a collection of principles and insights that could be applied by individuals in various ways in concrete situations, but was itself already concrete, to be interpreted by authorized community representatives in legal, judicial contexts. (Reminder: this is incarnational theology. The preexistent did not become a general "principle of humanitarianism" but a particular human being, the Aramaic-speaking Jewish ex-carpenter, second-career itinerant preacher Jesus of Nazareth.) Even so, the Torah was not thought of as only a list of laws or a collection of such lists. In the LXX and Hellenistic Jewish tradition, "the law" can mean the Pentateuch, the first part of the biblical canon, which is much more than catalogues of rules and regulations. The Pentateuch is a *grand narrative*, from creation of the world through the calling, formation, and deliverance of Israel at the exodus to their arrival at the border of the promised land. Within this narrative, laws as such are an extremely important part but are all inserted into this saving narrative of God's acts, the story that reveals God's own character as the covenant-making God. Designating this grand-narrative-that-includes-the-covenant-laws-of-Yahweh as "law" has thus been often challenged. Such challenges rightfully insist that *Torah* is best rendered as "instruction," "teaching," or "direction," without the "legalistic" overtones often associated with "law."[21] This understanding of the whole Pentateuch as law was extended to the Scripture as a whole, so that, for example, Paul could refer to the chain of citations from the Psalms, Ecclesiastes, Proverbs, and Prophets (Rom 3:10–18) as "whatever the *law* says" (3:19).

Dead Ends

Even if one cannot draw an accurate map of "Paul's teaching about the law," in uncharted territory it is helpful to mark some roads that lead nowhere.

Paul's understanding of the law is not a dismissal of law in itself. Christian life is not *anomia*, "lawlessness," already rejected in the LXX (224 times) and condemned throughout the New Testament (Matt 7:23; 13:41; 23:28; 24:12; 2 Cor 6:14; 2 Thess 2:3, 7; Titus 2:14; Heb 1:9; 10:17; 1 John 3:4). Resistance to legalism does not mean rejection of law as such, which is not freedom but anarchy, chaos.

Paul's understanding of the law is not a contrast between "Judaism" and "Christianity." First-century Judaism was not a monolith but a spectrum of belief and practice that included more than one attitude toward the law. There were some legalistic Jews, just as there are some legalistic Christians. Gerd Theissen, for instance, provides a helpful summary of the options among first-century Judaism in responding to the law's demands. "The law could also be felt to be a problem in Judaism." Paul and other New Testament authors should be seen as part of this spectrum, not merely as an alternative to "the" Jewish view of the law.[22]

Paul's understanding of the law cannot be understood as a reduction of the multitude of biblical regulations to a single "principle" of love or faith. The rabbis dedicated to carefully living by God's revelation counted 613 laws in the Torah, 248 positive and 365 negative commandments, but they, too, could summarize the law in a single command. Nor, despite Romans 7:6, is a Christian understanding of the law a matter of "letter of the law" versus "spirit of the law," as this phrase is commonly understood. Paul is not speaking of a general spiritual attitude that generalizes about the "point" of the law verses a literalistic devotion to "the letter of the law," but about two ages, the old age oriented to letters on the page that cannot give life in contrast to the new age in which the power of the Holy Spirit is the energizing force.

Paul's understanding of the law cannot be reduced to chronology or dispensations, on the analogy of constitutional law. For Paul, it is not the case that God once dealt with humanity by one constitution, the old covenant written in the Jewish Scriptures, but now deals with us by the new covenant that has superseded the old, in the way that the US Constitution superseded previous colonial and British law. Thus the line between law and gospel is not the line between the Old Testament and the New Testament, but a line that cuts through both parts of the Christian Bible, each of which has elements that can be understood as either law or gospel. New Testament affirmations of grace and faith, for instance, can be understood in terms of prideful legalism—"I am acceptable to God not because I can keep the 613 commands of the Torah (though the unrighteous don't) but because I believe in Jesus and trust in God's grace (though unbelievers don't)."

A serious and curious gentile once promised Hillel to become a proselyte if the famous rabbi could recite the whole Torah while standing on one foot. Hillel took the offer seriously and responded: "What is hateful to you, do not to your neighbor: that is the whole Torah, while the rest is commentary thereof; go and learn it" (b. Shabbat 31a).

Paul's View of the Law: Positive Theses

From the time of the Reformation, Paul's positive view of the role of the law has been expressed as the "threefold use of the law."

The first use of the law is to make life together possible in an ordered society. Paul thinks in terms of God's law given to Israel, which included personal and civic conduct without distinguishing between secular and sacred law (cf. even the Decalogue). As such, law is the gift of God in order to provide an orderly life. Although morality cannot be legislated, laws imposed on a society have a conditioning effect. Racism, for instance, cannot be eliminated by laws against racial discrimination, but children who grow up in a society with such laws will have a more wholesome view of what life together in the human community means, quite apart from religious convictions. Paul does not make this perspective on the law explicit but assumes it; it comes to expression in the context of his instruction to obey Roman civil law (Rom 13:1–10; see discussion below).

The second use of the law is to reveal the reality and power of sin and human inadequacy to resist it. The law confronts human beings with the will of God as a standard of righteousness that cannot be attained by human power alone. "Through the law comes the knowledge of sin. . . . If it had not been for the law, I would not have known sin" (Rom 3:20; 7:7). Of course, Paul, like us, understands that most people know that murder is wrong without reading it as the sixth commandment of the Decalogue, just as he is aware that sinful human beings are too easily satisfied with their own judgment that "nobody's perfect" and that by human standards they come off quite well. But Paul means that I would not know what sin is, its depth and power to separate me from God, from my fellow human beings, and from myself, apart from the revealed law of God. The law discloses that my act is not "inappropriate behavior," a violation of community standards, a hold-over from evolution, but *sin*, a personal violation and affront to the personal God, my Creator who holds me accountable. It is only when I seriously try to live by the will of God that I need a revelation, and what is revealed is not only that God's will is higher than I can attain on my own but also that the attempt itself can lead to a perverse pride, even that the law can stimulate and provoke sin.

Who Is the "I" of Romans 7?

The "I" of this struggle does not represent self-awareness of the pre-Christian or Christian self, but a "speech in character" giving voice to the situation of every morally serious person seen in the light of God's saving act in Christ, insight given by God's Spirit. The "I" is not autobiographical, does not represent Paul's own struggle to keep the law before he was converted, but is like the general human "I" of, for example, 1 Corinthians 13:11, "When I was a child, I spoke like a child, I thought like a child, I reasoned like a child; when I became an adult, I put an end to childish ways."

Beverly Gaventa has presented an insightful comparison with the "I" of the Psalter. Beverly R. Gaventa, "The Shape of the 'I': The Psalter, the Gospel, and the Speaker in Romans 7," in *Apocalyptic Paul: Cosmos and Anthropos in Romans 5–8*, ed. Beverly R. Gaventa (Waco, TX: Baylor University Press, 2013), 77–92.

Paul poignantly explores this dimension of the law in Romans 7:7–25. The struggle of one who knows what is right and wants to do it but ends up in failure represents not merely an internal battle between one's mind and body or one's "higher" and "lower" natures but the human situation generally; however, this struggle is not seen for what it is until one is delivered from it. This is something good, something I would not have apart from the law.

The third use of the law is that, after being converted and led and em-powered by God's Spirit, Christian believers receive moral instruction from the law when seen in the light of Christ. Paul has a variety of ways of appealing to the law of Moses as a vehicle of Christian ethical instruction. Not only does he cite specific commands of the law as directions for followers of Jesus (e.g., Rom 12:19–20 [Deut 32:35; Prov 25:21–22]; Rom 13:9 [Exod 20:13–16; Lev 19:18]; Rom 15:10–11 [Ps 117:1; Deut 32:43]; 1 Cor 1:31 [Jer 9:22–23]; 1 Cor 5:13 [Deut 17:7]), but he also appeals to the law in a variety of analogical and typological ways as guidance for Christian practice (cf., e.g., Rom 15:3 [Ps 69:9]; 1 Cor 6:16 [Gen 2:24]; 1 Cor 9:9 [Deut 25:4]; 1 Cor 10:26 [Ps 24:1]). When Paul became a Christian, he did not abandon his lifelong Jewish conviction that God's revealed Torah is a source of guidance in a life pleasing to God. This positive use of the law is the heir of the Bible's and Judaism's own joy in the law, the grateful celebration that God has not left us to go our own way but has revealed the meaning, purpose, and joyful fulfillment of life in the Torah. Even the "ceremonial law" could illustrate joyful human obedience to God's will, without insisting that the law first satisfy one's own rational explanations of its value.

Joy in the Law

"When people think of the law, they ordinarily imagine a religion for bookkeepers, who tote up the good deeds and debit the bad and call the result salvation or damnation, depending on the outcome. But life under the Torah brings the joy of expressing love of God through a cycle of celebration."

—Jacob Neusner, *The Way of Torah: An Introduction to Judaism* (Belmont, CA: Wadsworth, 1979), 97

There was a fourth use of the law, to mark off Israel as the people of God, to distinguish them as the covenant people God had called to be his witnesses and means of blessing the whole world. This function of the law applied primarily, but not exclusively, to the "ceremonial law," those identity markers that singled out Israel as a peculiar people with a unique mission. Faithfulness to these marks of the covenant such as circumcision, the Sabbath, the festivals, and the food laws kept Israel from blending into the rebellious world at large and pointed to God's ultimate purpose to save the whole creation. Israel's calling to faithful observance of these laws was not understood as a response to the question, "How can I, guilty sinner as I am, be accepted before God?" but "How can I fulfill my covenant responsibility if I relax the defining boundaries of the covenant people of God?"[23] Israel was called to be a "light to the nations" (Isa 42:6; 49:6), which required that they observe those boundary markers that identified them as a distinctive people with a mission, whose light must not flicker or be extinguished.

God's Good Law Was Hijacked by Sin

Paul declares that the law is holy, just, good, and spiritual, creating gasps ancient and modern (Rom 7:12, 14). If he is right, how then can God's law be associated with the slavery from which God's act in Christ has delivered us? Paul's answer is clear. God's good law has been commandeered by the enslaving power of sin (7:7–13). The law itself is not an evil power but the good gift of God, though it has been seized by the rebellious power let loose in the world by Adam/humanity's sin. Like God's good creation as a whole, God's good law now functions as an element of the rebellious creation. As Paul moves to his exultant portrayal of salvation in 8:1–39, he thus distinguishes between the Spirit-law (the original revelation of God's will, now seen in the light of Christ, restored in the dawning new age) and the sin-death-law (the law under the sway of this present age): "For the Spirit-law, that is, life in Christ Jesus, has set you free from the sin-death-law, that is, the law commandeered by the powers of sin and death" (my paraphrasing translation of 8:2; cf. REB, NIV).

The primal pattern of the saving act of God is clear: humanity sinned, but God did not abandon us. God made the covenant with Israel and sent the law, the revelation of God's will, into this sinful world as our guide. But the law, in becoming part of this world, was "weakened by the flesh" (8:3). This does not mean merely "because of human weakness" (REB) or "since it was weak because of selfishness" (CEB) and the like, but that the law, becoming part of this sinful world, was overcome by the sinful power rampant in this world. Instead of delivering from sin, in coming into the world and sharing its reality, the law itself became a victim of sin, sharing the lot of the creation itself. Just sending good and right teaching into the world did not solve the problem. The law was tested by the sinful power of the world, and failed, becoming itself a part of the problem. But this was not to be the last word. "For God has done what the law, weakened by the flesh, could not do: by sending his own Son in the likeness of sinful flesh, and to deal with sin, he condemned sin in the flesh, so that the just requirement of the law might be fulfilled in us, who walk not according to the flesh but according to the Spirit" (8:3–4). The pattern is retained: God sees the sinful, enslaved human condition and sends a deliverer. But whereas the law entered into the world of flesh and succumbed to and was overcome by the enslaving power, the Son was tested, but he overcame the testing and set free not only the law and humanity but also the creation itself (see further on Rom 10:1–13 below).

Salvation Is for the Universe—Including Me (Romans 8:1–39)

Revel in it—this is the only way to study Romans 8, the climax of Paul's evocative portrayal of the meaning of salvation. The following notes can only point to the fragmentary splendors of the biblical text. For Paul, Christian life is eschatological existence, the life of believers who still *exist* in the old world but already *live* in the new creation that is dawning. In this final scene, he pulls together the powerful metaphors he has already developed: justification, liberation, incorporation into the body of Christ, and participation in his life. He reverts to the courtroom imagery—no condemnation for those in Christ; it is sin that is condemned, not the sinners who had been held captive (8:1, 4, 33–34); but now the justification imagery is set in a cosmic framework. It is not only, or even primarily, sinful human beings who are saved but the creation itself. Two metaphors are given new prominence and intensity: the believers' life in the Spirit and their status as God's sons and heirs.[24]

Sons of God in the World of Flesh and Spirit[25]

Since the coming of Christ, the world has been a conflict zone of competing force fields, flesh and Spirit, the old world that is passing away and the new world that is dawning. Believers do not live ("walk," 8:4) according to the flesh, but according to the Spirit. As in Jesus's call to discipleship, this is a matter of repentance, mind-set, mental reorientation, depending on whether one sets one's mind on things of the flesh or on things of the Spirit, the world of human things or the divine things of God's world (8:5; 12:1–2; cf. Matt 16:23; Mark 8:33). Whoever does not have the Spirit of Christ does not belong to him (Rom 8:9). But "having the Spirit of Christ" does not mean only having a Christlike attitude. The choice between flesh and Spirit is not merely subjective and psychological but is objective and ontological. Thus Paul can not only call believers to *think* according to the Spirit but he can also insist that "[they] *are* not in the flesh; [they] *are* in the Spirit, since the Spirit of God dwells in [them]" (8:9). To be sure, Paul does not neatly divide the world into a fleshly world and a spiritual world or claim that Christians live only in the world of the Spirit. Even though believers are called not to live *according to* the flesh (*kata*), they still live in (*en*) the world of the flesh (2 Cor 10:3; Gal 2:20; Phil 1:22). For the present, they live in both worlds, subject to the conflicting claims of each world, and are called to orient their lives to the new creation rather than the old world that is passing away. Christian life is not a matter of personal spirituality but of living in the reality of the new creation—real, but still a matter of hope. This hope that already shapes the present is not wishful thinking but is grounded in the reality of events that have already happened, the death and resurrection of Jesus, God's firstborn Son who has already suffered, triumphed, and inherited the full glory of God's new world, guaranteeing that believers as Christ's fellow heirs will also receive the inheritance promised to all God's children (Rom 8:16–17). This is made doubly sure by their own experience of the Spirit, the down payment (*arrabōn*) of the full inheritance (8:16–17; 2 Cor 1:22; 5:5; cf. Eph 1:14).

The world is a world of death, but Paul's first-century world was more aware of this than ours, in which death is disguised and hidden away. Then, before more democratic health care, common to rich and poor alike,

- many children died at childbirth and of early diseases
- many mothers died at childbirth
- without modern antibiotics, an infected ankle on Monday might mean a funeral on Friday
- the stench and stiffness of death was not clinically removed from everyday life
- war was not a matter of media reports of distant tragedy but up close, personal, and bloody
- death as spectacle and entertainment (gladiatorial shows and such) made the imagery of death common
- mortality rates were far higher, life expectancy far shorter

Salvation as Cosmic and Personal

Paul has pictured salvation as liberation from all the powers that limit, distort, and destroy life: from *condemnation* (wrath), from *sin* (the power, not just personal peccadilloes), from *law* (God's good law itself commandeered by sin to become an instrument of slavery). The ultimate enemy of life is *death* (1 Cor 15:26), which is not only the shears that cut the thread at the end of our brief life but is itself a thread woven into the fabric of our lives from the beginning, weakening and distorting life, curving it selfishly in upon itself. In this climax of his portrayal of the meaning of salvation, God's liberation is from the power of death, a power that not only perverts our individual lives but has infected and corrupted the world itself. The cosmos, too, groans in its oppressed, unfulfilled state, standing on tiptoe and looking forward to the redemption of creation (Rom 8:20–23).

In the biblical picture, human sin unleashed the power of death that has infected all life, including the whole animal world. In this post-Eden world, all life is predatory, feeding on other life, requiring the death of other living things to survive. Every living thing lives by devouring other living things. So regarded, human beings are part of the food chain, and they are not even at the top. The biblical hope for salvation is thus not only salvation from death but also deliverance from predatory life. This profound vision that the law of the jungle is not the last word about human and animal life can only be expressed in the mythological language of texts such as those the community of faith reads at Advent, looking forward to the new creation in which lions and lambs shall lie down together, children shall play in the streets of New Jerusalem, and none shall make them afraid (Isa 11:6–9; 65:17–25; Ezek 34:28; Mic 4:4; Zeph 3:13; Zech 8:5).

> Earth felt the wound, and Nature from her seat
> Sighing through all her Works gave signs of woe,
> That all was lost. . . .
> Earth trembled from her entrails, as again
> In pangs, and Nature gave a second groan,
> Sky loured, and muttering Thunder, some sad drops
> Wept at completing of the mortal Sin
> Original; while Adam took no thought,
> Eating his fill . . .
> —John Milton, *Paradise Lost* 9.782–84, 1000–1004

The Bible's mind-stretching pictures of sin and salvation extend beyond human and animal life to the planet itself and to the whole cosmos. Human life is embedded in evil that is not only beyond human decision but also beyond nature. In Paul's biblical theology, earthquakes and tsunamis are not the evil that nature does but, beyond nature, the evil inflicted *on* nature, evil that nature *suffers* along with us. Along with us, the cosmos itself looks backward to the D-Day of God's decisive saving act and forward to the V-Day of the full liberation of God's children and God's creation. Paul's language of salvation is story language, the language of myth and metanarrative, the grand story in which all human thinking, deciding, and acting take place, the given framework and context for all our living. Within this framework, we are relatively free to make decisions for which we are accountable; we are not free to live in the framework of some other world, a world without God as Creator, a world in and for which Christ has not died, an as-is world that will last forever.

Romans does not use this specific vocabulary, but this is only incidental. Paul's theology in Romans is everywhere conceived within this worldview—the God who will bring salvation to the world (not just to individual souls) at the end, overcoming sin and death, establishing justice, granting eternal life, has already inaugurated the coming kingdom by raising Jesus from the dead. The resurrection is the vanguard of the new creation, the incursion of the new age into the present evil age. Believers live their lives between the *already* of Jesus's resurrection and the *not yet* of the final resurrection that means the salvation of the universe (Rom 11:11–36, esp. v. 15). This life is what Rudolf Bultmann famously called *eschatological existence*. Paul designates it the life of freedom, the glorious freedom of the children of God, a freedom the cosmos itself will experience and for which the universe itself scans the horizon in confident hope (8:21).

History: God's Eschatological Plan (Romans 9:1–11:36)

Sketch of the Content

The particulars of this dense and deep section must be explored with the help of good commentaries (see the bibliography at the end of this volume), but the overall thrust is clear: God, the God of all peoples, has chosen the one people Israel as witnesses to and agents of God's purpose to save all peoples. The Messiah promised to Israel has come, and many gentiles have become believers, but most Jews have not believed this good news. God's plan for history and the world seems to have gone awry, but God is faithful and will complete it in ways no one can foresee.

The section begins with an anguished protest and lament declaring Paul's willingness to be damned for the sake of Israel's salvation (9:1–5). But God's word has not failed, for Israel's election was never a matter of biological descent but of God's sovereign choice. With the coming of the Messiah, God's purpose in giving the law is fulfilled (9:6–10:4). "Christ is the end (goal, purpose, culmination, fulfillment; cf. NJB, NIV, CEB) of the law so that there may be righteousness for everyone who believes" (10:4). "There is no distinction between Jew and Greek; the same Lord is Lord of all and is generous to all who call on him. For, 'Everyone who calls on the name of the Lord shall be saved'" (10:12–13). Acceptance of gentiles into the people of God absolutely does not (*mē genoito!*) mean that God has rejected his people. Paul himself and other ethnic Jews who have become Christian believers (without, of course, ceasing to be Jews) are the guarantee of God's continuing faithfulness to Israel and the fulfillment of God's purpose for Israel and the creation (11:1–6). This remnant of Israel does not mean "leftovers" but is the "guarantee of God's future." Israel's widespread failure to believe that God has sent the Messiah is temporary and allows the gentiles to come into the chosen people Israel, like branches of other trees being grafted into the Israelite olive tree (11:11–24). When the full number of gentiles has come in, God will "'banish ungodliness from Jacob' . . . for the gifts and the calling of God are irrevocable" (11:26–29). Thus, when all people are included in God's chosen people, all Israel will be saved, for "God has imprisoned all in disobedience so that he may be merciful to all" (11:32). This is not something that could have been figured out. It is a revealed mystery, as in other apocalyptic theology (11:25; cf. Rev 1:20; 10:7; 17:5, 17).

What began as a sorrowful lament concludes with a paean of praise:

> O the depth of the riches and wisdom and knowledge of God! How unsearchable are his judgments and how inscrutable his ways!
> "For who has known the mind of the Lord?
>   Or who has been his counselor?"
> "Or who has given a gift to him,
>   to receive a gift in return?"
> For from him and through him and to him are all things. To him be the glory forever. Amen. (Rom 11:33–36)

The Problem: Paul's and Ours

These three chapters include fervent, forceful claims about election and predestination, including,

"I have loved Jacob,
but I have hated Esau,"

a statement indicating that God chose Jacob over Esau "even before they had been born or had done anything good or bad (so that God's purpose of election might continue . . .)" (9:13, 11). God's sovereign freedom to choose is illustrated by a potter who makes from the same lump of clay a special vase and an ordinary pot (9:21—on the pot's objection, see below on 10:1–12). We tend to back away from such images, which trigger our sense of autonomy and freedom, so that we read Paul's words as a not-very-successful effort to reconcile God's sovereignty and our freedom to make our own choices. The problem was discussed in Paul's time. A Pharisee himself (Phil 3:5), he probably shared the Pharisees' view that combined divine sovereignty and human free will, but he is not here composing an essay on the abstract problem of "determinism versus free will" that has exercised philosophers and theologians of every century. To understand Paul, once again we must enter his thought world. Before we can understand his answer, we must see the problem with which he was struggling, a problem that comes from his faith in Christ and his expressing this faith in terms of his Bible and his Jewish tradition—which then becomes the problem for later believers as well. If, as members of the Christian community, we own "Paul's" problem, we may ponder his answer with more appreciation.

Predestination and Freedom: First-Century Views

"At this time there were three sects among the Jews, who had different opinions concerning human actions; the one was called the sect of the Pharisees, another the sect of the Sadducees, and the other the sect of the Essenes.

"Now for the Pharisees, they say that some actions, but not all, are the work of fate, and some of them are in our own power, and that they are liable to fate, but are not caused by fate. But the sect of the Essenes affirms that fate governs all things, and that nothing befalls men but what is according to its determination.

"And for the Sadducees, they take away fate, and say there is no such thing, and that the events of human affairs are not at its disposal; but they suppose that all our actions are in our own power, so that we are ourselves the cause of what is good, and receive what is evil from our own folly."

—Josephus, *Antiquities* 13.171–73

Paul's problem is generated by conflicts among three fundamental convictions, none of which he is willing to abandon:

1. God the Creator has chosen Israel as his covenant people called to witness to this intention and be God's agent in God's work of salvation.
2. God has sent the Messiah as the climax of this saving history.
3. Though there are many individual exceptions, Israel as a people has rejected God's Messiah.

To Paul's mind, these are all events, not just ideas. The problems involved in understanding Romans 9–11 are not generated by tensions between ideas but by the collision of events that have happened—happened even though God the Creator is in charge of them all. For Paul, this was a matter of events in the real world; all who share Paul's biblical faith struggle with how best to think it through. Preachers and teachers wrestle with the difficulties of communicating it within the Christian community with clarity and conviction. We are not the first; we join the church's efforts, past and present, to be faithful to God, the Bible, the world, and itself. The following guidelines are distilled from this struggle.

Guidelines for Interpreting Romans 9–11

This section of Paul's theological teaching document is not an optional excursus. Readers of all theological persuasions have sometimes tended to jump directly from Paul's glorious picture of salvation at the end of Romans 8 to his instructions on Christian ethics in chapter 12. Paul does not. The issues he deals with in this passionate and dense theological section are integral to Christian faith. They can only be avoided by failing to take seriously one of the three components of the problem. That most Jews have not believed that the Messiah has come is empirical reality, in Paul's day and ours, and can't be avoided or dismissed. That "Jesus is the Messiah" is essential to Christian faith—it is its defining claim—and cannot be compromised. All who cling to these two affirmations are then faced with Paul's question: whether God's word, God's promise to Abraham and Israel, has failed, or God has rejected his people (Rom 9:6; 11:1; Gen 12:1–3).

Serious reflection on election and predestination is mainstream biblical theology. This question of God's election of Israel, its seeming arbitrariness, the apparent failure of God's purpose in view of Israel's sin and punishment, the gnawing question of whether God is unable or unwilling to fulfill the promise to his people, and through them, to the creation—this complex question is fundamental to Pauline theology (cf. 1 Thess 1:4). It is not, however, peculiar to Paul (or Luther or Calvin) but is rooted deeply in a variety of streams of biblical theology. What follow are a few sample texts.

Genesis 12:1–3. After the continuing prideful rebellion of humanity after the flood, and God's judgment on human arrogance by confusing and scattering humanity into various groups that no longer understand each other, God's salvific new beginning is the call of Abraham to found a new covenant people as the nucleus of God's blessing to all peoples:

> Now the LORD said to Abram, "Go from your country and your kindred and your father's house to the land that I will show you. I will make of you a great nation, and I will bless you, and make your name great, so that you will be a blessing. I will bless those who bless you, and the one who curses you I will curse; and in you all the families of the earth shall be blessed."

This text, of course, is fundamental to the rest of the biblical story.

> Exodus 19:5–6: "'Now therefore, if you obey my voice and keep my covenant, you shall be my treasured possession out of all the peoples. Indeed, the whole earth is mine, but you shall be for me a priestly kingdom and a holy nation. These are the words that you shall speak to the Israelites.'"

> Deuteronomy 7:7; 9:5: "It was not because you were more numerous than any other people that the LORD set his heart on you and chose you—for you were the fewest of all peoples. . . . It is not because of your righteousness or the uprightness of your heart that you are going in to occupy their land; but because of the wickedness of these nations the LORD your God is dispossessing them before you, in order to fulfill the promise that the LORD made on oath to your ancestors, to Abraham, to Isaac, and to Jacob."

> Deuteronomy 10:14–15: "Although heaven and the heaven of heavens belong to the LORD your God, the earth with all that is in it, yet the LORD set his heart in love on your ancestors alone and chose you, their descendants after them, out of all the peoples, as it is today."

Amos 3:1–2: "Hear this word that the LORD has spoken against you, O
people of Israel, against the whole family that I brought up out of the
land of Egypt:
> You only have I known
>> of all the families of the earth;
> therefore I will punish you
>> for all your iniquities."

Lamentations 5:21:
"Restore us to yourself, O LORD, that we may be restored;
> renew our days as of old—
unless you have utterly rejected us,
> and are angry with us beyond measure."

Isaiah 6:9–10: "Go and say to this people:
'Keep listening, but do not comprehend;
keep looking, but do not understand.'
Make the mind of this people dull,
> and stop their ears,
> and shut their eyes,
so that they may not look with their eyes,
> and listen with their ears,
and comprehend with their minds,
> and turn and be healed."

This passage, in which the failure of the elect people is not only the result
of their own disobedience but is the act of God, who hardens their hearts,
is cited in all four Gospels, Acts, and Paul (Matt 13:14–15; Mark 4:12; Luke
8:10; John 12:39–40; Acts 28:26–27; Rom 11:8).

> Matthew 24:22: "'And if those days had not been cut short, no one would
> be saved; but for the sake of the elect those days will be cut short.'"

> 1 Peter 1:1–2: "To the exiles of the Dispersion in Pontus, Galatia, Cappa-
> docia, Asia, and Bithynia, who have been chosen and destined by God
> the Father and sanctified by the Spirit to be obedient to Jesus Christ and
> to be sprinkled with his blood . . ."

Paul is here dealing with the historical lives of categories of people, not with God's sorting a box of individual name tags into "In" and

"Out" before history began. A part of the distance we modern Western types feel toward the doctrine of election in general and Romans 9–11 in particular is that we don't like for the groups to be accepted or rejected wholesale. It seems unfair to put the class as a whole on a pass/fail basis. We want deserving individuals to pass and slackers to fail. We know the reality of life is that at commencement, some graduate and some don't, but it is a matter of individual merit, not the class as a whole. In the Super Bowl of life there is no thrill of victory without the agony of defeat. We don't want to play a game in which everybody loses, not even a game in which everybody wins.

But Romans 9–11 is not about individuals and their decisions. Paul is here talking about Israel and the nations, about Jews and gentiles, about categories of people. He is responding to sincere, thoughtful Christian believers who, aware of their Bible and their Jewish heritage, ask if the inclusion of gentiles in the people of God means that God has rejected his people Israel. None of this is objectifying language about outsiders, but all is confessional language, affirmed by grateful insiders anticipating the day when all have become insiders.

Revelation by Flannery O'Connor

O'Connor's story must be read, and cannot, of course, be summarized, any more than Romans or Isaiah can be summarized. Here we offer only a contextual reminder to preface the searing conclusion.

Ruby Turpin, owner with her husband, Clyde, of a pig farm in early twentieth-century Georgia, sits in the doctor's waiting room, silently proud and grateful to Jesus that she is saved, that God had not created her white trash or Negro. As she waits, she notices with a sympathetic disdain those who are waiting with her. Among them is an overweight, unattractive college student named Mary Grace, reading a book entitled *Human Development*. Mary Grace has some sort of seizure, during which she yells at Mrs. Turpin, "Go back to hell where you came from, you old wart hog."

Later that afternoon, unable to forget the shaking experience, Mrs. Turpin asks God why he sent her such a message. She's a good Christian woman, so how could she "be saved and from hell too." She receives a vision of a fiery bridge of light extending upward, with a vast throng advancing from earth to heaven. The procession is led by white trash, black people, "freaks and lunatics" such as she considered Mary Grace, followed at the end of the line by respectable Sunday school attenders and church pledgers like Clyde and herself. Her stunned, indignant challenge is at once to God and to Mary Grace:

"Who do you think you are?"

Paul's affirmation of the biblical doctrine of election in Romans 9–11 does not abolish individual freedom and responsibility for our own decisions, nor does it apportion responsibility between "God's part" and "our part." Within this narrative framework of the real world, we are responsible, we can make decisions. What we cannot decide is to live in some other world, an unreal world not created by God, not in need of a savior and to which no Messiah has come, a world that perhaps goes on forever, or ends in some cosmic or human catastrophe, but not on its way to some sort of final goal. In regard to sin and condemnation, we are not merely victims. If the world posited by Christian faith is the real world, we are not free to select a world of our choosing. We human beings do have a certain kind of freedom, and are truly responsible, active in our own condemnation, not passive. But *at the same time*, we are somehow victims. Likewise, we also make crucial decisions about our salvation. But *at the same time*, we do not take the credit for being better or smarter than those who do not believe, for God chose us before we ever chose God.[26] In 10:3 Paul says with regard to Israel, which has failed to believe in Jesus the Messiah, "Since they did not know the righteousness of God and sought to establish their own, they did not submit to God's righteousness" (NIV; cf. KJV, REB, NJB, ESV, CEB versus RSV, NRSV, "the righteousness that comes from God"). This text is rightly understood as affirming human freedom, responsibility, and accountability for our decisions. It has been a category mistake, however, to use this text to contrast "Jewish self-righteousness" with "Christian trust in the grace of God." In any case, Jews, including the pre-Christian Jewish Paul, have never recognized themselves in this description. "No true Jew ever expected to obtain salvation by perfect law observance."[27] Paul is not here addressing the question, "What must I do to be acceptable to God?" as though he were claiming that Jews have failed because they tried to establish their own righteousness; he has already fully addressed that question and made it clear that God's salvation is not a reward for those who try hard (see on 3:21–4:25 above). Salvation is not a matter of rewarding either perfection or trying, neither actualized goodness nor good intentions—the difference between us and Sodom is not that they are bad and we are good, but God's choice (9:29–30). All this is beside the point, Paul argues in Romans 9–11, which addresses the anguished, existential question of the Christian readers in Rome: "Is the God who made promises to Israel and the world faithful?" It's not about me, my freedom and my decisions; it's about God.

Paul's theology here is not arbitrary or idiosyncratic but is expressed in the same pattern already revealed in the Jewish Scripture and Jewish self-understanding. Paul cites Deuteronomy 30:11–14, interweaving the Christian *kerygma* in such a way that the biblical pattern of God's gracious revelation in the law becomes transparent to God's definitive revelatory and saving act in Christ. From one point of view, this is seen as Paul's hijacking a beautiful text from Israel's Torah and claiming that it is really talking about Jesus Christ. Without denying the legitimacy of this protest, from Paul's point of view (and he believes he is speaking for all who believe that the Messiah is Jesus of Nazareth, crucified and risen), this text preserves the pattern of the saving act of the unchanging God, now ultimately represented not by God's giving the law but by God's sending his Son the Messiah. Humanity had rebelled against God and gone its own way. God could have let that be the end of the matter—"All right then, have it your way"— but instead, God's gracious, saving act responded to the human predicament by giving the Torah. Biblical and Jewish tradition rightly celebrates God's gift that revealed God's purpose and what God required of the people of God, saving them from ignorance, aimless self-centered wandering in their own darkness (Ps 119; etc.). But the law failed to resolve the problem and bring humanity back to their true status before God, not only because of human weakness but also because of the weakness of the law itself. The law entered into the world of flesh, was tested, and succumbed, becoming part of the problem (see on Rom 7 above). The problem is not only that we are weak and inadequate. The law is also weak, cannot save, cannot make us acceptable to God. "God has done what the law, weakened by the flesh, could not do: by sending his own Son in the likeness of sinful flesh, and to deal with sin, he condemned sin in the flesh, so that the just requirement of the law might be fulfilled in us, who walk not according to the flesh but according to the Spirit" (Rom 8:3–4).

Jesus entered into the world of flesh, not as a spectator from another world but as one who shared our life. He was tested. He was not overcome, but, alone among human beings, he remained faithful, lived a life of true trust and obedience to God (see above on Rom 5:12–21). We do not need to say, "Who will go to heaven and bring God's revelation down?" or "Who will descend into the abyss to bring God's revelation up?" It is already here, an event that has happened, before and apart from either our striving or nonstriving, already on our lips and in our hearts. And it is there for all, Jew and gentile (10:5–13).

It's all about God, the one God, the Creator, the God who is faithful and free. Paul appeals to his readers to let God be God (as though we had a choice). This is the hard part, that we don't get a vote on who is God, just as we didn't get to vote on whether there would be a world, whether there would be a me, whether there would be a you and a they. This God is the covenant God, who has made promises to Israel and the world. We did not get to vote on whether God would choose a particular people to be his agents and witnesses in this world. If we ask whether this is "fair," not only will God not answer the question but God will not allow the question in the first place. To pose it, to suppose that the Creator must answer the creature on the creature's own terms, is already to disavow the sovereignty that belongs to the Creator. To insist on the question is to refuse to worship God as the Creator, to suppose that Creator and creature are in some kind of given peer relation, or that God is subject to some higher authority to which appeal can be made. Such a God is no longer God; those who call God to account don't know their place (9:19–29), just as they don't know what it means to address God as *Creator*, and they lack awareness of being a *creature*. When we creatures insist on an explanation from God and are told that pots cannot call the potter to account, we naturally (*kata sarka* thinking) say, "But I'm not a pot!" True enough, but that's not the issue; the issue is, "Are you a creature, or independent of God your Creator?" This is not bullying of responsible, searching human beings by a transcendent Almighty but the word of the Creator to whom gratitude and worship are due, and who will not deny his identity in order to deal with us as less than he truly is. These are the rules of the game, and they must be. According to Paul, although God does not allow our questions on our terms, on God's own terms he declares that he has not rejected his people (11:1).

Returning to the race analogy from another direction, Paul explains that Israel has been tripped up by its own lack of faith and obedience but is not out of the race. Rather, their temporary stumbling opens the way for gentiles, who—in yet another change of metaphors—will be grafted into olive-tree-Israel in a way that both preserves God's faithfulness to the covenant people and includes *all* people in the *chosen* people (11:13–27). Israel will recover and cross the finish line. The victory celebration will include not only Jews and gentiles but also the resurrected dead and the whole creation. "The gifts and the calling of God are irrevocable. . . . God has imprisoned all in disobedience so that he may be merciful to all" (11:29, 32, another shift of imagery, destabilizing our lust for theological neatness). Paul emphatically denies that anyone could have figured this out—it is the revelation of God's mystery (1:25).

> "The imperative is around four verbs, 'seek, call, forsake, return,' good Lenten verbs. But this is not about generic repentance for generic sin. I believe, rather, the sin addressed concerns for Jews too eager to become Babylonians, too easy to compromise Jewish identity, Jewish faith, Jewish discipline—in order to get along in a Babylonian empire that had faith in other gods with other disciplines. The imperatives are summons to come back to an original identity, an elemental discipline, a primal faith.
>
> "I suggest, moreover, that these are just about the right imperatives for Lent among us Christians. For I believe the crisis in the U.S. church has almost nothing to do with being liberal or conservative; it has everything to do with giving up on the faith and discipline of our Christian baptism and settling for a common, generic U.S. identity that is part patriotism, part consumerism, part violence, and part affluence."
>
> —Walter Brueggemann, *A Way Other Than Our Own: Devotions for Lent*,
> Ash Wednesday (Louisville: Westminster John Knox, 2017), 2

This is confessional language, affirmed by grateful insiders, not objectifying language about outsiders. Even when disclosed, the revelatory language of the community's faith is beyond conceptual understanding and can only be apprehended in worship. Paul continues to think within the thought world of his Bible.

> For my thoughts are not your thoughts,
>   nor are your ways my ways, says the LORD.
> For as the heavens are higher than the earth,
>   so are my ways higher than your ways
>   and my thoughts than your thoughts. (Isa 55:8–9)

This was not an abstract issue of ivory-tower theological thinking. "Thoughts" and "ways" are inseparable. The divine indicative calls for human response:

> Let the wicked forsake their way,
>   and the unrighteous their thoughts;
> let them return to the LORD, that he may have mercy on them,
>   and to our God, for he will abundantly pardon. (Isa 55:7)

Before beginning his challenge to live a life based on the faith he has explicated, Paul echoes the words of the prophet:

O the depth of the riches and wisdom and knowledge of God! How unsearchable are his judgments and how inscrutable his ways!
"For who has known the mind of the Lord?
    Or who has been his counselor?"
"Or who has given a gift to him,
    to receive a gift in return?"
For from him and through him and to him are all things. To him be the glory forever. Amen. (Rom 11:33–36)

Ethics: The Saved Life in Action (Romans 12:1–15:13)

The "therefore" of 12:1 moves Paul's discourse from theology to ethics, from thought to action. This is a turn in Paul's thought, from the "what" of Christian faith and theology to the "so what" of Christian life.[28] But the two parts are two aspects of one inseparable reality. Paul could never have thought to himself as he began 12:1, "So much for theology, now, on to practical application." There is no theology without ethical implications, no ethics without a theological foundation.

Christian Ethics and the Transformed Mind

Paul communicates his call to the Christian life by his appeal for his readers to put into practice the transformation and renewal of their minds they received by being incorporated into God's new reality. This is not a new moralism but the acknowledgment and putting into practice of their new situation. They have reoriented themselves, recalibrated their perception of reality, radically revalued their understanding of what's important and what's not. This change of mind is more than adjusting their previous opinions in the light of new information. It corresponds to what Jesus and the prophets called "repentance" (*metanoia*), a matter of mind-set, where one's mind is "set." The believer has not merely added some new information or insights to the old mind-set but has a new "default setting" for the mind. Paul designates and characterizes the kind of life they are to live as their *logikē latreia* (traditionally "reasonable service" [KJV]; cf. "spiritual worship" [RSV, NRSV, NAB, ESV], "true and proper worship" [NIV]; perhaps best by CEB, "your appropriate priestly service"). Paul clearly does *not* mean that the Christian life is a matter of common sense, just what reasonable people do. The service is the priestly service of those who offer sacrifice—not animals, not even money, but themselves, their whole, everyday lives ("your bodies" means "your *selves*"). The only "common sense" involved is the sense that those who belong to the body of Christ have in common, which does not take its signals from the surrounding culture but is transformed by the constant renewal of its mind (12:1–2 as in Rom 8:1–5; cf. Jesus in Mark 8:33 par), living in tension with the surrounding culture—not a thermometer that merely registers the status quo but a thermostat that changes the way things are. Such a renewed mind, participating in the whole body of Christ, cannot read the will of God from the surface of the biblical text, from the prevailing cultural wind, or from internal prejudices and nudges of conscience, but must *discern* God's will from case to case, situation to situation. This is what Paul sees himself doing, as he thinks through Christian responsibility in contemporary situations foreseen neither in Scripture nor in the teaching of Jesus.[29] Paul's ethic is not an ethic of command but an ethic of insight.

Yahweh the Bear

A vacationer, picnicking in the Great Smoky Mountains National Park, paid no attention to the Do Not Feed the Bears signs. He tossed an apple to the large, friendly-looking bear that wandered through the picnic area. The bear gobbled it down and looked up expectantly. The vacationer tossed it his unfinished sandwich, which likewise quickly disappeared. The bear's expression said, "More!" The picnicker scrambled, found some cookies and a candy bar, and tossed them to the hungry bear one by one until they were gone. "More," said the bear's growl.

The vacationer began to understand the rationale behind the signs: bears don't understand when you're out of cookies.

With increasing panic, he called to a park ranger, who had been silently watching the whole episode. "I've given him everything in my basket! What does he want?"

"He wants you."

—Hosea 13:8

Through the generations, a number of theologians have pointed out that such discernment is analogous to the kind of improvising done by skilled actors and musicians, who improvise not because they are not prepared but because they are. Christian believers know that their little lives unfold their brief span within the framework of a grand narrative that stretches from creation to consummation. Believers know that they live in God's creation, a fallen and rebellious creation in which the Creator has called Israel to be his people, has sent the Messiah, has called the church into being in continuity with Israel. The first acts of this drama have happened and are mediated by the church's Scripture and tradition, to which the church is delivered (Rom 6:17), but the details of believers' present lives are not scripted. There are no prewritten lines for us to recite, no moves already programmed that we may passively enact. The church is called to improvise, and can do so, for in Scripture and tradition it is provided with the scripts and musical scores of the preceding acts and has internalized their stories, and their music resonates in their collective soul. To improvise is not to play out of tune or to go one's own way with no concern with what and how others have played and are playing. Christian believers do not play solo performances but make beautiful music together.

The Ecclesial Ethics of the People of God

As one body "in Christ," believers are so closely bound to each other that they can be called "members of one another." Christian ethics are personal, involving one's personal life, things one must do and not do, and Paul provides reminders and instructions on such duties. These include conventional morality that rejects not only criminal acts ("You shall not murder; You shall not steal," 13:9) but also the maxims of conventional civil behavior ("extend hospitality to strangers," "do not be haughty," "so far as it depends on you, live peaceably with all," 12:13, 16, 18). Reveling and drunkenness, debauchery and licentiousness, cannot characterize the lives of those who confess Jesus as Lord (13:13). Such marks of human decency are not to be trivialized, but they belong within the larger framework of the ecclesial ethics of the people of God. Though Christian ethics are personal, they are not private or individual. For believers, the framework for all ethical behavior is the reality of their new life "in Christ" (see on 5:12–21 above).

While later New Testament authors adopt and adapt variations of Paul's conceptuality of the believer's participation "in Christ," explicit *sōma Christou* (body of Christ) language for the church is found only in the Pauline tradition (Rom 12:5; 1 Cor 6:15; 10:16; 12:12, 27; Eph 4:12). Paul himself uses the image only in 1 Corinthians and Romans, with a different focus in each case. In 1 Corinthians he addresses Corinthian enthusiasm for charismatic phenomena by projecting the image of the church as Christ's body animated by Christ's breath/Spirit, in which every member participates. As a human

The Maypole

Several cultures have traditionally celebrated the budding new life of springtime with the maypole dance. A tall pole stands in the middle of a circle, festooned with long multicolored ribbons attached to the top of the pole. Each dancer holds a ribbon; each ribbon goes directly to the top. Church folk are tempted to see this as an image of Christian spirituality—each one must hold tight to one's own ribbon, and each goes directly to God. But in the festive dance, the music begins, the girls begin to circle the pole, and as they dance they weave in and out. At the end of the dance, each one is still holding her own ribbon, and each still binds the dancer to the top of the pole, but now only as they are interwoven with all the other ribbons. The result is beautiful. The music and dancing resonate with the music and celebration of Christian worship.

organization participating in the life of this world, the church develops appropriate structures to facilitate its mission. The church, however, is not primarily an organization but an organism, a living body. To be a "church member" is to be part of Christ's body (not merely a name on a list; think "membrane," "dismember"), and one must live appropriately (1 Cor 6:15!). Paul's later address to the Romans does not merely repeat this, as though it were a stock image, but reminds and instructs them that they are members *of each other*, that they are "in Christ," but not as separate individuals. They are not only incorporated into the body of *Christ*; they are one body of Christian believers.

In terms of ethics, this throws an important new light on the role of conscience in authentic ethical living. Believers cannot violate their own conscience. They cannot willfully engage in acts they believe to be wrong, that is, acts contrary to their understanding of the will of God (Rom 9:1; 13:5; 14:5–7, 14, 22–23). It is in this context that Paul presents his most radical understanding of sin: whoever does something he or she is convinced is wrong, that is, contrary to God's will, has committed sin, whether the act was "actually" wrong or not, for "whatever does not proceed from faith is sin" (14:23). "Faith" (*pistis*) here does not refer to the content of one's creed but to faithfulness, the life of trust and obedience to God. Though one's conscience is sacred and cannot be violated, Paul does not present the individual conscience as the guide to the content of the kind of life Christians are called to live. "Conscience is . . . a relational concept: it does not itself set norms but judges conformity to them."[30] To do something one believes to be wrong *is* wrong, always wrong, because such an act violates one's trust in God. What

I believe to be wrong is indeed wrong for me, because it drives a wedge between me and the one I confess as Lord. Even if I do something good and right but believe it to be wrong, I have sinned not only against conscience but also against God. I can also do something evil with no qualms of conscience, as Paul, the former zealous persecutor of the church, knew right well. Thus for the believer, the authentic ethical life is not a solitary compact between the individual and God but must be worked out in the communal life of the church. For Paul, "I just let my conscience be my guide" cannot validate the *content* of the Christian ethic, cannot legitimate particular acts as right or wrong, even "for me."

The Christian Ethic Embodies and Makes Real the Love of God

The Christian life is not only a matter of personal "being good." Nor is the responsible ethical life of the Christian community merely the application and enactment of reasonable humanitarian moral principles such as "tolerance," which too easily fades into indifference. The community of Christian faith, the body of believers "in Christ," is the expression of the new life generated and guided by the Spirit, "because God's love has been poured into our hearts through the Holy Spirit that has been given to us"—*God's* love, *our* hearts (5:5). Here we only point out three specifics of Paul's exposition of the love command in Romans, as illustrations of how his instructions to the Roman church of the first century can still speak powerfully to believers in a much later time and very different situation: (1) Love is the fulfillment of the law. (2) Love leads to radically new conduct within the Christian community. (3) Love leads the church beyond itself, to practice an ecclesial ethic in engagement with the world.

Love Is the Fulfillment of the Law (13:8–10)

Paul is not giving abstract explanations of the nature of either love or the law but writing a letter to believers in a specific situation. It is not our situation. In the Roman church, which had a deep awareness of its roots in Jewish Scripture and tradition, the whole question of biblical law still hovered in the background, along with their suspicion that Paul's version of the gospel set aside God's law. They listened, with more or less patience, understanding, and agreement, to Paul's exposition of his gospel, then asked, "What about the law?" (see above on Rom 7). In this form, the question hardly appears on the agenda of most contemporary Christians. But we are still plagued by the question of how God's love and God's law are related. How is loving concern for the welfare of other people related to "going by the book," whether "book" be the Bible, ecclesiastical canon law, the penal code, or the Constitution. Paul deals only with the aspect of the issue that concerns biblical law, though this has implications for the relation of law and love as such.

Paul's response is clear and confident. Christian life guided and empowered by the love of God does not set aside God's law but fulfills it. *All* the commandments of the law "are summed up in this word, 'Love your neighbor as yourself.' Love does no wrong to a neighbor; therefore, love is the fulfilling of the law" (13:9–10). This is not a definition of Christian love, the positive, proactive concern for the welfare of others, which cannot be reduced to not hurting people. Elsewhere, Paul details the nature of such Christian caring (e.g., 1 Cor 13, where love is the supreme gift of the Spirit). But the subject here is not love but law, and the question is, Does Paul's gospel set aside God's law? His answer: No.

What about Circumcision?

The absence of circumcision in this discussion is striking. Circumcision of gentiles as a condition for membership in the people of God was a key issue in Paul's sharp debate with the Galatians, but the issue there was different: not whether Jews should abandon circumcision but whether gentile Christians must be circumcised in order to be acceptable to God and be welcomed into the covenant people. Paul had dealt with this issue earlier in Romans, more moderately than in his harsh diatribe against the Galatian false teachers (Rom 2:25–3:1; 3:30; 4:9–12; cf. his concluding words of this section, 15:8–13). In Romans 14–15 Paul deals with practical issues currently dividing the Roman church; mandatory circumcision of gentile converts was clearly not one of them. Had that been the case, there can be no doubt of how Paul would have responded.

Love Leads to Radically New Conduct within the Christian Community

How can "liberals" and "conservatives" live together in one church (14:1–15:13)? Paul gives here one extensive illustration of how love acts in concrete situations. Again, he may at first surprise and disappoint us, for he addresses a problem that is not our problem. Its radical challenge to modern readers only emerges when we come within hearing distance of the text in its original situation, which may be briefly described as follows. The problem focused on dietary and calendar rules—for Christians who take seriously what their Bible says, what can be eaten and drunk, what special holy days are to be observed. Specifically, can Christians eat meat that may be ritually unclean, drink wine that may lead to drunkenness, ignore holy days prescribed in the Bible and hallowed by tradition (14:2, 5, 21)? These were pressing issues for Roman believers who had grown up in the synagogue and still valued the kosher kitchen and Sabbath observance, as well as for new gentile converts who took seriously the commands they found in the Scripture that was now their own Bible and wanted to live faithfully by doing "what the Bible says." They were pressing for gentiles too, who, when converted, had kept valued elements of their previous religious life concerned with diet and calendar and continued to observe them. Being faithful to God's law was being interpreted in two contrasting ways, equally serious and sincere. The issues that threatened to divide the two groups are not the items that plague the unity and mission of most congregations we know, but Paul's response—*his most extensive instruction on a specific ethical issue in Romans*—overflows with educational guidelines for congregations that (rightfully!) include, or want to include, committed Christian believers from across the broad liberal-conservative spectrum. Can liberals and conservatives live together in one church? Paul's response has five facets.

First, "Welcome one another, therefore, just as Christ has welcomed you, for the glory of God." We begin with Paul's bottom line (15:7). Each group is to welcome the other, for God has called both. As throughout Romans, the imperative is based on the indicative, practice is based on theology, and the theology is theocentric. It's not about us but about God, the glory of God that radiates from Christ's welcome of all peoples into the one church of God. "Welcome one another" is a gracious act of love. Not "tolerance." Certainly not merely "putting up with" them. The condescending translation of the NRSV and NAB at 15:1, "put up with the failings of the weak," is unfortunate. The verb *bastazein*, literally "bear, carry," does not here even mean "bear with" (NIV), which is better. The word is used for Jesus as the Servant of the Lord who bears our sickness (Matt 8:17), for a mother who bears/carries a child (Luke 11:27), for Jesus's bearing the cross (John 19:17), for followers of Jesus called to share his mission by bearing his cross (Luke 14:27), and by Paul himself in Galatians 6:2, "Bear one another's burdens, and in this way you will fulfill the law of Christ."

Second, "Let all be fully convinced in their own minds" (Rom 14:5). No one is to be bullied into conformity by peer pressure, subtle or overt. To influence people to act against their own conscience is to lead them into sin against God (see above). The problem here for the conservative is to respect the conscience of the liberal, to avoid insisting liberals go by rules they don't believe in; the problem for the liberal is to respect the conscience of the conservative, to avoid pressuring conservatives into violating rules they *do* believe in. But how can this be, in actual practice, in one congregation? It never occurs to Paul to "solve" the problem by suggesting, "Easy. Just form two congregations, one for liberals, one for conservatives." While this would allow everyone to be comfortable, for Paul such a "solution" would violate the very nature of the church. His instruction zeroes in on the particular inclination of each group.

Third, "Those who abstain must not pass judgment on those who eat" (14:3). Judgment is in fact very important for Paul; indeed, it is axiomatic, not only for Paul but also for Jesus and New Testament theology in general. Paul is not about to say, "Don't get worked up about it; these things don't matter anyway." They matter. It's not about just having a "nonjudgmental attitude," which can be only half a step from indifference. To love is to care; not-to-care is to abandon love of the neighbor and violate the fundamental law. Judgment is important, but God is the Judge. The loving, good-willed conservative is inclined to say, "I just don't see how someone who goes against the plain teaching of Scripture can be acceptable to God." Paul's response: "You don't have to see this. That person has been accepted by God, welcomed by God into the covenant community. You don't have to change your own convictions or practice, but the liberals in the congregation belong to God as God's slaves (see on Rom 6:12–23 above). It is before their own Master that they stand or fall, and God can make them stand. *You* don't have to be able to explain how" (see 14:4).

Fourth, "Those who eat must not despise those who abstain" (14:3). "Despise," of course, does not mean "hate." Liberals, who love and accept everybody (except, sometimes, conservatives), are not tempted to hate, and hatred is not what Paul forbids. The word *exouthenoō* here means "disdain"—its primary meaning in the standard Greek lexicon. *This* is the liberal's temptation, to assume the superior, enlightened stance of one who has been liberated from tradition, society's conventions, the scruples of the unenlightened. It is not clear that Paul himself has altogether avoided this temptation. He does not use the liberal/conservative terminology but labels the liberal group "the strong," the conservative group "the weak." In his defense, however, he may have been adopting the labels he knew were current in the Roman debate, where *each* group considered itself "strong" and its opponents "weak." Conservatives considered their rigid adherence to the rules strong and thought of their opponents as compromising, watering down, not willing to do what it takes to "go by the Bible." Liberals considered *their* understanding of Christian freedom strong, and they thought of being bound by tradition and convention as submitting to weakness. Paul makes it clear that he takes his stand with the liberals—"we who are strong" (15:1)—he does not try to be the noncommittal and neutral counselor who is merely trying to help people work out problems *they* find important or looking for a pragmatic "win-win" solution. He models the loving care to which he calls the liberal group, embracing the conservatives as fellow members in the one church of God, respecting their convictions and theology without agreeing with it.

Fifth, the burden is in fact on the liberal. Even though Paul agrees, in theology and practice, with the strong, both factions are urged, "Let us then pursue what makes for peace and for mutual upbuilding" (14:19). This means taking the conscience of the *other* person seriously. "I know and am persuaded in the Lord Jesus that nothing is unclean in itself; but it is unclean for anyone who thinks it unclean. If your brother or sister is being injured by what you eat, you are no longer walking in love. Do not let what you eat cause the ruin of one for whom Christ died" (14:14–15). We are not talking about trivialities here (as the liberal is tempted to think); this is serious business. It must be noted that Paul is *not* necessarily instructing the liberals to refrain from practices the conservatives find bothersome. This would mean that the practice of the whole congregation would always be bound by the tender conscience of its strictest conservatives, which can become a kind of smug tyranny. Altering one's practice on eating, drinking, or holy days because it is bothersome to the conservatives is not the kind of sacrifice to which Paul is calling the liberals. "Offending" brothers or sisters is not a matter of irritation. "Offending" means "cause to stumble," that is, by subtle pressure leading *them* to do something *they* think is sinful. This is what the liberals must by all means avoid, and it may sometimes mean refraining from exercising their own freedom about eating, drinking, and observing special holy days if their more liberal practice leads the more conservative brothers or sisters to violate their conscience. The burden (in the sense discussed above) is indeed on the liberal; it is the "burden" of loving care for the other, not the insistence on one's own rights. It is to be done without condescension. It is an acknowledgment that liberals have a kind of freedom that conservatives do not have; they are free to give up their legitimate "rights" in the service of the church's mission. They are not *bound* to always assert their convictions but are truly free, free enough not to worry about their liberal image, even if it might sometimes mean being taken as more conservative than they actually are.

Outwitted

He drew a circle that shut me out—
Heretic, rebel, a thing to flout.
But love and I had the wit to win:
We drew a circle and took him In!

—Edwin Markham, 1852–1940

This is a radical challenge for both liberals and conservatives, then and now. Paul's lengthy instruction is not about what one eats and drinks or what one does or does not do on days that some consider holy. The radical thing about it all is the idea that anyone should suppose that these are not just each individual's personal business, that belonging to the church means such decisions should be made in the light of how they affect the church and its mission. Each must decide for himself or herself, but not by himself or herself. "We do not live to ourselves, and we do not die to ourselves. . . . We are the Lord's" (14:7–8). Learning to think of their "private life" in this way is a radical decision for both conservatives and liberals; it recalibrates their place in the people of God, who have a mission to the world.

Love Leads the Church beyond Itself,
to Practice an Ecclesial Ethic in Engagement with the World

Christian love, like God's love of which the church is a channel, extends to the whole world. To respond to God's call to belong to the church means to find oneself part of a loving community where members care for and serve each other, *belonging* in the deepest sense. Not only in regard to liberal-conservative issues but in all the nitty-gritty of life, Christians are called to "love one another" (12:10). But just as love is not only a vertical relationship, directed upward to God ("Love God with all your heart"), but a horizontal dynamic directed outward to others ("Love your neighbor as yourself"), this outward dynamic is not restricted to the insiders of the Christian community. Love for the neighbor that fulfills the law extends to all (13:8–10). Even the insider love-one-another has in view the outsider: "Take thought for what is noble in the sight of all" (12:17). Although the familial love of brothers and sisters in the church is directed to *them*, not looking past them as a tactic to entice others into such a fellowship, it nonetheless has an inherent evangelistic, missionary dimension. "Overcome evil with good" (12:21) is neither an inspirational motto nor a strategy, but the christological redefinition of winning, practiced for the benefit of others, insiders and outsiders, by those who believe in the crucified and risen Man for Others.

Most of the maxims in 12:9–21 apply to human relationships in general, not only to fellow church members. As in the teaching of Jesus, even enemies are to be loved, and that actively, their needs provided for (12:20). The love of God the Creator embraces all people and the whole world, but it does not run on two separate tracks, one to the church and the other to the world. Though the church is by no means the only channel of God's love to the world, God's love for the church flows through the church into the world. When God calls Christians to be instruments of this love, this is not merely my individual responsibility as a believer, as though I might go to church, love and help out there, and *also* do some good things for needy people in the community and even in other countries. Christian service to the world is neither general humanitarianism nor an individualistic end run around the church, but integral to what it means to say, "I belong to the church." The church has a mission to the world: in word and deed to share the gospel of what God has done in Christ for the whole world.

Christian love determines the believer's stance with regard to the state (13:1–7). Paul's explications of Christian ethics are all specific, elements of a letter addressed to concrete issues in the church of Rome circa 57 CE. This paragraph is no exception. It is not an essay on "Christian civic responsibility" or "How to come to terms with an imperialistic government" but addresses the Christian gospel to a particular problem. Again, it is not our problem, for we live in a different situation. And again, if we come within hearing distance of what the text wants to say, we may find it has something to say to us, and through us, to the world.

First, it is important to remind ourselves of the cultural situation. Paul, his Roman readers, and New Testament authors in general took the system of imperial government for granted. Within this general context, a particular development in first-century Rome is important for understanding Paul's letter as a whole and Romans 13 in particular: in 49 CE, eight years before

Paul writes, the emperor Claudius expelled all Jews from Rome. This was not merely anti-Semitism, evil enough in itself, but they were removed "for constant rioting at the instigation of Chrestus," probably a garbled reference to disturbances among the Roman synagogues resulting from Christian preaching (Suetonius, *Claudius* 25.4). At that date, Roman officials did not distinguish Christians as a separate group within Judaism but categorized them as a particular kind of Jews. Jewish Christians such as Aquila and Priscilla had to leave Rome not because they were Christians but because they were Jews (Acts 18:2). The gentile element in the new Christian community in Rome remained; the remnant of the Roman church that had originated in a Jewish context and had retained strong Jewish traditions had suddenly become virtually a gentile church. At Claudius's death in 54, only two or three years before Paul's letter, the decree was rescinded, and many Jews, including Jewish Christians, returned to Rome and were more or less reintegrated into the church they had been forced to leave. Such a church was wary of any behavior that would call the government's attention to them again. Diaspora synagogues, including those that had Jewish Christians among them, had worked and suffered long to attain a level of acceptance by the Romans. They were likely leery of Paul's own track record of disruption and needed reassurance that his arrival in Rome would not create new problems for them with the authorities. Romans 13 is spoken into *this* situation.

At the opposite end of the political spectrum, there may have been church members who understood the present-and-coming kingdom of God as a political alternative to Roman imperial rule, shortly to be replaced by the returning Christ, and who were hesitant to pay taxes or engage in other activities indicating submission to Roman rule. What was to become the Zealot movement in Palestine that eventuated in the rebellion of 66–70 was already simmering, and was to result in the destruction of Jerusalem, the devastation of Judea, and the restructure of Judaism. In his letter, Paul not only wants to firm up the Roman Christians' understanding of the Christian faith but he also wants to counsel them in how better to understand their faith and how to live it out in the capital of the empire, to help them avoid further devastating and unproductive conflicts with the authorities, and to assuage suspicions that, when he arrived, he would provoke further government attacks on the church. We thus have neither an abstract essay on "the Christian understanding of church-state relations" nor a compromising capitulation to the imperial rule good Christians should resist, but clear instructions for responsible Christian conduct in the present situation. The instruction could be elaborated and nuanced when Paul arrives personally, on the analogy of 1 Corinthians 11:34. This is the nature of *letters*; it reminds us that all the New Testament documents reflect concreteness of the incarnation rather than abstract general principles.

Specifically, Paul tells them the following:

1. Christians are to obey the civil authorities, for God is the ultimate authority. Their choice was Roman government or anarchy, and Christians cannot be anarchists. Paul does not instruct the followers of Jesus to withdraw from the political scene into an interior spirituality of the heart or of the church, nor does he give divine legitimation to any particular government or form of government. Faith in the one God, the Creator, not only sets believers free to participate in relative and temporary human governments, but it compels them to do so, for the world—not only the church—belongs to God.

2. Do what is good and right, and you need not fear the government, for government has been established by God. Thus, responsible obedience to civil law is not merely pragmatism and fear of punishment but a matter of conscience and obedience to God.

3. Christians are to pay taxes like everyone else. Romans were generally tolerant of all sorts of religious and ethnic customs, so long as people paid taxes and were not disruptive of public order. Paul instructs Christians to be compliant on both counts, not only for pragmatic reasons but also on the basis of faith and conscience.

Like John the prophet of Revelation (who indeed had a different perspective on Roman rule—and who likewise wrote a *letter*), Paul is not propounding a theory of government but offering pastoral instruction for believers in a particular situation. We do not know what he would have said in other situations in which he might have perceived that the believer's choice was to obey God or yield to the pressures of a human government, or if he had not believed in the near parousia.

While Paul is not explicitly teaching theology in Romans 13:1–7, his instruction is founded on and in line with the teaching of the great biblical prophets. A comparison with Deutero-Isaiah reveals the following: First, God the Creator is sovereign over all the nations, even if they do not know him as the one true God. A monotheistic faith carries with it the conviction that "there is no authority except from God" (13:1). Second, this is the message of Paul's Bible, especially of prophets such as Deutero-Isaiah who saw their own time as the dawning of the fulfillment of God's eschatological purpose. The later prophets, who thought in the apocalyptic categories that had emerged in response to oppressive governments, were more specific—the kings and emperors who seem to govern the world are actually tools in the hands of God, who has appointed them. Paul thinks within the apocalyptic stream of such prophets, whose apocalypticism addressed oppressed peoples, assuring them that the powers that seemed to dominate the world were not out of control but were subject to the ultimate power of God, tools in the hand of the Almighty. Paul shares this apocalyptic worldview but does not explicate its details in the manner of Daniel or Revelation. Third, in this very context, Paul indicates that his instructions are for Christian believers who live in the waning darkness of the old age and the dawn of the new. Like the apocalyptic thinkers of his Bible, he does not see himself writing a theology of the state for all time to come but pastoral encouragement to Christian believers called to work and witness within an empire that is soon to yield to the kingdom of God that is already dawning (13:11–14). Paul does not specifically appeal to the brief interim before the end as an argument for his instructions on how believers should live in the (last) empire, but his eschatology hovers in the background of all his thought. This is inherent in the theology of anyone whose basic conviction is that the Messiah has come and the new world is already dawning.

The Church in Auschwitz

In 1994, en route to a meeting of biblical scholars in Prague, I and two friends and colleagues visited Auschwitz. As we stood on the platform where victims were unloaded from the boxcars and the selection was made, we asked,
  "How could this happen?"
  On a quiet street in the town, not too far outside the walls, we could clearly see a church tower.

Through the centuries, Romans 13:1–7 has been understood in many different ways (see the commentaries and books and essays on "church and state"). It has been cited to support the divine right of kings and to discourage revolution and civil disobedience. In modern times this text has become an embarrassment to some streams of liberation theology, who sometimes condemn Paul for encouraging collaboration with the evil empire. A few have considered this text a post-Pauline interpolation and eliminated it from consideration. We will not here attempt any generalizing hermeneutic—Christian preachers and teachers must attempt to hear the text as it addressed its original situation, translating and conveying its claim on other, later situations. But this cannot mean that whatever totalitarian "powers that be" have been established by God must always be obeyed, that people of Christian faith must always stand idly by and submit to, or even justify, government-sponsored terrorism or atrocities such as the Holocaust. However Romans 13 is understood, it must be read within its contexts, ancient, canonical, and modern—the contemporary reader's own context as well as the ancient historical and canonical contexts. "In New Testament times political responsibility was only a live option for the Christian in rare and exceptional cases and in areas of subordinate jurisdiction. If Paul limits his scope to the requirement of obedience, this corresponds with reality [i.e., the reality of his situation]; there was normally no other means of political expression for the stratum of society out of which early Christianity arose. For this reason it is impossible simply to transpose our passage into our modern situation."[31] These words, written in 1956 by a leading German exegete who had served some years as a pastor, Ernst Käsemann, are one of the most influential and helpful treatments of this text, honestly engaging both the original context of Paul's mission and the contemporary mission of the church. Käsemann was a member of the Confessing Church that resisted Hitler, was a pastor in the mining town of Gelsenkirchen, was arrested and briefly jailed by the Gestapo, and then was drafted into the German army. He was captured and spent time as a POW. Upon his release, he resumed his New Testament scholarship at Göttingen and Tübingen. His daughter, Elisabeth Käsemann, was abducted by security forces in Argentina during a military dictatorship and disappeared, apparently murdered, in 1977. His New Testament work is not only carefully historical but also hermeneutical, theological, and personal. He has a right to be heard on this text.

The common denominator of Paul's "then" and our "now" is thus that Christians, God's redeemed slaves (see Rom 6:12–23 above), are called to obedience to their one true Master. "With regard to the secular government, it is not the right to resist but the duty to obey that is the task of Christian worship in the everydayness of the world."[32] This text calls us to see our everyday life of involvement in the world as the expression of the love and justice of God, of a piece with Christian worship in the secularity of the world. The world, not only the sanctuary, is the place we are called to serve God. "Christian obedience [to government and cultural powers] comes to an end where further service becomes impossible—and only there."[33]

It is striking that this profound, mind-wrenching theology, this exposition of, and call to, a radically transformed life, concludes with an almost chatty list of personal greetings. Twenty-six individuals are named, along with several others Paul has met here and there in his missionary travels, who now live in Rome (16:1–16). This list was once seen as evidence that chapter 16 was not originally written to the Roman church, which Paul had not yet visited, but was a fragment of a letter to another church, probably Ephesus. This theory, always without extant manuscript evidence, is now generally abandoned. The complex, profound theology of this letter is for "ordinary" people, that extraordinary company of believers who are incorporated into the community of Christian faith that extends through the centuries and around the world.

Chapter 4

The Emerging Church: On the Road
to the One Holy Catholic Apostolic Church

When Paul was martyred in Rome circa 64 CE, he left behind a number of congregations he had founded and influenced in what is now Greece and Turkey, congregations that had looked to him for leadership. Some developments within churches in the Pauline tradition after Paul's death have sometimes been regarded by modern interpreters as a step backward, a decline from the dedicated "eschatological existence" of the original followers of Jesus to the "early catholicism" of the "institutional church."[1] Much recent New Testament scholarship now regards this approach as overdone and one-sided. While there are significant differences between Paul's theology and that of his followers, it is now seen more clearly that the "institutionalization" of postapostolic Christianity was a development rooted in Paul's own theology and practice.[2]

Pauline Churches, Pauline School

After Paul's death, the core of colleagues and teachers he had trained, the women and men who had been partners with him in founding and instructing the new churches, continued his teaching, adapting it to new situations within the Pauline congregations of Roman Asia. This *Pauline school* served as an informal network of teachers within the churches in the Pauline community of congregations, analogous to the *Johannine school*. In the generations after Paul, teachers who claimed Paul as their leader produced an abundance of literature intended to represent the message of Paul in their later situation, including not only the deutero-Pauline letters included in the canon but also such texts as the Letter to the Laodiceans, the Acts of Paul and Thecla, and the Apocalypse of Paul.[3]

Paul's understanding of the church embraced unity in variety. While not every kind of theology could be included, as evidenced by his strug-

PAULINE CONGREGATIONS: We are here concerned with the churches founded in Roman Asia by Paul and his coworkers in the 50s of the first century CE and their successors in the Pauline tradition through circa 130 CE.

PAULINE SCHOOL: An informal network of teachers in the Pauline tradition, presumably centered in Ephesus.

PAULINE CORPUS: The seven undisputed letters of Paul written in the 50s, in the order 1 Thessalonians, Philippians, Philemon, 1 Corinthians, Galatians, 2 Corinthians, Romans, collected and circulated by the Pauline school near the end of the first century CE. These were augmented by letters written by teachers in the Pauline school:

> Colossians, circa 70–80 CE
> Ephesians, circa 90 CE
> 2 Thessalonians, circa 90–100 CE
> Pastorals (1–2 Timothy, Titus), circa 100–125 CE

ADDRESSEES: The network of churches in the stream of tradition associated with Paul, in the province of Asia.

PROVENANCE: A central location of the Pauline stream of tradition in Asia, most probably Ephesus.

LITERARY SOURCES: Each of the deutero-Pauline letters shows an awareness of at least some of the previous letters in the Pauline tradition. Colossians is heavily dependent on Philemon. Ephesians knows and uses the whole Pauline corpus, especially Colossians, which is used as a template. Second Thessalonians is heavily dependent on 1 Thessalonians, using it as a template. The Pastorals know previous Pauline writings well but manifest minimal explicit dependence. For evidence and argument for the above conclusions here presupposed, and alternative views, see the bibliography at the end of this volume.

gles with false teachers in Galatia and Corinth (e.g., Gal 1–3; 2 Cor 10–13), the one church united under the lordship of Christ could include a variety of types of leaders and theologies (1 Cor 1–3, esp. 3:21–23). Paul's interpreters, including those found in the canonical New Testament, were not of one mind as to how Paul's understanding of the faith should be communicated to later generations. Unlike the teachers in the Johannine school, the Pauline school never adopted the gospel genre that would have allowed them to present the Christian faith by retelling the story of

Jesus's life and teachings. We shall here make exploratory soundings in two representatives of deutero-Pauline Christianity that offer differing, somewhat conflicting, and yet complementary views: Ephesians and the Pastorals.

Ephesians: The Church at Its Best, En Route to Become the Universe

We remind ourselves again that the New Testament documents were not composed for silent reading by individuals but were written for reading aloud in the community's worship and instruction. This is especially evident in Ephesians, which is filled with liturgical materials and resonates throughout with thanksgiving and praise. In Ephesians, theology is to be sung and prayed; it is more a matter of praise than conceptual analysis, more to be pondered upon than thought through. To grasp and be grasped by the reality to which such language points, one must enter this circle of prayer and praise. The message any biblical document conveys happens through direct engagement with the text itself, as a whole, not by spotty references to commentators or summary analyses such as are presented here. Such resources are intended to facilitate entering the circle within which the voice of the text itself can be heard.

"Theology Is Prayer"

When Karl Barth declared, "The first and basic act of theological work is prayer," he meant not only that our theological ponderings are made in a prayerful attitude but that they are made before God—whether made in our private study or explained in a sermon or lesson in the congregation or Bible study group. Theological reflection, preaching, and teaching are all in the personal I-Thou mode addressed to God, not the impersonal I-it mode in which God is talked about as an object. See Karl Barth, *Evangelical Theology: An Introduction*, trans. Grover Foley (New York: Holt, Rinehart & Winston, 1963), 160.

Our procedure for enhancing our ability to study the theology of Ephesians will be two-pronged. First, we will explore diachronically the narrative world projected by Ephesians. We will then venture a brief synchronic synthesis of Ephesians' interwoven theology of God/Christ/church.

The Grand Narrative of Ephesians

Biblical theology is narrative theology. The early followers of Jesus who became Christian evangelists/missionaries/preachers/teachers did not invite their hearers to "join them in a spiritual quest," expound "the enduring ideals of Jesus," or offer *good advice*, but presented their testimony to be *good news* of the saving act of God in Jesus Christ. New Testament authors expressed this faith not in systematic essays but by telling stories, with all the little stories incorporated in the big story. Ephesians is exhibit A in this regard; it not only intuitively adopts the narrative mode of theological expression but also explicitly calls attention to the grand narrative of God's saving acts (e.g., 1:8–10).

In the last thirty years or so, several New Testament theologians have drawn our attention back to the essentially narrative mode of biblical theology.[4] I commend this approach to all as a helpful way of getting one's mind around a biblical text. Here I can offer only a streamlined summary of the approach and its results when applied to Ephesians:

- Real letters assume a narrative world shared by author and readers and refer to events, mostly incidentally, in the past, present, and future.
- Perceiving the narrative world of a letter means focusing on a particular text, not on the author's worldview, some of which can be known from other information outside the text. Thus a New Testament author such as Paul or the author of Ephesians may have a particular event in his own worldview but may write several texts that make no reference to it (an example is the Last Supper in 1 Corinthians, which is not specifically mentioned in any of Paul's other writings or the deutero-Paulines). The issue is, which events occur in the narrative world of a particular text, and how they function there, not their reality or meaning in other texts or the extratextual world.
- The serious reader can work carefully through any such letter, listing every event mentioned or implied. The list will be in the "plotted order," that is, the order in which the events occur in the text.
- When the list is complete, the events can be arranged into the "referential order," that is, their order from earliest to latest, from past through the present into the future, in the world projected by the text. These chronological periods can then be subdivided into sections corresponding to the perspective of the letter. The result is the events of the narrative world projected by the letter.

- The author is not overtly "teaching a grand narrative" but assuming a world he or she considers to be the real world. The readers of the letter enter this world as an aspect of understanding the letter; they may or may not agree that the events of the narrative world are real. Readers of New Testament letters find themselves in a world often different from their everyday assumptions about the "real" world, and must decide whether to continue in the world they have constructed, as influenced by their social setting, or whether the world projected by the letter is in fact real (even if its imagery must be interpreted in other categories in order to be apprehended at all).

- New Testament letters function to mediate the transformative call of God and instruction in the Christian life not only, or even primarily, by explicit affirmations or by lists of dos and don'ts. As in Jesus's parables, the letters function most powerfully in the mode of indirect communication, by what is presupposed as the reality of God's world. This indirect challenge to the readers' assumptions about what is real and important works transformatively, reshaping the minds of open and willing hearers/readers to live in step with the biblical faith.

The following outline lacks some of the helpful subtleties possible in a more extensive presentation but includes all the essentials of the narrative world of Ephesians. It allows readers to ponder the grand sweep of the narrative projected (but not explicated) by Ephesians from *creation* through God's *covenant* with Israel, sending the *Christ*, and calling the *church* into being as the continuation of God's mighty acts that will be *consummated* at the eschaton. A few notes are inserted to illustrate how such study evokes, illuminates, and sometimes answers exegetical questions. It is hoped that readers will pursue more careful and detailed studies, utilizing this approach along with other historical and literary methods, to come within better hearing distance of biblical texts.

. . . Before Creation

1. God has a plan for the world, a mystery hidden for ages in God who created all things (Eph 3:9). This plan (*oikonomia*) extends from before creation to beyond the eschaton and is centered in Christ, under whose lordship all things will finally be fulfilled. This is the plan into which our little lives are fitted.

2. God chose us in Christ before the foundation of the world (1:4).
3. God destined us for adoption as his children (1:5).
4. We have been destined according to the purpose of the one who accomplishes all things according to the counsel of his will (1:11).
5. God prepared good works beforehand in which we should walk (2:10).

I. Creation (and "Fall"/Rebellion)

6. The world was created/founded (1:4).
7. God created all things (3:9). The universe is not a given, is not just "there," has not always existed, but was created. The creation is not narrated, pictured, or elaborated. That the world is God's creation is what is essential, not what this involves or how it was done.
8. Every family and social group (*patria*) in heaven and on earth takes its name from God the Father, who is the Creator and Father of all human beings (3:15).
9. The good world of God's creation was somehow hijacked by the cosmic power of evil—Ephesians gives no explanation, no narrative of a "fall" or rebellion, but presupposes that the present world has been usurped by evil. These powers continue to be active throughout the times of Israel, Christ, and the church, until the consummation (6:12).
10. The world came to be ruled by the aeon ("course") of this world, identified as the ruler of the power of the air, the cosmic evil spirit that is now at work among those who are disobedient (2:2).
11. All of us once lived among the passions of our flesh, following the desires of flesh and senses, and were by nature the children of wrath (2:3).
12. The gentiles—prior to the covenant, all people were "gentiles"—live in the futility of their minds, darkened in their understanding, alienated from the life of God because of their ignorance and hardness of heart (4:17–18).
13. Such human beings have lost all sensitivity and have abandoned themselves to licentiousness; they are greedy to practice every kind of impurity (4:19).
14. The readers' old selves belonged to this world and were corrupted and deluded by its lusts (4:22).
15. People live in darkness and do evil things in secret (5:11–12).

II. COVENANT

16. The transcendent spiritual powers of evil, the cosmic powers of this present darkness, were active in the time of Israel, just as they are in the later time of the church (6:12).

17. In a world under the domination of cosmic evil, a world not consciously seeking God, God acted to create a covenant people (2:12). This covenant is primarily the covenant with Israel, so the plural in verse 12 likely includes the covenant with Abraham (Gen 12:3; etc., not specifically mentioned in Ephesians), in which Israel became a participant in the covenant at Sinai.

18. God's act in creating a covenant people necessarily created the distinction between "insiders" and "outsiders." The covenant people Israel were called "the circumcision," circumcision being the mark of the covenant. It was a physical circumcision made in the flesh by human hands. Insiders of the covenant community called outsiders, to whom the readers of Ephesians belong, "the uncircumcision" (Eph 2:11).

19. Humanity was divided into Jews and non-Jews, those in the covenant with Israel and those outside. A dividing wall of hostility separated Jews and gentiles (2:14).[5]

20. The world did not know the mystery of God's plan to reunite all people, Jews and gentiles, under the lordship of Christ (3:5).

21. During the time of the covenant with Israel, Scriptures were given that promised future saving events (1:13; 3:5; 4:8).

22. The Holy Spirit was promised (not clear to whom) (1:13).

23. The promise of Christ was given (3:5).

24. The Scripture promised that Christ would "ascend on high" (4:8).

III. CHRIST

25. God "has made known to us the mystery of his will, according to his good pleasure that he set forth in Christ, as a plan for the fullness of time, to gather up all things in him, things in heaven and things on earth" (1:9–10).

26. God has carried out his eternal purpose in Jesus Christ our Lord (3:11). The affirmations in 1:9–10 and 3:11 illustrate that the author thinks of

the Christ event as a whole, not only as the life and death of Jesus of Nazareth. God's act in Christ embraces precreation; the historical reality of the universe and all humanity; the covenant history of Israel; the incarnation, death, resurrection/exaltation of Jesus Christ; the formation of the church and its history; and the eschatological consummation of God's purpose. Christ is both the revelatory center and the comprehensive reality of universal history, manifest in the incarnation and death/resurrection/exaltation of Jesus. God's act in Christ set forth the mystery of his will, a plan for the fullness of time (1:9).

Prehistory

27. The preexistent Christ descended to the "lower parts" (4:9) of the universe, namely, the earth (4:10).

History: The Earthly Life and Death of Jesus

28. Christ came and proclaimed peace to "you who were far off" and to "those who were near" (2:17). Is this the historical event of Jesus's preaching, or the post-Easter transcendent event of the proclamation of the risen Christ through the church? Cf. #34 below, on 2:16.
29. Christ loved us and gave himself for us (5:2).
30. Christ loved the church and gave himself up for her. As in the Old Testament (e.g., Israel's confessions in such texts as Deut 26:5–10 and Ps 66:6, and the exhortation in Deut 5:1–7), the author switches easily from objective talk about the church to confessional talk about us, using the same vocabulary (Eph 5:25).
31. Christ was killed; he shed his blood (1:7).
32. In the shedding of Christ's blood, we have redemption, the forgiveness of our trespasses (1:7).
33. Christ's blood was shed, which had the transcendent effect of bringing the far-off readers near. It is a transcendent event. Christ was crucified. This historical event was also a transcendent event. In the death of Jesus, those who were "far" (the gentiles) were "brought near." They did not "come" near but "were brought near" by the blood of Christ. It is not the earthly Jesus but the transcendent Christ who does this, yet it is done in/by his flesh and blood (2:13, 16).

Resurrection and Session

34. God raised Christ from the dead and seated him at the right hand in the heavenly places (1:20).

35. Christ ascended on high, as the Scripture had promised (4:8). For Ephesians, it is not clear whether references to the resurrection (e.g., 1:20) and the ascension/exaltation (e.g., 4:8) refer to one event or two. Does Ephesians (like other parts of the New Testament) identify resurrection and ascension as the same event? At least we must say the author is not concerned to keep them distinct. Ephesians has nothing like the chronology of Luke 24–Acts 1, nor does Paul or any other New Testament author.

36. Christ ascended far above all the heavens, so that he might fill all things. Here, Christ fills all things, as previously the church fills all things. Ontologically, the risen Christ and the church seem to be identified (4:10).

37. God put all things under the feet of the risen Christ and made him head over all things for the church. Again we must ask whether this is thought of in Ephesians as one event or two. Likewise, is becoming head over *all things* and head of the *church* one event or two (1:22–23)? Furthermore: Should this be combined with 1:20, so that the "four" events of resurrection, ascension, head of the church, and head of all things are all one event—or two, or three, or four?

38. The church as the body of Christ is the fullness of the one who fills all in all. This seems to be a past, present, and eschatological process or series of events, as the reality of the body of Christ in the church expands to fill the universe (1:23).

39. Christ has, in his flesh (2:13 says "blood"), made both groups one, breaking down the dividing wall of hostility that separated them (2:14). 2:15 calls the result "one new humanity." It is a transcendent event. They did not "come" near but "were brought near" by the blood of Christ. It is not the earthly Jesus but the transcendent Christ who does this, yet it is done in/by his flesh and blood (2:14).

40. Christ has abolished the law. This was a transcendent event (2:15).

41. Christ has reconciled both groups to God (2:16).

42. Christ came and proclaimed peace to "you who were far off" and to "those who were near." It is not clear whether this is the historical event of Jesus's preaching or the post-Easter transcendent event of the proclamation of the risen Christ through the church, or whether the author of Ephesians makes such distinctions (2:17).

43. Christ has become the cornerstone of the church (2:20).

44. When Christ ascended on high, he made captivity itself his captive (4:8).

45. The church struggles against the transcendent spiritual powers of evil, the cosmic powers of this present darkness. This means the (defeated) powers still continue in the time after Christ (6:12).

IV. Church

Paul and the Apostolic Ministry

46. Paul was called to be an apostle by the will of God (1:1).
47. Paul has become a servant/minister of this gospel (3:7).
48. God gave Paul a commission for the sake of the gentile readers of Ephesians (3:1).
49. God's grace was given to Paul by the working of his power, which made him a minister (3:7).
50. The mystery was made known to him by revelation (3:3).
51. Paul came to an understanding of the mystery of Christ revealed to him (3:4).
52. The church ("in Ephesus") was founded, by Paul or others (1:1).
53. Paul became a prisoner for the sake of the gentile readers (3:1).
54. Paul has been imprisoned and is a prisoner for the Lord (4:1).
55. Paul suffers (in prison) for the readers of Ephesians. These sufferings are the readers' glory (3:13).
56. As Paul writes Ephesians, he is a prisoner, an ambassador in chains (6:20).
57. Paul hears of their faith and their love for all the saints. This refers to the whole church, those they have not seen but yet love (1:15).
58. Paul bows his knees before the Father and prays for the readers this beautiful and extended prayer (3:14–21).
59. Paul writes to the church ("in Ephesus") (1:1).
60. Paul sends Tychicus with the letter to the readers ("in Ephesus"), to let them know how he is doing (6:22).
61. The church receives and preserves the letter Paul writes—otherwise, we would not have it (1:1). The series of events in which Ephesians was edited and gathered with other letters to be included in the corpus within which we read Ephesians might also be listed (1:1).
62. The readers of Ephesians perceive Paul's understanding of the mystery of Christ by reading the (first part of) the letter (3:4).

Conversion of the Readers, the *Ordo Salutis*, "Order of Salvation"
The steps in the process of conversion from "outsider" to "insider" are not absolutely clear chronologically, nor is there a crisp distinction between God's action and human response.

63. The readers were once gentiles, alien from Israel, strangers to the covenants of promise, without God and hope (2:12).

64. The readers previously had lost all sensitivity and have abandoned themselves to licentiousness; they are greedy to practice every kind of impurity (4:19).

65. The readers were once dead, committing trespasses and sins. They were dead through and through, flesh and mind/spirit. There is no anthropological dualism (2:1).

66. They followed the course of this world, the ruler of the power of the air, the spirit that is now at work among those who are disobedient (2:2).

67. All, Jews and gentiles, were this way (cf. Rom 1–3). Israel/Jews were different, but soteriologically, all were equally in need (Eph 2:3). The readers then "heard Christ" or "heard about him" (4:10). Several translations have a form of "heard Christ," for example, KJV, ASV, NAS95, NKJV, NJB. Most others have some form of "heard of," "heard about." Does this text speak of what Christian preachers say about Christ, or does it picture Christ himself speaking in the church's message about him? (See commentaries on Rom 10:19.)

68. The readers were taught about him, taught the truth as it is in Jesus—prior to or after baptism, or both (4:21).

69. God has called the readers to a sure hope in which they now live (1:18; 4:1, 4).

70. The readers heard the word of truth (1:13).

71. The readers believed the word of truth (1:13).

72. God made the readers alive with Christ (2:5).

73. God raised the readers up with Christ (2:5).

74. The readers were baptized (4:5).

75. The church was washed by water by the word (5:26).

76. The saints have been placed in Christ Jesus (1:1).

77. The readers were marked with the promised Holy Spirit (1:13).

78. People in the church were sealed by the Holy Spirit from God, marked for the day of redemption (4:30).

79. God adopted us as his children (1:5).

80. God has enlightened the eyes of the hearts of the readers (1:18).

81. The readers were once far off but have now been brought near. This is a transcendent event. They did not "come" near but "were brought near" by the blood of Christ (2:13).

82. The readers have been baptized (4:5).

83. The readers were converted from the life they once lived as gentiles. They "learned Christ," were taught the truth as it is in Jesus, were taught to put away their former way of life, their old selves, corrupt and de-

luded by lusts (4:20–22). Was this teaching prior to or after baptism, or both?

84. The readers were renewed in the spirit of their minds (4:13).

85. The readers were changed from darkness to light (5:8).

86. By grace you have been saved through faith—not by your own doing (2:6).

87. Slaves have been converted and have become members of a local congregation (6:5).

Situation, Character, Life, and Mission

88. The church continues to struggle against the transcendent spiritual powers of evil, the cosmic powers of this present darkness, which means the (defeated) powers still continue in the time after Christ (6:12).

89. People set their hope on Christ (1:12). "We" were the first to set our hope on Christ. The readers now live in the hope into which God has called them (1:18; 4:4). It is not clear who the "we" are. Are they contrasted in verse 13 with "you," the readers of the letter? Then "we Jewish Christians," "you gentile Christians"? Then, do only these live/be "for the praise of his glory"? Or is "we" the Christians of all time, who are the firstfruits who set their hope in Christ, including the "you" of verse 13? The church lives for the praise of God's glory, the God who will ultimately bring all into the one body. The repetition of "to the praise of his glory" in verse 14 suggests a contrast/continuity between now and then, not between "we Jewish Christians" and "you gentile Christians" (1:12).

90. The saints live faithful lives in Christ Jesus (1:1).

91. God has blessed us in Christ with every spiritual blessing in the heavenly places, the present transcendent location of believers' lives (1:3).

92. God freely bestowed his grace on us in the Beloved (1:6).

93. God made known to us the mystery of his will set forth in Christ, a plan for the fullness of time (1:9).

94. We have obtained an inheritance (1:11).

95. The readers have come to love all the saints. This refers to the whole church, those they have not seen but yet love (1:15).

96. The church as the body of Christ is the fullness of the one who fills all in all. This is a past, present, and eschatological event or series of events, as the reality of the body of Christ in the church expands to fill the universe (1:23). The church is in the expansive process of "filling all things." Christ ascended far above all the heavens, so that he might fill all things. Here, Christ fills all things, as previously the church fills all things. The

risen Christ and the church seem to be identified in some ontological dimension (4:10).

97. God made the readers now sit in the heavenly places with the ascended Christ (2:6).

98. God broke down the dividing wall, joining Jews and gentiles. This is not *only* a matter of removing the barriers of prejudice. Also, and primarily, it is the incorporation of gentiles into the ongoing people of God. It is not two streams uniting to become a third, new stream, but an ancient stream flowing into another, more ancient one; gentiles joining Israel, not Israel and gentiles uniting to form something discontinuous, entirely new (2:11–18).

99. Christ has made both groups into one body (2:16).

100. Christ has put the hostility that separated Jew and gentile to death through the cross (2:16).

101. The apostles and prophets became the foundation for the church (2:20).

102. The whole structure of the church is joined together into a holy temple in the Lord, a dwelling place for God. The readers are built into this structure (2:21–22).

103. The gentile readers of Ephesians have heard of the commission given to Paul (3:2).

104. God has revealed this mystery to humankind by the Spirit to his holy apostles and prophets (3:5).

105. The gentiles have become fellow heirs, members of the same body, sharers in the promise of Christ through the gospel (3:5).

106. The wisdom of God in its rich variety is now being made known through the church to the rulers and authorities in the heavenly places (3:10).

107. We have access to God in boldness and confidence through faith in Christ (3:12).

108. Each of the readers has been given grace according to the measure of Christ's gift (4:7).

109. When Christ ascended on high, he gave gifts to his people (4:8). Christ gave gifts to the church to equip it for its ministry: apostles, prophets, evangelists, pastor-teachers (4:10).

110. The ministry Christ gave the church builds up the body of Christ (4:12).

111. The whole church is in the process of coming to the unity of the faith and knowledge of the Son of God, to maturity, to the measure of the full stature of Christ (4:13).

112. The church is currently children, tossed to and fro and blown about by every wind of doctrine, by people's trickery, by their craftiness in deceitful scheming (4:14).

113. Speaking the truth in love, the church is growing up in every way to Christ, who is the head of the church (4:15).
114. The whole church is knit together with itself and with its head, and supplied with ligaments; it grows and builds itself up in love (4:16).
115. The readers clothe themselves in their new self, created according to the likeness of God in true righteousness and holiness (4:24).
116. People in the church lie to one another, though they are urged not to do so (4:25).
117. People in the church steal from one another, though they are urged not to do so (4:28).
118. The kingdom of Christ and of God has been/will be established; the present aspect of this kingdom is manifest in the church (5:5).
119. The readers worship, singing psalms, hymns, and spiritual songs, giving thanks (5:19–20).
120. Some readers have gotten married and had children (5:22–6:4).
121. Some church members have obtained slaves (6:5–9).
122. Christ nourishes and tenderly cares for the church (5:29).
123. The church struggles against the transcendent spiritual powers of evil, the cosmic powers of this present darkness (6:12).
124. Tychicus was converted and became a member of a local congregation (6:21).
125. Tychicus became a dear brother and faithful minister in the Lord (6:21).
126. The readers have come to belong to a (universal) community that has an undying love for the Lord Jesus Christ (6:22).

V. Consummation

127. There will be a coming age. This is the only explicit reference in the New Testament to the common Jewish doctrine of two ages, "this age" and "the age to come" (1:21).
128. The kingdom of Christ and of God has been/will be established (5:5).

Judgment, Separation, and Wrath
129. No fornicator, no impure person, or no greedy person (idolater) has any inheritance in the kingdom of Christ and God (5:5).
130. The wrath of God comes/is coming on the disobedient (5:6).
131. All, slave and free, will be recompensed for what each has done (6:8).

Salvation for the Church

132. God's own people will be redeemed, to the praise of his glory. This is apparently future, for it occurs after being sealed with the Holy Spirit (1:14).

133. There will be a day of redemption for those who have been sealed by the Holy Spirit (4:30).

134. In the ages to come, God will show the immeasurable riches of his grace in kindness toward us in Christ Jesus (2:7).

135. The church, the bride, is presented to Christ in splendor, holy and without blemish (5:26).

All (*Ta Panta*)

136. God's plan for the fullness of time is to gather up all things in him, things in heaven and things on earth (1:10).

137. The "we who were first" (1:12) does not mean Jewish Christians who preceded gentiles into the church but contrasts all present Christians with the future reconciliation of all people.

138. The church as the body of Christ is the fullness of the one who fills all in all. This is a past, present, and eschatological event or series of events, as the reality of the body of Christ in the church expands to fill the universe (1:23).

139. Christ ascended far above all the heavens, so that he might fill all things. Here, Christ fills all things, as previously the church fills all things (1:23). The unity of the risen Christ and the church seems to have an ontological dimension (4:10).

Ephesians on God/Christ/Church

We have seen that the major topics of theology can be separated for discussion but in reality are all woven together, are all subheadings of the doctrine of God. The above list of 139 more or less distinct events, arranged in a general chronological order, is helpful in bringing the sweep and contours of the letter's narrative world into sharper focus, but we must remember that the list only brings out facets of one jewel. We will briefly sketch major elements in Ephesians' doctrines of God and Christ (including salvation and eschatology), then look more carefully at the letter's breathtaking understanding of the church.

God

God is our Father (1:2), the Father of Jesus Christ (1:3, 17), the one and only God (4:6), the Father and Creator of all, the universe and everyone in it (*ta panta*, "all that is," 3:9, 14; 4:6). God continues through universal history to be the Creator, who holds the universe in being, energizing all things (1:11). As throughout the Bible, "God" is not "defined" abstractly in terms of God's being or essential characteristics (almighty, omniscient, omnipresent, etc.) but by his acts, his work in history. God's work of salvation is not patching up the old world or delivering saved souls from it but the generation of a new creation, that is, a renewed, transformed creation in continuity with the present world (2:10, 15; 4:24). Salvation is 100 percent the gift of God, the result of God's initiative and call of those who were chosen in Christ before the foundation of the world (1:4, 18; 2:8; 4:1, 4). God's reality and purpose cannot be deduced by observation; such knowledge has come through God's own revelation (1:17; 3:3, 5). This is the significance of "mystery" (*mystērion*) in Ephesians' theology—not only has the love of God that surpasses merely human knowledge been made known in Christ (3:19), but also that which *could* not have been discovered by human thought has also been disclosed, the mystery of the gospel that must be proclaimed (1:9; 3:3, 4, 9; 6:19), the uniting of all God's people into one community. The one God has a plan for the universe that stretches from creation to the eschaton, when all things will be summed up in Christ (1:10–11). The meaning of universal history and of individual human lives is already revealed and experienced in the Christ event and its continuation in the church. Such a God—though monotheists cannot seriously use such phrases that imply a category of gods into which the God of Israel fits—"such a" God cannot be explained or discussed but only worshiped and praised. Ephesians is theology sung and confessed, more at home in the sanctuary and set to music than pondered in the seminar room, library, or laboratory (3:14–21!).

Christ

Throughout the Pauline school as represented by Colossians, Ephesians, and the Pastorals, Jesus of Nazareth was the incarnation of the heavenly Son of God. This Christology is simply assumed and no longer needs to be spelled out—see the absence of specific references in section III of the narrative world outlined above and the omission of the profound Christ hymn in Colossians 1:15-20, even though the author has adopted Colossians as a template for his own composition and follows this earlier exposition from the Pauline school very closely in both structure and content. Nonetheless, the Christology of Ephesians is shaped in terms of the U-shaped event characteristic of Paul. As in the hymn of Philippians 2:5-11, Christ is the preexistent one,[6] who came to earth and shared our life to the point of death and was exalted to heaven at the resurrection, where he reigns not only as Lord of the church but also over the universe and all its powers (Eph 2:20-23; 4:7-9). The author does not conceptualize this reign or present images by which it may be imagined, but it seems to be analogous to the "shared throne" of Revelation (cf. Rev 1:6, 9; 3:21; 5:10-13; 7:9-11; 14:3). The earthly life and human death of Jesus were the means of redemption, forgiveness, and reconciliation between God and humanity, just as they effected the reconciliation and unifying of fragmented humanity (1:7; 2:13-17).

In all this, Christ is not identified with God as in, for example, John 1:1, but Christ is inseparable from God. For Christians, Jesus cannot be spoken of apart from his relation to God; God cannot be spoken of apart from his revelation in Christ. Thus Christians as servants of *Christ* are doing the will of *God* (Eph 6:5-6). Though it is fundamental for the author that there is "one Lord" (4:5), this does not conflict or compete with faith in the "one God" (4:6).[7] The author uses "Lord" for both Christ and God, contrasting "Lord" with human beings, but the author also uses the title for the human being Jesus (1:2-3, 15, 17; 3:11; 5:8; 6:7-10). Christian ethics is "imitation of God" (5:1), which is no different from understanding and doing "the will of the Lord," "what is pleasing to the Lord" (5:17, 10). Like Paul, the author thus does not illustrate Christian ethics with examples from the life and teaching of the earthly Jesus but refers to the love of God manifest in the Christ event as such.

The saving act of God in Christ is thought of in cosmic terms. To be sure, salvation is for individual persons, who experience acceptance by God's grace as forgiveness of their sins (1:7; 2:1, 5), but salvation is not the saving of individual souls out of an evil world. Paul's understanding of sin as an enslaving power (e.g., Rom 6) is represented by the "cosmic powers of this present darkness, . . . the spiritual forces of evil in the heavenly places" (Eph 6:12; cf. 1:21; 2:2). Developing ideas already present in Paul (Rom 8:19-24) and expanded in Colossians (Col 1:15-20), the author pictures the Christ event as including the church and ultimately all creation. Christ has already come, the saving event is already under way, and believers already participate in it, but the fullness of salvation is still to come, for both the individual and the world. Eschatology is both presently realized and the firm future hope. The already/not yet of Jesus's original preaching of the kingdom of God is continued in the church, in the same dialectical mode. The "one hope" shared by all believers (Eph 4:4) is universal: one church, one humanity, one cosmos, including the human, animal, plant, and material universe. As in Revelation, here is a theological foundation for ecological responsibility without self-interest or pragmatic ideology. The world is to be cared for because it is God's, who does not abandon it but has a glorious future for it.

Much of what Ephesians has to teach us about God, Christ, salvation, eschatology, and ethics is woven into its doctrine of the church, to which we now turn.

Church

Ephesians has the most exalted view of the church in the New Testament. The author's narrative world of universal history includes 82 of the 139 events in the two generations of church history from the resurrection to his own time. The church was in the mind of God before creation, is already enthroned with Christ in the heavenly world, and extends into the eschatological future, linked inseparably with the destiny of the universe itself (1:4–10, 22–23; 3:8–11; 5:27). In such thinking, loyalty to the church does not, of course, compete with faith in God or Christ. "It is not so much that Christology is swallowed up by ecclesiology as that ecclesiology is thoroughly christological."[8] Just as God cannot be thought of apart from Christ, so Christ cannot be thought of apart from the church and the Holy Spirit at work in it. The author writes a circular letter to be read in particular congregations but always thinks of the church in catholic terms. All nine references to *ekklēsia* are to the universal church (1:22; 3:10, 21; 5:23, 24, 25, 27, 29, 32).

The church already participates in the glory of God. The saints are already enthroned in heaven (2:6; cf. the transcendent dimension of the church discussed at 1 Thess 1:1 above and in Rev 2–3). There is no tendency in Ephesians toward idolization of the church, for the glory of the church is ascribed to God. The very existence of the church in the world as the called and chosen people of God redounds to God's glory (Eph 3:21). This exuberant celebration of belonging to the united people of God is expressed in a broad spectrum of terminology and imagery, including the following.

The church is the body of Christ, who/which is filling the universe. In mind-stretching images that resist harmonization, the author adopts and goes beyond Paul's own imagery of the church as the body of Christ (1 Cor 12:4–31; Rom 12:1–8). The deutero-Pauline author of Colossians had already given cosmic dimensions to Paul's metaphor of the church as the body of Christ (Col 1:20–24; 2:19; 3:15). The author of Ephesians has adopted Colossians as the template for his own letter, and here, too, he expands the imagery: Christ is not only head of the church but also head of the cosmos. Within the cosmos, the church is the body of Christ, the people of God within the whole of humanity, that exhibits and facilitates the working out of God's purpose for the whole creation.

The church is the leading edge of God's new creation. Ephesians' primary image is not only that gentiles have been incorporated into the ongoing history of Israel as God's people (as in Rom 9–11) but that God has initiated a new creation in which the distinction between Jew and gentile is dissolved. This in principle breaks down the divisions between all tribes and peoples. The root metaphor is "new creation" rather than "incorporation into Israel, the people of God." Nevertheless, the author, like Paul, understands Christian believers as now belonging to the "commonwealth of Israel," one new humanity created by God, who has "made both groups into one and has broken down the dividing wall" of hostility (Eph 2:12–16). Paul's insistence that "works of the law" cannot justify is now virtually replaced by a theology that salvation is entirely by grace, apart from human works of any kind (2:1–10). In the first generation, when Paul's theology of salvation by grace apart from works of the law was in danger of being misunderstood as a kind of lawlessness that rejected God's Torah as such, Paul had been careful to insist that the Christian gospel does not abolish (*katargoumen*) the law but in fact establishes it (Rom 3:31). The later perspective of Ephesians regards this danger as past and does not hesitate to use a form of the same word to declare that Christ *has* in fact abolished (*katargēsas*) the law with its commandments and ordinances (Eph 2:15). In the new creation, one's relationship to God is not a matter of law. Period.

The church is the people of God, the bride of Christ. The churches addressed by Ephesians were already familiar with bridal imagery for the church, since both the Pauline and Johannine Christians in Roman Asia had taken up the Old Testament image of Israel as the bride of Yahweh (Isa 50:1; 54:5–8; 61:10; 62:5; Jer 2:20–25; 3:1–14; Ezek 16; Hos 1–3; cf. 2 Cor 11:1–3; Rev 19:7, 9; 21:2, 9; 22:17; John 3:29). In Paul and Revelation, the present life of the church is the time of engagement, with the grand wedding to be celebrated at the parousia. Ephesians' use of the image is more complex, reflecting the already/not-yet dialectical eschatology of both Pauline and Johannine theology. On the one hand, the bride has been ceremonially washed in preparation for the wedding, the bridal bath symbolizing the "washing of water by the word" of Christian baptism (Eph 5:26–27) as believers look forward to the consummation of the marriage at the wedding, as in Paul and Revelation. On the other hand, the biblical "the two shall become one flesh" of Genesis 2:24 seems to be applied to the present experience of the believer; it is applied boldly to the image of the church as already the bride of Christ, living in intimate union with him. In the light of the nearness of the parousia, Paul had advised church members already engaged to be married to continue in their unmarried state unless compelled by irresistible passion, and marriage comes off as a second-best for true believers perceived to be living in the final generation of human history (1 Cor 7:8–9, 25–31). In postapostolic times, the author of Ephesians has a different, more exalted view of marriage, which is symbolized by the unity of Christ and the church (cf. Eph 5:22–33).

The church is the temple of God (2:21–22). Israel's conviction was that the living God does not live in a fabulous temple in far-off heaven while migratory Israel lives in tents in the desert, but he himself has a tent among his people. Then, when Israel settled down in the promised land and built houses, God, too, finally commissioned the building of a splendid house in Jerusalem, where God dwelt among his people. The Jerusalem temple had been destroyed by the Romans in the war of 66–70 CE. Faithful Jews struggled with how they could continue to be faithful to the Torah when the temple no longer existed and found more than one answer. Even before the temple's destruction, the sectarian Jewish community at Qumran had come to regard the Jerusalem temple as corrupt, not following the correct calendar and ritual, and viewed the community itself as God's true temple (1QS 8.5–9)—but the Qumran community was destroyed by the Romans along with Jerusalem and its temple. Analogous to the new covenant community at Qumran, significant streams of Christian tradition also came to understand the church itself as the house of God, the new temple that represented the continuing presence of God in this world (John 2:19–21; 1 Cor 3:9–17; 2 Cor 6:16). Ephesians adopts and adapts the image of the temple to express the reality of the church, uniquely combining it with the image of the body of Christ. The body is not yet mature and complete but is on the way to fulfillment. The temple is still under construction; it is built on the foundation of apostles and prophets; Christ himself is the cornerstone or capstone (Eph 2:18–22); and all members are being built into this temple where God is real and present.

The Church Is One, Holy, Catholic, and Apostolic

We have briefly explored only a few of the many images utilized by early Christian teachers to portray the nature of the church.[9] The Nicene Creed will summarize the variety of New Testament imagery as unity, holiness, catholicity, and apostolicity. The roots of this creedal statement are already in the New Testament. Our discussions of both Johannine and Pauline theology have shown that all versions of Christianity in Roman Asia 90–130 CE were concerned with the church's unity, holiness, catholicity, and apostolicity. These four rubrics serve admirably to express the ecclesiology of Ephesians.

The Church Is One

For Ephesians, there is a unity God gives and a unity we attain (think indicative/imperative, already/not yet). The priority belongs to the unity God gives. The church's unity corresponds to the unity of the one God. The author does not exhort the church to become one, does not speak in terms of "ought," "should," or "ideal," but simply declares: "There is one body and one Spirit, just as you were called to the one hope of your calling, one Lord, one faith, one baptism, one God and Father of all, who is above all and through all and in all" (4:4–6). The sevenfold declaration sounds formulaic and may correspond to other heptads circulating in the churches of Roman Asia (Revelation!). It begins with the "one body," the church. The one church is a reality given by God.

Looking out from whatever congregation in whatever city in Roman Asia the author is located (probably Ephesus), he does not see a united church but a variety of Christian groups, some of which would later be judged heretical by the emerging mainstream. Affirming the essential, God-given unity of the church as a reality that already exists, the author of Ephesians sees the present state of the church as provisional. The church is a body that, so long as it manifests divisiveness in spirit and in its corporate life, is still immature (to use Ephesians' imagery of the body growing toward maturity, 1:23; 4:16) or still under construction (to use Ephesians' image of the temple, 2:21). The church is one, but it is a work in progress, an unfinished poem composed by the divine author (cf. *poiēma*, 2:10, rendered "what he has made us" [NRSV], "God's work of art" [NJB]).

The unity of the church is the prolepsis of the unity of all humanity. Ephesians deals with a large issue that continues to be important for thoughtful Christians: In the multicultural, religiously pluralistic world in which a fragmented church strives to be clear about its identity and mission, are the people of the church all on the same road or are there several roads? Are people that belong to other Christian groups than mine to be regarded as "we" or "they"? What about human beings who belong to non-Christian religions, or to none at all? Wherever and however the line is drawn, is the us/them mentality an irreducible component of human being as such? The us/them mind-set does seem to be inherent in unredeemed human nature (cf. 2:3, 15). Babies are not born with this built-in apparatus, but distinguishing "us" from "them" is one of the earliest reflexes society imprints on the souls of babies and little children. This social conditioning is apparently a necessary aspect of the survival mechanism for family, clan, tribe, state, and nation. It is not necessary as an essential part of human being, but in this fallen world it is inevitably transmitted to all of us by cultural conditioning. Archaeologists and social anthropologists inform us that when the earliest hunter-gatherers settled down on the banks of great rivers and founded the Sumerian cities such as Sumer, these first cities had walls. These walls were too small and flimsy to have been constructed for defense—that came later. These primordial walls had a ritual, symbolic function; that is, they were identity markers, separating insiders from outsiders, those who belonged from those who didn't, "us" from "them." Later walls would be more effective militarily, but they continued to signal the same symbolic world: the Great Wall of China, Hadrian's wall, the Pale, the Maginot Line, the Iron Curtain, the Berlin Wall, White Only signs, the glass ceiling.

Krikkit

In one of Doug Adams's wildly entertaining science fiction novels, *Hitchhiker's Guide to the Galaxy*, billions of years in the future and many galaxies from here is the planet Krikkit. It had been encased for millennia in a dark, impenetrable cloud. No light came in. No sun, moon, stars, planets could be seen. The residents of Krikkit supposed they were the only beings in the universe—did not even know there was a universe. The time came when they built a spaceship; went through the enveloping cloud that separated their planet from everything else; saw sun, moon, stars, a vast universe; and realized they were not alone. Their first words: "It'll have to go." On the way back home they sang a number of tuneful and reflective songs on the subjects of peace, justice, morality, culture, sport, family life, and the obliteration of all other life-forms. They then built warships to destroy everything outside their wall.

Ephesians saw the issue in terms of the church's religious history, a church that had been born in the context of Judaism that understandably divided all human beings into Jews and gentiles. In the biblical narrative, Israel is chosen for the sake of others, the people of God with a special mission to all God's people, a priestly community chosen to be holy and separate but existing for the sake of all the rest of God's people (Gen 12:3; Exod 19:6). They sometimes rightly understood their priestly role but often had to be forcibly reminded by God's prophetic messengers that they were chosen for the sake of the world, to be the light to the nations, who would all finally be insiders (Isa 42:6; 49:6; cf. also the unimaginable 19:25!). Biblical and historical Jerusalem had been a city with a wall. Ephesians was written within a churchly context where the imagery of Revelation was known—the first of the messages to "the seven churches of Asia" was to Ephesus (Rev 2:1–7). Revelation concludes with the vision of the city of God, the new Jerusalem, a city with walls, insiders and outsiders. But the gates of this city are always open, and the gentiles finally bring the glory and honor of the nations into the city of God. And Ephesians insists that God in Christ has already broken down the dividing walls (Eph 2:13–18).[10]

The Church Is Holy

"Holy" means "separate." It is strange to read in the Bible that *holiness*, separateness, is an essential quality of the church. After all, the Bible presents the church as the people of God called and dedicated to God's program of breaking down the walls that separate people and uniting the universe under the rule of the one God, the Creator and Redeemer of all. Yet the first line of Ephesians directs the letter's message to the "holy ones" (*hagioi*, "saints," as designation for the people of God, 1:1, 15, 18; 2:19, 21; 3:8; 4:12; 5:3, 26, 27; 6:18; see above on 1 Thess 1:5–6).

"Holy" does not mean "pious." God is the Holy One not because God is pious but because God is other, the Wholly Other, the Creator, different and separate from every created being. Holiness is not a subjective attitude but an objective reality. The church *is* holy. The church's holiness is not an ideal to be striven for but a reality to be lived out, the ethic of a transformed community not conformed to this world (Eph 4:23–24; Rom 12:1). The church's holiness, its separateness and distinctiveness, is an essential mark of the church in the here and now, on the way to the final kingdom of God when the insider/outsider distinction will be erased. This side of the parousia, the church must maintain its distinctiveness, not simply fade into the world. The Jewish Scriptures and tradition often represent this concern. Some elements of the Torah are for the purpose of keeping Israel separate—the Israel whose ultimate purpose is the blessing of all peoples, the ultimate erasure of the distinction between all "God's people" and the covenant "people of God" (see Rom 9–11). There will be a time in God's ultimate future when the insider/outsider distinction will be finally overcome, and all will be insiders. In the Holy City there will be no temple, no distinction between sacred and profane (see *Hearing John's Voice* on Rev 21–22).

Win-Win

"What we need here is a win-win solution." We have all heard such attempts to be helpful in conflicted situations, and we know what such language means, that is, how the phrase functions, that it is a temporary distortion of language to make a valid point. "Win" by definition requires "lose" as its corollary. There cannot be winners without losers; if everybody wins, "win" has lost its linguistic valence. So it is with insider/outsider language. The present and temporary reality experienced by insiders will ultimately be universalized, and everyone will experience the meaning of belonging, being accepted, being an "insider."

The church's holiness is manifest in ethics, in the way its members live their lives. This does not mean withdrawal from the world but living a transformed life in the midst of the world, no longer "as the Gentiles live" (Eph 4:17; 5:8). This is said to people who are themselves gentiles. Ephesians' readers are not ethnic Jews; they once did not belong to Israel (2:12), but they now have a new self-understanding of their own identity—they belong to the holy people of God, are fellow citizens with the saints, members of the household of God (2:19). This ethic requires, of course, that they, too, live by the moral standards given in the traditional Jewish ethic, which to a large extent overlaps and is identical with the ethics of human decency and respect found in gentile ethics. Just as Jews and gentiles are taught not to steal and lie, so Christians are not to steal and lie (4:25, 28). The ethic to which Ephesians calls the followers of Jesus also manifests distinctive aspects of the Christian faith. We note five.

The ethics of Ephesians is a *church ethic*, mainly directed to insiders, concerned with life within the people of God. This focus does not mean that Ephesians is unconcerned with ethical issues beyond the boundaries of the church, but that this teaching document is directed to insiders who share

Christian faith, to equip them for its mission. This includes its relation to outsiders, both corporately and as individual members (4:12!).

The ethics of love, justice, and respect for others not only advocates what is true and right in itself; it offers a *testimony*.[11] The way Christians live their lives witnesses to the truth of their faith, the basis of all their conduct. As in the teaching of Jesus, Christian conduct does not merely honor Christians as good people but is done in the service of others, pointing away from them to God (Matt 5:16).

Despite the exalted view of the present reality and final destiny of the church, the ethics of Ephesians is a down-to-earth *road ethic*, the way of life of those who walk together along life's road. Once again, the Jewish metaphor of movement along a road is used to picture life and behavior (Greek *peripateō* represents Hebrew *halak* = "walk"; *halakah* = way of life, the commandment, the revealed will of God about how to live one's life). The Jewish metaphor for life, "walk," is found eight times in Ephesians (*peripateō*, 2:2, 10; 4:1, 17; 5:2, 8, 15), rightly rendered as "live" or "life." Ephesians' view of the transcendent nature of the church does not lead the author to disdain everyday decisions that must be made along the this-worldly road of life.

There is an emphasis on the *linguisticality* of ethics. The Christian life is evidenced in the way one speaks. Christian faith brings a new respect for words, their destructive power and their healing power. Admonitions to avoid obscene, frivolous, and vulgar talk are not mere prudishness but reflect an awareness that words reveal and communicate the depth of life (4:29; 5:4).

The holiness of the Christian life is manifest in the *family*. When Ephesians gives specific instructions for Christian family life (5:21–6:9, to wives and husbands, children and parents, slaves and masters), the author is not composing off the cuff but taking up a traditional element of Christian instruction that became common not only in the Pauline school but also in most of the streams of Christian tradition in the Christianity of Roman Asia 90–130 CE. Paul himself had given specific instructions to family members, including slaves, but they were based on the expectation of the first Christian generation that the parousia would occur during their lifetime (cf. 1 Cor 7:1–40). When the end did not come as expected, Christian teachers of later generations adopted and adapted the household codes circulating in the Hellenistic world, including those already adopted by Hellenistic Judaism as authoritative guides for Christian family life (since Martin Luther, often called *Haustafel*, "table of household duties"). The earliest extant example is Colossians 3:18–4:1, elaborated with more theological interpretation by the author of Ephesians in 5:21–6:9. Other examples from the same general period, all with contacts with Pauline school tradition, are 1 Timothy 2:1–15, 3:1–15, 5:1–21, 6:1–2, Titus 2:1–10, and 1 Peter 2:13–3:7. Patristic writings continued this pattern of ethical instruction for the Christian household, though there are no exact formal parallels to New Testament household codes (e.g., Didache 4:9–11; Barnabas 19:5–7; 1 Clement 1:3; 21:6–9; Ignatius, *To Polycarp* 4.1–6.1; Polycarp, *To the Philippians* 4.2–6.3). Literal compliance with these codes has been urged in some streams of contemporary Christianity as a biblical protection of "family values," but many readers of the Bible in the mainline churches find them objectionable and repressive, especially instructions on the subordination of women. The subject is important, not only for these codes' particular content but also as a key illustration of listening to the Bible in its own terms before integrating its message into our own understanding of Christian faith and life. We will continue this discussion below in the context of the Pastorals, probably the most challenging instance of the New Testament household code for Christian believers who want to be faithful both to the Bible and to the world—which continues to be God's world.

The Church Is Catholic

The word "catholic" (*katholikos*) was not used by the author of Ephesians or any other New Testament author, but the idea is there, commonly expressed by *oikoumenē* (cf. "ecumenical"), referring to the whole inhabited earth. In our extant literature, the common adjective *katholikos* ("general, whole, universal") was first applied to the church in Ignatius's letter to the church at Smyrna 8.2 (ca. 110 CE): "where Jesus Christ is, there is the catholic church," written about the same time as Ephesians, Revelation, and the Johannine letters, in the same area of Roman Asia. Though "one" and "catholic" are related, to believe the church is "catholic" is not the same as believing the church is "one." The opposite of "one" is "two or more." The opposite of "catholic" is "local." God did not call two or more churches into being, but one. Whoever belongs to the church belongs to the *same* church as every other member of the church. God did not call a local church into being. Whoever belongs to the church belongs to a community manifest throughout the world and the centuries. This church is catholic, not local, regional, national, denominational, ethnic, or anything less than universal. Some members of the Christian community in Roman Asia 90–130 CE were tempted to think of the church as a local, denominational, or sectarian group. Then as now, the religious landscape was polka-dotted with churches representing a variety of traditions. Their members did not all look alike, think alike, or speak alike, and did not all have the same theology or structure. The author of Ephesians calls the churches of the Pauline tradition to broaden their horizons, to see the one church of God as the catholic-universal-ecumenical church, including all its manifestations, even if they are sometimes uncomfortable with each other.

The magnificent vision of the catholicity of the church is misunderstood if it disdains a particular, always imperfect, local manifestation of the church, as though one could say, "I belong to the universal church but don't participate in the life and work of any particular denomination or congregation." This would be analogous to claiming to be a good member of the human race without belonging to a particular nation and ethnic group. Nor can one claim to be a good US citizen without belonging to a particular state. "Think globally, act locally" represents Ephesians' view of responsible membership in the one holy catholic apostolic church.

The one church has unity in variety, variety in unity. Just as God has given every believer a gift to be used in building up the whole church (Eph 4:6; cf. 1 Cor 12:7, "To each is given . . . for the common good"), so each group of Christians has a contribution to the life of the whole Christian community. The often-repeated maxim, "Unity is not the same as uniformity," must not become a cliché. Neither the unity God gives nor the unity a fractured church should try to attain means reducing the church's refreshing variety to a standardized uniformity. Such unity manifests a *limited variety*. Uniformity is easy, conceptually and in practice—only one thing goes. Likewise, unlimited variety is easy, conceptually and in practice—anything goes. Limited variety is difficult, conceptually (it is not conceptually neat) and in practice (it requires sensitivity to others and their ways of thinking, and discerning pastoral care). In thinking and talking about the church and its faith, more than one thing goes, but not just anything. Such open-ended tolerance inclines toward indifference. Unity-in-limited-variety is manifest not only in early Christianity but also in the biblical canon that emerged. It is conceptually and practically easy, for instance, to have only one normative gospel, and some early church leaders lobbied for that view (Marcion!). It is conceptually and practically easy to have an open-ended canon that accepts all comers, from Mark to the Gospel of Judas. After much struggle, the church accepted more than one gospel, but not just any of the texts that claimed to be "Gospels," as normative, that is, bearing authentic testimony to the meaning of the Christ event. The church celebrates unity and variety. The church can celebrate its life-giving variety only if it identifies itself as *apostolic*.

The Church Is Apostolic

The church as such is a commissioned, missionary church. An "apostle" (*apostolos*) is one commissioned and sent (see below). As in Matthew 28:16–20, so also for Ephesians, all disciples are commissioned and sent. To be a member of the church is to be involved in a community with a mission. To be sure, there is no specific command in Ephesians to evangelize the nations or the neighborhood, but this is everywhere implicit. By its very being, the church has a ministry and witness to the cosmos, from the neighbor (Eph 4:25) to the "rulers and authorities in the heavenly places" (3:10). The church does not exist for itself but is integral to God's mission of reconciling the world. Within the universal church, God has given the gift of specialized ministries to equip the church for its mission. Different church traditions in Roman Asia 90–130 CE described the church's ministry with differing terminology. Ephesians lists apostles, prophets, evangelists, pastors, and teachers (or pastor-teachers, 4:11–12).

The understanding of apostles and apostleship is related to the question of church ministry in general. The author addresses a situation in which a special class of clergy is emerging. He affirms this new development, considers the emergence of new forms of specialized ministry to be the gift of God through the risen Christ, and appeals to Scripture to support this new development (4:7–16). Specialized ministries do not remove the task of mission and ministry with which the whole church is charged—the church's evangelists and pastor-teachers are to "equip the saints for the work of ministry" (4:12).

The Famous "Misplaced Comma"

The KJV seemed to assign "the work of the ministry" to the clergy: God's gifts were "for the perfecting of the saints, for the work of the ministry." Virtually all later translations correctly render the phrase to mean that God has given apostles, prophets, evangelists, and pastor-teachers "to equip the saints for the work of ministry" (RSV, NRSV), "to prepare God's people for works of service" (NIV).

As the whole church is called to what came to be designated the "ministry of the laity," so the whole church is called to participate in the church's apostolic mission. Here it is important to remember that "apostle" is the transliteration (not translation) of an ordinary Greek word, referring to one who is *sent*. Both in secular and in biblical Greek, *apostolos* can refer to the representative of some person or group, sent to perform a particular task. The verbal cognate, *apostellō*, is found dozens of times in the LXX in this ordinary sense (e.g., Gen 8:8, Noah's sending the dove from the ark; Gen 21:14, Abraham's sending Hagar into the desert; the noun *apostolos* is not found in the LXX). The New Testament uses *apostolos* in this ordinary sense of "messenger," "envoy," "delegate" (e.g., John 13:16; Phil 2:25; 2 Cor 8:23). A rough analogy in English is the use of "secretary," which can refer to anyone charged with writing, typing, filing, and other office work, or to a specialized, high-ranking government official such as secretary of state. Ephesians understands that within the apostolic mission and ministry with which the whole church is charged, there is a special class of ministers. So also, within the large group of the church's missionaries, there was a specific group of apostles authorized by the risen Christ to found new churches and be leaders for the church as a whole. During the first generation, these apostolic leaders guided the life and mission of the church by their personal presence and by apostolic letters, as represented in Acts and the letters of Paul.

Like us, both the author and readers of Ephesians live in postapostolic times. The Pauline churches in Roman Asia 90–130 CE looked back on the history of their churches founded by Paul and his associates in a previous generation (2:20). With the death of the apostles and those who had personally known them, the churches faced the question of how the authority of God and the living Christ was to be mediated to them as they expanded and entered new situations, and they asked how they were to understand their faith and mission. All Christian communities addressed by Ephesians were asking this question. The New Testament canon preserves more than one answer to this question, with which the church continues to struggle. Our task here is not to resolve this issue but to improve our hearing of the biblical witness by reviewing the possibilities we have found in canonical texts.

Colossians presents the church as guided by Paul, its sole apostle. In the chronology assumed here, the letter was written to the Pauline churches within a decade or two of the death of Paul, who continues to instruct the church by this letter. No other apostles are mentioned. No new revelations through inspired prophets are mentioned. The letter does not mention the Holy Spirit and is wary of "spiritual experiences." If we had only Colossians, we would suppose that Paul was the sole apostle and that the revelation given through him is the church's only guide. In the next century, this view in fact became a central understanding of Marcion and his followers.

Revelation, written circa 95 CE, pictures the church as guided by prophets who receive new revelations from the risen Lord. No other congregational or regional leaders are mentioned. There are numerous references to "elders," but they are all in the heavenly temple, not ministers in earthly congregations. The vision honors and looks back to the "twelve apostles," whose names will be inscribed on the twelve foundations of the wall of the new Jerusalem (Rev 21:14). The churches are commended for rejecting those "who claim to be apostles but are not" (2:2), but the book does not identify the true apostles, nor explicate how their leadership and teaching function in the church.

Second Thessalonians, written in the name of Paul in the latter part of the first or beginning of the second century CE, rejects both the resurgence of near expectation of the end found in Revelation and the emergence of a special class of paid clergy found in Ephesians and the Pastorals, referring to them as the "disorderly."

The Johannine letters, written around the turn of the century about the same time as Revelation, portray the congregations as guided by elders, at least some of whom have extracongregational authority.

The early edition(s) of the Gospel of John, from the concluding decades of the first century CE, pictures the Holy Spirit, the Paraclete, as the church's guide, both keeping alive the memory of Jesus's life and teaching, and guiding the church into new truth. The Paraclete seems to have worked through Christian teachers in the tradition of the Beloved Disciple, without formal authority.

The narrative world of 1 Peter presents Simon Peter, writing from Rome, as teacher and leader for churches in provinces in other parts of the empire (1 Pet 1:1–2; 5:13). The bishop of Rome does not yet claim ecumenical authority, but the symbolic figure of Peter exercises church leadership through the circulation of his pastoral letter.

In the final, canonical edition of the Gospel of John, probably written in the early second century, charismatic authority is not rejected but coordinated with and subjected to the emerging clerical leadership symbolized by the figure of Peter, who is made the church's shepherd by the risen Christ (John 21).

Luke-Acts, probably written (also from Rome?) in the same general period as the canonical edition of the Fourth Gospel, has local congregations directed by elders (*presbyteroi*), who in the early period of the Jerusalem church also function as leaders for the wider church in conjunction with James the Lord's brother. Both Peter and James exercise leadership in the churches of Judea and Syria but pass off the scene, leaving Paul in Rome, preaching and welcoming all who come to him (Acts 28:30–31, the last scene of Luke's story of Jesus and the church); no "official" ecumenical authority is ascribed to him, and he is not called an apostle comparable to the Twelve.

The Pastor will later, in 1–2 Timothy and Titus, support an emerging system of ordained bishops, presbyters, and deacons (including women?), guided by the heritage and letters of Paul and his disciples and students, as the teachers and leaders of the church in its struggle against heresy (see below).

Second Peter, probably the latest canonical document, represents ecumenical leadership from Rome, opposes heresy in Peter's name, but embraces (the writings of) Paul as "beloved brother," whose writings are valuable but difficult to understand and can be perverted by ignorant people, "as they do the other scriptures" (2 Pet 3:15–16).

Within this conflicted situation—when Ephesians was written, the final edition of the Fourth Gospel had not yet appeared, nor had Luke-Acts, the Pastorals, or 2 Peter—as the churches struggle to find their way forward in the postapostolic situation, the author of Ephesians sets forth his own understanding of the apostolic church, which we may summarize in the following theses.

The church is built upon the foundation of the original apostles and prophets given it by God (Eph 2:20). As in Colossians, Paul is the key apostle, the one through whom the mystery of God's plan for history is revealed, focused on the unity of Jews and gentiles in the one church (3:1–13). In contrast to Colossians, Paul is not the only apostle, but, as he himself had insisted, was an authorized member of the apostolic group (1 Cor 9:1–23; 15:3–11; Gal 1–2). The apostolicity of the church means it is guided *not only by Paul* but by a limited plurality of apostles.

Apostles are closely associated with church prophets. The prophets of Ephesians 2:20 and 3:5 are not the biblical prophets of Israel but the Spirit-inspired prophets of the early church, whose new revelations led the church into new truth given by the risen Christ. This included the key revelation of the admission of gentiles to the one church, a post-Easter process of revelation through the Holy Spirit in the life of the church narrated in Acts 1–15. The distinction between apostles and prophets is not sharp—Paul, for instance, exercised the functions of both—but apostles are associated more with the authentic interpretation of the Christ event and consolidation of the tradition in the first, founding generation, while prophets interpret the tradition and give new revelations for later times, keeping the tradition relevant. The Pauline school represented by Ephesians resembles the teachers of the Johannine community, which insisted that the church affirms both authentic tradition that goes back to the beginning (1 John 1:1–3) and subsequent direction by Spirit-guided prophets and teachers (John 14–16; Revelation).

Both apostles and prophets belong to the foundation period of the church. The author of Ephesians knows of no contemporary apostles and reports nothing about new revelations from the heavenly Lord in his own time. Thus, *like* his contemporary, the visionary prophet-author of Revelation, he looks back to a foundation period established by the original apostles but is *silent* about the kind of continuing revelation claimed by the seer John of Patmos. The author of Ephesians is already approaching the later view of a deposit of tradition from the first generation that must be faithfully handed on and interpreted by the church's teachers, a view to be explicated in the Pastorals.

The present, emerging ministers of the church, whom the author designates as evangelists and pastor-teachers, are in continuity with the original apostles (Eph 4:11). It is not clear whether "pastors and teachers" refers to one group or two. Likewise, there is no sharp distinction between "evangelists" and "pastor-teachers." As in Paul's lists of spiritual gifts and "fruits of the Spirit," the functions are not crisply separated but are overlapping (1 Cor 12–14; Rom 8:23; 12:6–8; Gal 5:22). The author would have probably considered himself and other teachers in the Pauline school to be both pastors and teachers as well as evangelists. The distinction, if any, between ministers in the "local congregation" and more general ministers to the church at large is also vague.

Ephesians 4:11 places the past ministry of apostles and prophets and the present ministry of evangelists and pastor-teachers in the same category, as gifts of God through the Spirit for the equipment of the church for its mission. The contemporary ministry of the church is responsible for mediating the past revelation given by apostles and prophets. Evangelists and pastor-teachers are pictured as the bearers and preservers of the tradition, a bridge between the apostolic and postapostolic periods. The author of Ephesians, like the author(s) of the Gospel of John, would presumably identify himself with this group of evangelist-pastor-teachers, whose task is to nourish the congregations in their growth toward maturity. The church is the one holy catholic people of God, but it is not perfect. Ephesians does not label this imperfection sin; it labels it *immaturity*. It moves—rather, is being moved—toward the ultimate goal of the reconciliation and restoration of the universe as God's good creation. It has not arrived; it is on the way; and the road it is on will bring it to the destination God intends. The author of Ephesians offers the church a magnificent vision of its own identity and glorious future but has little practical instruction about how the church should be structured to be faithful to its mission. He (possibly "she"; cf. next section) affirms the new developments in which the Spirit of God is at work and acknowledges new forms of ministry and leadership but has no organizational structure to propose. As we now turn to the latest canonical document of the Pauline school, we meet the Pastor, the author of 1–2 Timothy and Titus, who presents firm instructions for the faith, structure, and life to guide the church through changing times. It is a challenging encounter.

1–2 Timothy, Titus: The Pastor as Radical

Faith, Order, and Mission

It was renewed awareness of the church's *mission* that generated the modern ecumenical movement, which sprang from the International Missionary Conference held at Edinburgh in 1910. After World War I, the ecumenical movement generated two organizations, the Life and Work Movement, concentrating on the practice of Christian faith in everyday life, in all its personal, social, economic, and political aspects, and the Faith and Order Movement, focusing on the essential beliefs and polities of the member churches, the convictions that identified them as churches, convictions that both united and separated them. In 1948 the two movements merged at the first assembly of the World Council of Churches.

Word, World, Mission

"The Word of God which was given in Jesus Christ is a unique historical fact, and everything Christian is dependent on it; hence everyone who receives this Word, and by it salvation, receives along with it the duty of passing this Word on; just as a man who might have discovered a remedy for cancer which saved himself, would be in duty bound to make this remedy accessible to all.

"Mission work does not arise from any arrogance in the Christian Church; mission is its cause and its life. The Church exists by mission, just as a fire exists by burning. Where there is no mission, there is no Church; and where there is neither Church nor mission, there is no faith."

—Emil Brunner, *The Word and the World*
(London: SCM, 1931), 108

The Pastor's instructions on faith and order are in the service of the church's mission, a call to its life and work. Like all New Testament authors, the Pastor affirms and shares the Christian faith in the sense of obedience-in-personal-trust (see above), the preconceptual, pretheological personal trust in the living God, *fides qua creditur* (faith as believing, the faith with which one believes). But faith must have content, an object; Christian faith is not mere believing but believing *something* (*fides quae creditur*, the faith that is believed). Though one can distinguish faith-as-personal-trust and theological content as expression of this trust, in concrete reality they cannot be separated. One cannot first "believe" and then only later, as a second act, inquire as to what one believes. As an individual believer, a congregation, or a denomination matures in the faith, the way they understand and state what they believe may change, without diluting—perhaps even strengthening—faith as personal trust in God. The Pastor expresses a profound Pauline personal faith in God (2 Tim 1:12), but his letters are concerned with faith in the sense of the "faith and order" of the churches, the church's theology and structure.

The Pastor: Profound Theologian?

Although we are making soundings in the theology of the Pastorals, not attempting a comprehensive statement of the theology of these letters, these letters do represent a faith both deep and broad. To be sure, no interpreter known to me considers the Pastorals the zenith of New Testament theology, and that claim is certainly not made here. On the contrary, for some interpreters of the New Testament, the Pastorals compete with Revelation for the dubious distinction of the low point of New Testament thought, the furthest from the message of Jesus and the theology of Paul. The critique may be misplaced; it may judge the Pastor by inappropriate criteria. Like us, and like all the New Testament authors, the Pastor is a theologian. He is, however, not a creative theologian of the first generation, like Paul. He is even less a systematic theologian than the other writers in the Pauline school. He presupposes the Pauline tradition in which he stands, supplementing the other letters already circulating under the name of Paul. Like them, all that he has to say has substantial theological presuppositions, but his writings are not intended to provide theological instruction as such. He assumes his readers already know the substance of what he refers to as "the teaching" (*didaskalia*, the authentic doctrines of the church, used twenty-six times in the New Testament, of which, fifteen are in the Pastorals), just as he presupposes they know the identity and beliefs of the false teachers threatening the church. Most of what he says to "Timothy" and "Titus" is evoked as a defense against this threat. Working through his response, we frequently see tips of what may be theological icebergs projecting above the surface of the text. We note only a few.

There is one God, the Creator and Savior. This is no abstract doctrine. The author presents God as the Creator, and the world as God's good creation, to refute the false but popular "rigorous spirituality" of those who reject the world, who "forbid marriage and demand abstinence from foods, which God created to be received with thanksgiving by those who believe and know the truth. For everything created by God is good, and nothing is to be rejected, provided it is received with thanksgiving" (1 Tim 4:3–4). "God our Savior" appears seven times in this brief corpus; it is the author's favorite title for God (1 Tim 1:1; 2:3; 4:10; Titus 1:4; 2:10, 13; 3:4). The saving God has a saving plan (*oikonomia*, 1 Tim 1:4) that includes "all people, especially . . . those who believe" (1 Tim 4:10). The author feels bound to affirm both that God's grace saves all and that it applies especially to those who respond in faith, but he makes no effort to integrate these affirmations into a systematic whole.

There is one mediator between God and humanity, the human being Jesus Christ (1 Tim 2:5). The Pastor opposed a spectrum of views, varieties of proto-gnosticism that apparently taught a complex hierarchical system of heavenly beings that separated the utterly remote, true God from the material world. In this view, Jesus Christ was one of these mediating divine beings: more than human, less than God, neither truly human nor truly divine. For the Pastor, Jesus Christ is the sole mediator between the one God and humanity. Just as the God who created the world was not a downscale heavenly being who bumbled the job but the one true God, so Jesus Christ is not merely a member of the heavenly hierarchy who came or was sent to earth. There is no sharp line between the Pastor's "doctrine of God" and his "Christology." In step with the other later New Testament documents, he can use God language of Christ, speaking of Christ in ways that do not distinguish Christ from God (e.g., Titus 2:13 can be translated either "our great God and Savior, Jesus Christ," or "the great God and our Savior Jesus Christ"; cf. John 1:1, 18; 20:28; Heb 1:8, 9; 2 Pet 1:1[?]; 2 Thess 1:12[?]). The Pastor also speaks readily of "God our Savior" and has no hesitation in distinguishing between the "two persons" of "God the Father and Christ Jesus our Savior" (Titus 1:4). Against the docetism that had become popular in the Christianity of Roman Asia, the Pastor insists that the one mediator is "the man Christ Jesus" who was "revealed in flesh" (1 Tim 2:5; 3:16). He is a descendant of David who truly died and was raised from the dead (2 Tim 2:8). The Pastor thinks of the saving event as the U-shaped event of the Pauline *kenosis* pattern, which has no room for stories of saving miracles during the life of Jesus. Though Gospels had been written and circulated in Roman Asia by the time the author writes, including the Gospel of John as the crowning theological achievement of the neighboring Johannine school, the author shows no appreciation for the gospel genre and no inclination to teach Christian doctrine by narrating incidents or expounding teaching from the life of Jesus. As in Paul, the saving love and power of God are manifest in the Christ event as a whole, not in particular incidents in the life of Jesus. There is no suggestion that Jesus worked miracles or citation of the teaching or example of the earthly Jesus, and only minimal points of contact with traditions picturing the pre-Easter life of Jesus.[12]

Pauline soteriology is to be preserved and elaborated. Salvation is not a matter of heavenly spiritual beings trapped in human bodies who return to their heavenly home. Nor is salvation a matter of human achievement, not by "works of righteousness that we have done," but by God's mercy and grace. Paul's doctrine of justification by grace through faith is represented and summarized in 2 Timothy 1:8–10 and Titus 3:3–7. There is no decline into a "works righteousness." It is assumed that this theology is already known and affirmed by the readers.[13] Paul himself is incorporated into the saving event, as in Colossians (2 Tim 2:10; cf. Col 1:24).

Eschatology is preserved but is no longer intense, and it is not elaborated in apocalyptic detail. The saving event is designated the "epiphany" (*epiphaneia* the noun, *epiphainō* the verb), found seven times in the Pastorals, usually translated as "manifestation" or "appearing." Epiphany is the Pastor's term for "revelation" (*apokalypsis*), which does not appear in the Pastorals. The saving event is the epiphany of Jesus Christ in this world, which has already occurred: "the goodness and loving kindness of God our Savior appeared" (Titus 3:4; cf. 2 Tim 1:10; Titus 2:11). But the epiphany/ manifestation is in two acts, the second of which is still to come (1 Tim 6:14; 2 Tim 4:1, 8; Titus 2:13). The church lives between these two epiphanies of Jesus Christ, the one as the crucified and risen Jesus of Nazareth to which the church looks back in memory (2 Tim 2:8, "Remember Jesus Christ . . ."), the other to which the church looks forward in hope (1 Tim 1:1, "Christ Jesus our hope . . ."; cf. Titus 2:13). Christ's resurrection is an event of the past, but the believers' resurrection is still to come. Paul himself had spoken of baptism as being united with Christ's death and resurrection, with the "eschatological reservation" that present Christian life is identified with the cross, lived in the "power of the resurrection" by the dynamism of the Spirit, with the believer's resurrection still in the eschatological future (Phil 3:7–11; 1 Cor 15). Though some of his contemporary Christian teachers in Roman Asia spoke of already being risen with Christ (Col 3:1–4; Eph 2:6; John 11:17–27), they, like Paul, continued to look forward to the resurrection at the consummation of history. Nonetheless, the Pastor considered this too close to the gnosticizing ideas he opposed, advocated only by the false teachers who had "swerved from the truth by claiming that the resurrection has already taken place" (2 Tim 2:18; cf. the insistence of Rev 20:5 that the *future* resurrection is the *first* resurrection). For the Pastor, this does not mean that the present is an empty interim, a parenthesis in the saving plan of God. The present, the time of the church, is the time of the continuing act of God in history, in and through the church, led and empowered by the Spirit. As in the other writings of the Pauline school, particularly Ephesians, the Pastor focuses and elaborates his theology as an understanding of "the church of the living God, the pillar and bulwark of the truth" (1 Tim 3:15).

Present Life as "Resurrection" in the Gospel of Thomas

"His [Jesus's] disciples said to Him, 'When will the repose of the dead come about, and when will the new world come?' He said to them, 'What you look forward to has already come, but you do not recognize it.'"

—Gospel of Thomas, Saying 51

The Pastor's Understanding of the Church

The Pastorals have sometimes been considered negatively as the parade example of the institutionalization of the "Jesus movement," transforming the countercultural dynamic of the first generation or its "eschatological existence" into "early catholicism" (see above) and shrinking radical Christian commitment to the conventions of bourgeois lifestyle that too easily accommodated itself to the values of the surrounding world. The vitality of Paul's "body of Christ" imagery (not found in the Pastorals) is supposed to have suffered an institutional hardening of the arteries. In particular, the Pastor's specific instructions to women regarding dress and keeping silent in church, and his general call to submission to authority, have often been ignored, rejected, or met with disdain (1 Tim 2:8–15; 5:3–16; 2 Tim 3:6–7; Titus 2:3–5). As is the case with Revelation, with which *Hearing John's Voice* began, the Pastorals, which conclude *Hearing Paul's Voice*, constitute a daunting challenge to one who is committed to biblical preaching and teaching. Instead of ignoring problematic or distasteful biblical texts, or co-opting them for our own agenda, this perspective on the task of the preacher and teacher in the church strives to come within hearing distance, attempting to understand the texts in their own terms, cultivating the same kind of nonjudgmental listening skills refined in pastoral counseling.

Agenda and Dialogue

"*Agenda* is a Latin word, the plural of *agendum*, which is the gerundive form of the verb *agere*, meaning what ought to be done. It is a neutral term, and need not be understood in the sinister or manipulative sense of 'hidden agenda.' . . . Every reader approaches the text with a particular agenda or set of agendas. I may be a racist or antiracist, a pacifist or a militarist, a feminist or male or female chauvinist, a nationalist or one with a commitment to the larger human community. My agenda is what I am concerned with, what I consider important and true and how to implement it, that-which-is-to-be-done. I have my agenda, and I cannot do otherwise. 'Let the one who is without an agenda cast the first stone.'"

—M. Eugene Boring,
An Introduction to the New Testament: History, Literature, Theology
(Louisville: Westminster John Knox, 2012), 69–70

Perhaps the key term here is "agenda." Though nowadays "agenda" is sometimes used with negative connotations, having an agenda is inherent in having a mission. To be sure, the Pastor has an agenda, as does every reader. Responsible biblical interpretation involves dialogue between the agenda of the biblical text and the interpreter's own agenda. Dialogue involves listening. What is the Pastor's agenda?

From the beginning, those who believed that Jesus of Nazareth was the Messiah sent by God had a spectrum of options in relating their new faith to the culture in which they lived, and which they inevitably shared. H. Richard Niebuhr proposed a typology that has become a classic starting point for discussing this issue. Niebuhr outlined five views of the relation of Christ and culture that have appeared in the long history of the church. All five are still with us.[14]

1. *Christ against culture*—Christian faith is inherently opposed to the culture. Christ's call to Christian believers means they are not to be "worldly" (Tertullian, Tolstoy, sectarian Christian groups, some monasticism, much fundamentalism).

2. *Christ of culture*—Christian faith sees Christ as inherently in continuity with the world, representing the highest cultural aspirations and achievements. The mission of the church is to promote "Christian values" (liberal culture-Protestantism of the nineteenth and early twentieth century, represented by, e.g., Adolf Harnack's *What Is Christianity?*).

3. *Christ above culture*—Christ transcends culture, which points beyond itself to the divine (Aquinas and much of the Roman Catholic tradition).

4. *Christ and culture in paradox*—Both Christ and culture are from God, but an irreducible paradoxical tension always exists between them. In this world, Christians always live within this tension, citizens of two worlds at the same time (Luther and much of the Lutheran tradition).

5. *Christ the transformer of culture*—Human culture is inherently sinful but was originally God's good creation, and it can become an expression of Christian purpose (Calvin and much of the Reformed tradition).

Although Niebuhr's analysis is valuable and has been widely influential, one weakness of his typology is that it allows—contrary to his own intention—"Christ" and "culture" to be thought of as two independent entities that can then be related in a variety of ways. But no one, and no group or stream of theology, ever has an understanding of "Christ" in some pure way that then, as a second step, can be related to "culture." Every understanding of the meaning of the historical Jesus or God's act in Christ is inevitably already perceived through the filter of some human culture. Even the English word "Christ" (Hebrew *mashiach*, "Messiah," Greek *christos*, each of which means "anointed," "smeared" with oil) reflects a particular culture in which leaders installed in certain offices or designated for certain functions (prophet, priest, king) were smeared with olive oil as part of the inauguration ceremony (e.g., Exod 28:41; 1 Sam 2:10; 15:1; 2 Sam 2:4; 1 Kings 19:16; 1 Chron 16:22)—just as altars and sacred rocks were anointed to set them apart for some holy purpose (e.g., Gen 31:13; Exod 29:36; 40:9). The basic confession of Christian faith is already expressed in a cultural medium strange to us (post)moderns, and inevitably so. The same is true of "Son of God," "Lord," and every other expression of faith, though less obviously so, allowing us to read our own understanding, from our own culture, into them, rather than hearing them in their own terms.

Two Radicals: John the Baptist and Jesus of Nazareth

Niebuhr's five types hardly exist in "pure" forms, but they can serve as a helpful grid for sorting out the actual options that face believers. Two such options have confronted Christian believers from the very beginning. Both John the Baptist and Jesus of Nazareth were "radical" in the sense of "foundational," "getting to the root of the matter" (etymologically, "radical" is related to Latin *radix*, "root").

John the Baptist

John the Baptist was an example of withdrawing from the culture and opposing it in the name of God. From a sociological point of view, this apocalyptic Jewish prophet shared the sectarian orientation Israelite groups such as the Rechabites (Jer 35:1–19), Kenites (Judg 1:16; 4:11–5:24; 1 Sam 15:6; 27:10; 1 Chron 2:55), and Nabateans (Diodorus Siculus, *Bibliotheca historica* 19.94.2–3) are supposed to have had. They had disengaged from the settled Israelite population and retained the nomadic, somewhat ascetic lifestyle of Israel during the wilderness wanderings, living the life of the pure Israel before they settled in Canaan and adopted many features of corrupting Canaanite civilization. John the Baptist had not compromised with the prevailing culture. He paid no taxes and did not wear the clothes, eat the food, or drink the wine of the cultured world (Matt 3:4; Luke 7:33). He did not fit into society, lived on its fringes, and could speak of the evils of society as what "they" were doing. He was a courageous prophet who spoke truth to power, and it cost him his life (Mark 6:17–29). He organized no institutions. His ministry provided one option of how the life faithful to God should relate to the corruptions of civilization. People rejected his separatist way of keeping himself "holy" and said he was crazy ("has a demon," Luke 7:33). In a situation where everyone had long since known that responsible citizenship and a respectable religious life meant fitting into the normal standards of "the world," John, who stood apart and called for repentance, was a radical.

Jesus of Nazareth

Jesus of Nazareth was baptized by John (Matt 3:13–17), was his disciple for a while (4:12–17), and, even after separating to form his own movement, continued to hold John in highest respect (11:7–15). Jesus, too, called for radical, full commitment. As remembered in the New Testament, Jesus did not marry, left his home and family to fulfill the mission to which God had called him (Mark 3:31–35), and formed a small group that he encouraged to do the same (Mark 1:16–20; 3:19; 6:7–13; 10:28–31). No priority, not even family, could be higher than devotion to God (Luke 14:25–27). But he was no ascetic, did not withdraw from society, and did not encourage his followers to do so. He participated in society, paid taxes to an imperialistic pagan government, and instructed his followers to do so (Matt 17:24–27; 22:15–22). He went to dinner parties, associating with religious groups to the right and left, and was criticized by the other side (Mark 2:15–22; Luke 7:36–50). When Jesus ate with sinners and associated with those deemed unacceptable in conventional society, this did not mean that he was simply a more liberal, tolerant person than most others, including John the Baptist, but that he had a different theology of God's mission in the world. It also meant he had to decide on whether and how to "compromise" with the given structures of society. Both John and Jesus were apocalyptic preachers, but neither advocated his way of life as an "interim ethic," valid only in the brief period before the end of the world. Jesus had an eschatological mission *in* the world, not just *to* the world as one who remained an outsider. He entered fully into the life of the world and, as a truly human being, could think of its political, economic, social, and religious life as what "we" do. Some deeply religious people rejected his way of entering into the life of the world, accommodating himself to its given structures, and said he was "a glutton and a drunkard, a friend of tax collectors and sinners" (Luke 7:34). In a situation where John was admired for his uncompromising lifestyle and true religion meant noninvolvement in the world, Jesus the partygoer and friend of sinners was a radical.

The Pastor: A Radical, after All?

When Martin Luther left the monastery, got married, raised a family, and participated in normal life, buying into the thought and culture of conventional society, in the context of sixteenth-century religious culture, this was a radical act. He did this for the sake of the church and the Christian faith, not as a personal lapse or individual protest.

When the Pastor commended Christian existence as life within the conventional social structures of the world, necessarily accommodating Christian commitment to it, in the context of Roman Asian religiosity, was this, too, a radical move, done for the sake of the church and its mission?

Though John the Baptist still had his followers in Roman Asia of 90–130 CE (Acts 19:1–7), the Pastor commends a kind of responsible accommodation to the given structures of society more in step with Jesus's own life.

Household Codes, the Christian Home, and the Church as the Household of God

Paul himself did not adapt the conventional household codes for his first-generation readers. He believed he and his readers were living in the last generation of human history and was concerned that he and they be faithful witnesses to the faith during these last times (see, e.g., 1 Cor 7). When the end did not come as expected, Christian teachers in the next generation followed the lead of Hellenistic Judaism in adapting the conventional household codes of the Hellenistic world as instruction for Christians shaping their lives and the church's mission to the realities of the ongoing world. The Pastor represents the latest and most rigorous example of this adaptation, but he found its roots and foundation in Paul's perspective on Christian ethical responsibility represented, for example, in Romans 14. He considered his instructions in the post-Pauline situation to be an authentic representation of Paul's own view; we cannot know what Paul would have thought, nor did the Pastor himself know. As a faithful interpreter of the tradition given him, in a church context guided by the Spirit, the Pastor had to take responsibility for faithfulness both to the tradition and to its interpretation for his later situation. So do we preachers and teachers in the church of the twenty-first century. We have both Paul and a spectrum of later canonical interpretations. We cannot know what either Paul or the Pastor would make of our interpretations. Though the Pastor's world was very different from our own, we stand in the same situation as the Pastor, charged to bridge the gap between the world of Scripture and our own world, being faithful to both. We need neither repeat him nor disdain him. We can consider him a fellow minister, preacher, and teacher, and we can learn from him. Whatever we decide to do, we must first listen to him. Here, we can only present some guidelines that might help us come within hearing distance of these texts that still have something to say to our own times.

There can be no direct transfer from biblical texts to contemporary instruction. Just as no one today can quote "Tell slaves to be submissive to their masters" (Titus 2:9) to justify the institution of slavery, so no one today can legitimately cite Titus 2:5 on the duty of younger women to be "submissive to their husbands" as justification for patriarchal marriage. In neither case can we claim to "just do what the Bible says." We must hear all such instructions in their own historical and cultural context before we attempt to interpret them for our own situation. The word "slave" in our ears naturally evokes racist and violent images of the forcible importation of Africans to be sold and exploited on American plantations. We naturally tend to understand instructions to family members in terms of modern Western nuclear families. Likewise, when we hear the Bible's instructions regarding political and economic action, we must keep in mind that they were not given in a democratic, capitalist, middle-class society where the church had long been an established institution. We must hear all these biblical instructions in their own historical and cultural contexts before we can appropriate them in any legitimate and meaningful way as a guide to our own decisions and actions. There are, of course, commentaries and historical studies that help us overcome our tendencies to read our own views into the biblical text (see suggestions for further reading at the end of this volume), but this does *not* mean that such historical study will solve all theological problems, and that once we hear the Pastor's word to the church of his time, we can welcome it and obey it. But whatever we decide is an authentic response to the biblical text for our time, we must *hear* it first. That is what we are about in this book. It may require some study.

There can be no abolition of all rules and authority. Since the people of God, from Moses and Aaron onward, have always been called to oppose oppression of the weak and vulnerable by the strong and privileged, interpreters have sometimes seen the basic problem as thinking of God as "king" or "emperor," with absolute authority, and have attempted to conceive Christian faith in ways that avoid all such language and imagery. In such a framework, it is claimed, the call to "obedience" to God or Christ is patriarchal, hierarchical, imperial, and oppressive in ways incompatible with Christian faith. The "kingdom of God," even if such language is replaced by such gender-neutral terms as "divine sovereignty," still represents top-down authority and the human responsibility of obedience. This objection is to be taken seriously, but we must ask whether in this world there can ever be a society without rules, order, and structure, which always call for interpretation and enforcement by violence or the threat of violence. At least for all biblical authors, anarchy is never an option in this world, where we always find ourselves already enmeshed in some particular social structure, all of which have, and must have, rules and enforcement as the price of community. Instead of the abolition of structure and power, the definitive biblical revelation redefines the nature of power. Many Christians in Roman Asia had come to know the image of the Lion King who had revealed himself as the Lamb, the one who does not abdicate his throne with its authority but who rules in self-giving love, calling his followers to do the same (Rev 5). Instead of rejecting the imagery and language of kingship, the Bible continues to think of God as Creator and Lord, and human beings as God's creatures who find their fulfillment not in autonomy but in obedience to the One in whose service is perfect freedom (see above on Rom 6:12–23).

Mission has the priority. The Pastor shares with all New Testament authors the conviction that the church is a commissioned church. We must again remind ourselves that the self-understanding of belonging to the community of faith, the people of God with a mission to the whole world, was not typical of Hellenistic religion. All members of the Christian community, whether master or slave, male or female, old or young, are called to live their lives with the mission of the community to the world as a higher priority than individualistic rights. Mission, not submission, is the focus of New Testament household codes.

Social responsibility is a part of the Christian mission. Christians of the twenty-first century have a kind of power to improve laws and social conditions that the churches addressed in the New Testament did not have and could not have imagined. We rightly think of our social responsibility as bringing Christian faith to bear on social issues, striving to eliminate injustice in community, city, state, nation, and world. We rightly see this as part of the church's mission. Teachers in the Pauline school could not have envisioned the possibility of applying the dynamism of Christian faith to social and political structures to move them toward a more just world. They did see the way their lives and congregations were perceived by the world at large as a matter of Christian mission. The Pastor tended to regard the breaking down of social conventions in the name of the new life of the Spirit as a danger to this mission. Early Christian communities needed patterns and models for ethical conduct that both manifested the newness of the Christian life to which they had been called and exhibited to the world that their manner of life conformed to general social expectations. He understood this as a call to "do what is appropriate"; common human decency and courtesy is a matter of respect for others and their opinions. Already Paul's profoundly theological letter to the Romans regarded the cultural criterion, the ethos of "what is done" (*ta kathēkonta*, Rom 1:28), as a valid ethical principle. One dimension of authentic human existence before God is the awareness that some things "just aren't done," an awareness that can communicate the radical demand of

God (cf., e.g., Gen 34:7; 2 Sam 13:12; and the prophetic remonstrance against violations of common human decency such as Amos 1–2). To be sure, Paul had called for a transformation of the mind that did not simply allow the world to press believers into its own cultural mold (Rom 1:28 is in the same letter as Rom 12:1!), but the extensive discussion in Romans 14 argued that Christian responsibility, especially for the liberal, "enlightened" believer, sometimes called for the formulation and adoption of cultural standards of behavior precisely in the service of the Christian message. Accommodation to cultural models had both the internal purpose of providing needed ethical norms and the missionary purpose, both evangelistic and apologetic, of showing to the world that the Christian faith did not undermine family and society but affirmed their highest values. The household codes taught insiders and reassured outsiders that Christians did not flee from the world but assumed a responsible place within it. This was not the approach of John the Baptist, as it did not fit in with the proto-gnostic proponents of "rigorous Christianity" opposed by the Pastor. It was in step with Jesus's own life.

Mission is local and particular. The New Testament codes are always presented in the context of letters addressed to a particular situation, do not purport to give valid rules for every time and place, and must be re-interpreted anew in every situation. The household codes are a reminder that faith does not lift one out of the givenness of one's historical situation, and that the life of faith must always come to terms with the realities of a particular society and history rather than fleeing into internal individualism or eschatological extremism. The specific social and political structures themselves are neither justified nor condemned but are accepted as the given historical reality of their time and place. God the Creator is the God of order. God the Creator is pictured in Genesis 1–2 as bringing life-giving order out of life-threatening chaos. Commands to be subordinate affirm the order God the Creator has established in the world, which is always better than chaos. The commands do not establish any particular social order as given by God.

Hierarchy includes mutuality and personal responsibility. It is historically understandable that the New Testament household codes reflect the hierarchical understanding of order and power assumed in the times, including the institution of slavery. The aspects of mutuality and personal responsibility, not part of the conventional codes but included in the New Testament adaptations, represent not merely a surrender to prevailing cultural understandings but also an interpretation and adaptation of the codes in the light of Christian faith. Commands are given not only to wives, children, and slaves but also to husbands, parents, and masters. All are directly addressed and called to personal responsibility for the decisions they must make, not merely to submission to cultural expectations. Such decisions need not mean the surrender or dilution of the radical call to discipleship, but they may be its courageous expression.

Christian faith applies to all of life, including the household. The household codes are not part of the teaching of Jesus nor the earliest Christian tradition, but they are adopted and adapted from the culture. This does not mean that the church always lives by the cultural conventions in which it finds itself. Such conventions change, and the church's understanding of the way of life to which it is called also changes, but this does not mean that the church simply goes with the flow of cultural change. We might think, for example, of the changing cultural mores regarding divorce, pre- and extra-marital sex, the use of tobacco and alcohol. Can Christian ethics simply say, "Well, times have changed"? There can be no doubt that as times change, and cultural mores change, responsible Christian ethics also change. But the church has its own ethical anchor points in Scripture, tradition, experience, and sanctified reason. The ethics of those who belong to the people of God are not always prescribed in advance, nor do they simply mirror the culture in which they find themselves. The New Testament household codes are not intended to be the law of all Christians in every age, but they do illustrate the church's mandate to live out the meaning of the gospel in every walk of life, including its understanding of family life. *That* this is the case is given in Scripture. *What* this is to be from case to case must be worked out by the Christian community in every situation. Responsible, intelligent, and informed Christian people might well change their understanding of what is right and wrong, influenced by dialogue with different times and cultures. But Christian believers cannot simply appeal to the changes in the culture around them as justification for an ever-changing "new morality" that only reflects the changing culture. Readers of the biblical household codes are given models of churches in other times and places who interpreted the Christian gospel in the context of their particular culture. We belong to the same church they did, but we modern Christians need not replicate these instructions as rules for our time and place, but neither can we ignore them. The gospel applies to all of life.

Household responsibility is expanded to include the social and political world. The social and political world was thought of as an enormous family. The emperor was the *paterfamilias* of an enormous and diverse family (cf. George Washington as "father of the country"). Civil servants were called members of "Caesar's household" (Phil 4:22). As had long been the case in the Jewish community in the Hellenistic world, Christian members of the people of God are instructed that "supplications, prayers, intercessions, and thanksgivings be made for everyone, for kings and all who are in high positions, so that we may lead a quiet and peaceable life in all godliness and dignity" (1 Tim 2:1–2). The radical Pastor joins the radical prophet John of Revelation in making it clear that Christian believers must draw the line at joining their neighbors at worship before the temple of the divine emperor, for there is only one "King of kings and Lord of lords" (1 Tim 6:15; Rev 19:16). Like their Jewish fellow members of the people of God, Christian believers may not pray to the emperor but will pray for him.

Since churches met in private homes and households required order to function for the welfare of all concerned, it is natural that the metaphor of the "Christian home" provided the perspective, images, and vocabulary within which the structures of church leadership were coming to be understood.

The Gift of Ministry

The Pastor shares the conviction of the author of Ephesians that the structure of the church is not merely a pragmatic necessity but that the church's ministry is God's gift to the church, important for the mission of the church to the world. What the Pastor has to say is neither descriptive nor prescriptive for all times and places.

The Pastor's instructions on ministerial office are not *descriptive*. The Pastor is here understood as a third-generation teacher in the Pauline school, whose letters are launched into a church context that already has a varied, growing, and disputed tradition of what church leadership should be. The Pastor presupposes that readers are aware of the meaning and function of the terms he uses. "Widows," "bishop," "elders," "deacons" are not explained. The issue is not the legitimacy of the offices, or what they are, but the related question of the qualifications of those who fill these roles. The history of interpretation confirms this. Through the centuries, interpreters of sound mind and good will have not been able to agree on the structure envisioned and advocated by the Pastor.

The Pastor's instructions on ministerial office are not *prescriptive*. The Pastor does not hesitate to give authoritative commands, but there are no commands to implement offices the church does not already have. The Pastor assumes that certain offices are already in place or in the process of implementation, at different phases in different locations or congregations, and addresses his instructions to a situation where the readers already understand something of the issues involved in putting into practice more than one tradition of church leadership. The letters probably circulated as a unit but were read in a variety of congregational situations, where there was some variation in both the patterns of congregational structure and how the congregations and their leaders related to other congregations. "Timothy" appears to address congregations where these offices are already established (1 Tim 3:1–13; 5:3–22); "Titus" is charged with the task of instituting new church offices in churches that did not previously have them (Titus 1:5–9).

The Pastor adapts a familiar, appropriate, and powerful strategy of communication to present his vision of church leadership. The author does not present his argument in the form of a manual of church order or an essay on church leadership, but as *letters from Paul*. Paul is gone. "Timothy" and "Titus" have been "left behind" to continue the Pauline mission (1 Tim 1:3; Titus 1:5). The second- and third-generation Pauline congregations were accustomed to hearing the letters Paul wrote to other churches, for collections of Paul's letters had been made and were circulated among the churches of Roman Asia, and were read in the worship and instruction of the churches alongside the reading of Scripture. When the Pastor wrote, Christians in Ephesus had for years heard Paul's letters to the Corinthians and others read in their own worship and instruction. They already faced the issue of not-written-to-us/written-to-us. In these letters, Paul had addressed the members of the congregations directly, in the second person. The Pastor chooses the literary form of letters to Timothy and Titus, his colleagues, assistants, and subordinates, who are then to instruct the churches. The form corresponds to the content and already suggests a certain hierarchical understanding of church leadership: Paul instructs Timothy and Titus on the formation of church leadership, and the letters' auditors overhear this instruction. Later interpreters listen, listen *in*, to the Pastor's instruction, and structure their congregations accordingly, congregations that will then authorize and equip faithful leaders to equip others (2 Tim 2:2).

The Pastor envisions an effective, functioning ministry to nourish the church in the faith, protect it from false teaching, and enable it to fulfill its mission. The commissioned church needs qualified and authorized leaders. Who are these leaders, what are their qualifications, who authorizes them, and how? The church is thought of as the "household of God" (1 Tim 3:5, 15, as already Eph 2:19); it is not insignificant that the phrase is found in the

New Testament only in these three deutero-Pauline texts, where church leadership and management are thought of in the same terms as the extended household addressed in the household codes. This means that God is the head of the household and the various leadership and management roles are all subordinate to God the Father (*paterfamilias*). This also means that we cannot suppose we already know the meaning of such terms as "widow" and "elder." Of course, we know the meaning of these terms in our own culture and church tradition. We may have to listen carefully to understand what the Pastor means by these terms, whether he is using them of the household or of the ministry of the church. The Pastor has a general vision of church structure he is advocating, but he addresses a situation somewhat in flux. Even though the details of the Pastor's vision of church leadership for the Pauline churches in Roman Asia in the early second century are no longer entirely clear to us, listening in on the Pastor's instructions can enrich our own understanding of the mission of the church and its ministry in our own time. The original readers could fill in the gaps from their own knowledge of the actual situation. We later readers must use our informed historical imagination to get the picture. The following is one reading; church history reveals it is not the only one.

The New Testament on the Way to the Papacy?

We have seen that the Pastor is not the only Christian teacher of his time who is attempting to consolidate the churches by firming up the order of ministry. First Peter and 1 Clement from Rome, Ignatius's letters from Antioch to Asian churches, and the Didache from Syria are among works advocating a firm authorized structure for congregations, integrating them into the larger structure of the ecumenical church, a church of which the risen Christ continues to be Lord, a church in which the Holy Spirit continues to be active, leading the church forward. Just how this was to be done was already a contentious issue in the Pastor's time. The Pastor's vision of Paul as the sole or principal teacher for the (whole) church will not become the dominant view of the emerging early catholic church. Like the Johannine community's vision of a church led by the Holy Spirit though symbolized by the Beloved Disciple, and the combination of Pauline and Petrine traditions under the image of Pauline leadership in Luke-Acts, the Pastor's vision will lose out to Petrine authority represented by leaders in the Roman church (1 Peter; 1 Clement, see 4.4.9; John 21). Like the traditions and texts of the Johannine community, the Pastor's insights and the witness of the Pauline community will be merged in the limited plurality of the canon and limited plurality of the monarchical episcopate, shepherded by the "first among equals," the bishop of Rome. But that is some generations after the Pastor's time.

The congregation lives under the authority of God. No one, then or now, would dispute that for all concerned, God is the ultimate authority in the church, the household of God. Paul, Timothy and Titus, the bishop, elders, deacons, widows, and prophets are all members of the household, who function with *delegated* authority. God is the *paterfamilias*, the ruler of the household. God's authority is mediated through the *risen Christ*, but just as the Pastor cannot think of Christ apart from God nor God apart from Christ (see above), the one God/Jesus Christ is the sole authority for the individual believer and for the church's life and mission. The *risen Christ* called and authorized the *apostle Paul* to represent God's authority in founding and directing the church. No other apostles are mentioned. For the Pauline churches as understood by the Pastor, there is no plurality of apostles (contrast Rev 21:14; Eph 3:5; 4:11). The three-word rendition of some English translations, which includes the indefinite article, "Paul, an apostle" (1 Tim 1:1; 2:7; 2 Tim 1:1, 11; Titus 1:1), represents the two words of the Greek text, *Paulos apostolos*. The Greek language, like Latin and some other languages, ancient and modern, has no indefinite article. The anarthrous usage represents the official claim to apostleship, not one of a group (cf. REB, NJB). Other claims to apostleship circulated in the churches of Roman Asia in the Pastor's time (e.g., 1 Pet 1:1). The Pastor could hardly have been unaware of them; he does not dispute with them but simply ignores them. He is interested in the Pauline churches in which he is a pastor-teacher and shows little interest in the wider Christian community. For this community, Paul is *the* apostle, period. One God, one Lord, one apostle. In this, he agrees with the emerging Marcionite movement. In this perspective, the issue is not how the church is to be guided by a plurality of apostles but how to interpret the one apostle Paul. Various interpretations are abroad in the Pastor's context, all appealing to Paul. The Pastor makes it clear that Timothy and Titus are the legitimate heirs and interpreters of Paul (*gnēsios*, "legitimate," 1 Tim 1:1; Titus 1:4). The chain of authority is thus God → Jesus Christ → apostle Paul → Timothy and Titus (cf. the analogous chain of command in Rev 1:1-3, in which God's authority is represented by the Spirit, who guides the church through charismatic prophets). None of the links in this chain are tangibly present in the congregations of Roman Asia in the Pastor's time. God, Christ, the apostle, and his first-generation assistants do not speak directly. Who or what is present to represent this authority?

God's authority is made present in the congregation in four concrete ways. First, the Jewish Scriptures were now heard as the Word of the God definitively revealed in Jesus Christ. Second, the Pastoral Letters themselves mediated the authoritative word of the apostle to the later generation. Third, the bishop and elders were established as legitimate teachers of the church. Fourth, the Pauline tradition that circulated in the churches as the collection of Paul's letters and the interpretation was becoming firm authoritative tradition. These are the church's teachers, serving as their guides for what it means to be an authentic church in uncertain times.

In the narrative world of the Pastorals, the letters are not addressed to the bishop and elders or to the congregations—further down the hierarchical "chain"—but to "Timothy" and "Titus," figures in the narrative world of the letters. When read in the congregation, the letters speak not only to bishop and elders but also to the congregation, who listen in on what "Paul" said to "Timothy" and "Titus." The next link in the chain after the apostle Paul → Timothy and Titus is not, therefore, the bishop and/or elders, who then relay their contents to the congregations, but the assembly of believers itself, the Christian community at large. The community of believers in the Pauline churches hears Paul's instructions on ministry and church order and is instructed on effective church leadership.

Bishop and Elders

The Pastor deals with bishop (singular) and elders (plural) together, as though they constitute one group. The instructions in 1 Timothy 3:1–7 deal with the bishop, presumably belonging to or overlapping the group of elders who rule, preach, and teach in 5:17. Titus 1:5–9 uses the terms interchangeably. Both "bishop" (*episkopos*) and "elder" (*presbyteros*, "presbyter") are used in secular Hellenistic Greek of household managers, supervisors of the affairs of an extended family. In the household, elderly men (*presbyteroi*) were respected for their experience and wisdom, and naturally assumed a leadership role in the extended family. When speaking of the church, the household of God, the Pastor's use of the term seems to vacillate between the conventional meaning and ecclesial usage for a church office. The functions often overlapped, for those who had shown themselves to be experienced men of mature wisdom in the household would tend to become prime candidates for church elders. Likewise, the Pastor sometimes distinguishes between elders (*presbyteroi*, always plural) and the bishop (*episkopos*, always singular), which may represent the variety of usage in the congregations he addresses (1 Tim 5:1, 17, 19; Titus 1:5).

The Pastor's instruction focuses on the kind of people the church needs in the position (1 Tim 3:1–7; Titus 1:6–9). These lists of qualifications correspond closely to the lists of qualifications for secular roles in Roman culture, such as city administrators and admirals in the navy. The church's leaders are to be quality people, respected by outsiders by their own standards. This is not only a matter of the church's need for competent leaders and part of its effort to gain respectability in society; it is also a function of the evangelistic mission of the church, which must not project the wrong image to the world by having leaders that get in the way of its message. The elder must "be well thought of by outsiders" (1 Tim 3:7), and all church members must be circumspect about violating the accepted standards of society "so that the name of God and the teaching may not be blasphemed" (1 Tim 6:1). "I don't care what people think" may sometimes be an authentic expression of Christian commitment. Applied in the wrong way in the wrong circumstance, it may sometimes be a hindrance to the mission of the church, just as it may be petty egocentrism. Romans 14 again.

The elder's actual role and function in church life receive little direct attention; the congregations the Pastor addresses already knew about that. The two key responsibilities mentioned somewhat incidentally are *ruling* and *preaching and teaching* (1 Tim 5:17), neither of which is assigned to deacons. Those who perform these tasks well are worthy of "double honor" (*diplēs timēs*). "Honor" (*timē*) here is best understood to refer not only to respect but also to financial support (cf. English "honorarium"). Elders have become at least a semiprofessional class of paid clergy.

In Ignatius's letters, approximately contemporary with the Pastor's letters and written to churches in the same area, the bishop (*episkopos*) holds an office distinct from that of the elders and is superior to them. The bishop is the supervisor of the work of the church in an area with several congregations, each of which has elders and deacons. We have seen in the Johannine community that an elder could claim to exercise teaching authority in other congregations, and that this was disputed. It is not clear that this development is already part of the Pastor's vision for the church. The bishop seems to be distinct from elders and deacons, but he may be the "first among equals," the moderator or chair of the board of elders in a congregation or city. The office of bishop requires the same qualifications as that of the elders, and has the same functions. In the Pastor's time, practice probably varied from place to place, but one can imagine a number of house churches that considered themselves one church in a town or area, some or all of which would have elders (*presbyteroi*), led by an elder who was the teacher, supervisor, and coordinator of the churches' mission. By circa 110 CE, Ignatius and the author of 1 Clement are clearly advocating a hierarchically structured threefold ministry of bishop → presbyters → deacons. This may also be the case in the Pastorals, but it is not so clear.

Deacons

The generic term *diakonos* means "one who serves" but has a broad range of connotations and designates a variety of functions, formal and informal. In the household structure, the *diakonos* can be charged with various responsibilities. When used in the church context, *diakonos* means "minister" in the broad sense, denoting administrative and service functions. Paul can designate himself and others as *diakonoi*, meaning simply "ministers," those who serve God in the church's mission (e.g., 2 Cor 3).

The grammatical gender of the Greek term *diakonos* is both masculine and feminine. Phoebe can be designated a deacon/minister of the church in Cenchreae (Rom 16:1). This presents a difficulty in understanding how the Pastor intended the reference to "the women" included in the instructions regarding deacons (1 Tim 3:8–13; cf. v. 11), which technically could refer to the deacons' wives but in context more likely includes women in the role of deacons. Since nothing is said about preaching or teaching as the responsibility of deacons, this would still fit within the Pastor's perspective: women may be deacons but not elders or bishops.

Widows

The extended household included women whose husbands had died. Since the average life span was not nearly as long then as it is now, such widows would often be relatively young. Households in the Pauline churches seem to have followed the cultural norm, incorporating widows within the family living under one roof, where they received material support and performed domestic duties, including teaching children and other women in the family. This pattern was extended to the church, where "widow" meant not only a woman whose husband had died but also members of a special class of women who made a "pledge" and were enrolled on a list (1 Tim 5:9–12). They seem to have been given some sort of ministerial responsibilities in the church that included not only constant prayer but also pastoral visitation. In the Pastor's situation and from his perspective, this prerogative seems to have been abused, and the church is being asked to provide financial support for widows that should have been the responsibility of a family. In the Pastor's view, the "widows" had become a problem, in that some women, now freed from domestic responsibilities, were "gadding about" as "busybodies," and their pastoral visits had raised eyebrows in the congregations and beyond. He gives strict rules. Only elderly women in genuine need, whose families are unable to support them, qualify as "real widows" (5:3–15). Such women may teach in the church, but only other women (2:12). Younger widows are not to aspire to a church career but to find their salvation in getting married and raising a decent family (2:9–15; 5:14–16). Such widows seem not to have been an "order," analogous to the later nuns, but provide a starting point for the later development.

Order and Ordination

The Pastor has a high view of ministry and ordination. It is a hierarchical, from-the-top-down perspective. As in Acts, elders are not elected but appointed.[15] Paul, the apostle, is not a volunteer but is chosen and called by God. With apostolic authority given by God, Paul chooses and ordains his successors, represented in the narrative world of the letters by Timothy and Titus. The Pastor is concerned that the church have a "legitimate" ministry, informed by the Pauline tradition and true to it as his legitimate heirs.

Timothy is ordained by the laying on of Paul's hands (2 Tim 1:6), but he also receives the charisma of ministry by the laying on of hands by the presbytery (*presbyterion*), the council of elders (1 Tim 4:14). The presbytery presumably represents the elders of the churches in a given city or area, not merely the leaders of a house church. Presumably this refers to one occasion, not two: when the presbytery ordains, this is the conferral of the gift and status of ministry authorized by the apostle. In the narrative world projected by the letters, Timothy also ordains others (1 Tim 5:22). In the hierarchical chain envisioned by the Pastor, God → Jesus Christ → apostle Paul → Timothy → presbytery → others, only the presbytery is physically present in the churches of Roman Asia of the Pastor's time, but through this "chain of command" God's authority is made present in ordination by the presbytery. The Pastor's letters are neither describing nor prescribing a church order for the readers, who were already acquainted with the details he presupposes. It is thus difficult for the modern reader to clearly discern the picture of church leadership he assumes. Through the centuries, the efforts to interpret these instructions as canon law have been frustrated by the nature of the Bible, which is not written in legal terms.

After reading the Gospels (especially John 1–20), Acts, and the undisputed letters of Paul, one might legitimately ask, "Where is the Holy Spirit in all this?" The Pastor is noticeably reserved in his talk of the Holy Spirit. Unlike Paul, who warned against unbridled spiritual enthusiasm but spoke often and passionately of the work of the Holy Spirit in the life of the church, the Pastor rarely mentions the Spirit (only in 1 Tim 4:1; 2 Tim 1:14; Titus 3:5 clearly speak of the Holy Spirit; "spirit" is mentioned also in 1 Tim 3:16; 2 Tim 1:7; 4:22). Yet it is clear that the Pastor, too, regards ministry as a gift and function of the Holy Spirit in the life of the church, guiding, empowering, and equipping it for mission. In the Pastorals, the Spirit tends to work through channels. The prophetic gift is still present, but prophecies point to the ordained ministry and function in the ordination procedure itself (1 Tim 1:18; 4:14). The Pastor pictures a Christian prophet of Paul's day, that is, a generation or two before the Pastor's own time, predicting the evils to come, which are now being experienced in the Pastor's time—including "deceitful spirits," that is, the claims of Christian prophets to receive direct revelation outside the legitimate stream of tradition (1 Tim 4:1–3). Even the pagans have their prophets (Titus 1:12). For the Pastor, God's word that instructs and nourishes the church is not found in claims to inspired revelations of new truth but in Scripture and tradition, interpreted by qualified and authorized ministers.

The Pastor's vision of a Pauline church order seems not to be enjoying numerical success, even among the Pauline churches of his time. While he, like the Johannine teachers in his neighbor churches, does not identify success with statistical growth (John 6:66–71!), he bewails the decline of congregations in his own tradition, picturing the aging Paul lamenting that even among his own followers, "all who are in Asia have turned away from me" (2 Tim 1:15). The future of the church and its mission cannot rest on each group of churches merely cultivating its own tradition.

God has given the church not only ministers but also Scripture and tradition. The minister's calling is to guide and nourish the church by communicating the life-giving Word of God, by interpreting the church's Bible and tradition.

The Gift of Scripture

The Pastor launched his letters amid a vigorous discussion already in progress regarding the role of Scripture in the formation of Christian faith and life. Some Christian teachers inclined toward proto-gnostic views that avoided, minimized, or rejected the Scriptures of Israel (so, e.g., Marcionism), while others adopted them as authoritative but interpreted them from a gnosticizing perspective. The church in Roman Asia had begun as missionary congregations of a community that had a biblical canon as part of its very being, although the canonical boundaries were not entirely firm. The earliest Christian congregations in Jerusalem and Judea were messianic believers within Judaism, and from the beginning they assumed the role and authority of the Scripture, along with all other Jews. The Jewish canon was not completely decided for all Jews by 100 CE, but the core of the Law and the Prophets was clear, surrounded by a penumbra of Writings that still had fuzzy edges. The Law and the Prophets were read every Sabbath in every synagogue (Acts 13:15; 15:21). The church began within a community that assumed that the life of the people of God was inseparably related to Scripture.

As believers in Jesus as the Messiah separated or were expelled from the synagogues, they took this pattern of church life with them. Churches had the Jewish Scriptures, now interpreted in the light of their Christian faith and adopted as their own Bible. When gentiles were converted into the Christian community, they came into churches that already had the Bible as a firm element in their life: the church has not always had a New Testament, but it has always had a Bible. Belonging to a religious community in which sacred writings played a formative and normative role was not typical of Hellenistic religion. For believers in Roman Asia, it was a new aspect of religious life to gather in worship and read sacred writings through which the word of God came, writings that were normative both for the believer's personal life and for the life of the religious group. The Hellenistic religions from which they had been converted had nothing like it.

Some Christian writings from the Pastor's setting make no explicit use of the Bible. The earliest extant letters of Paul himself (1 Thessalonians, Philippians, Philemon) make no specific appeal to Scripture. After the legitimacy of Paul's apostleship and his authority as an interpreter of the biblical faith were challenged, Paul made massive and explicit appeal to the Scripture, so that, beginning with 1 Corinthians, all his letters make intensive use of Scripture. After Paul's death, the writings of the Pauline school manifest considerable variety in their stance toward Scripture. Colossians, though opposition to heresy is a major element in its agenda, has no biblical quotations and never appeals to the Bible but focuses entirely on Paul's own authority. Ephesians makes massive use of Colossians but reintroduces scriptural proof as support for true doctrine. Ephesians 6:2 explicitly appeals to Exodus 20:12 and assumes that readers accept Scripture as "commandment" (cf. also Eph 4:8 = Ps 68:18; Eph 5:31 = Gen 2:24).

Teachers in other streams of Christianity in Roman Asia were likewise not of one mind regarding the role of Scripture in the life of the church. The prophet-author of Revelation lives in the world of biblical language and imagery and expects his readers to resonate with the *hundreds* of biblical allusions in his text, but he never cites Scripture directly or appeals to biblical authority to support his message. His appeal is not to written texts but to the direct authority of the risen Christ, who speaks through him. The Johannine community had Jewish roots, but it appears that the stream of Johannine Christianity reflected in the letters had relaxed its grip on the Scripture characteristic of its initial phase and was forgetting or intentionally avoiding biblical categories as the means of expressing and communicating the Christian faith. All three Johannine letters are silent about the covenant with Abraham, the revelation to Moses, the deliverance of the covenant people from Egypt, and Israel as distinct from the nations. They contain no quotations from the Scripture and only one clear allusion, the contrast between Cain and Abel (Gen 4:8/1 John 3:12), the two categories of human beings from the earliest days, long before the call of Abraham. The final form of Johannine theology represented in John's Gospel reappropriated and reaffirmed the Scripture as a key witness to the meaning of Christ and the church. Jesus was "the one of whom Moses and the prophets wrote."

The Pastor, like the Fourth Evangelist, reasserts the validity and necessity of Scripture for the life and nurture of the church. We will briefly note three texts in which this conviction comes to expression.

> "Until I arrive, give attention to the public reading of scripture, to exhorting, to teaching." (1 Tim 4:13)

A few translations such as the NKJV read "Give attention to reading," but virtually all modern translations read as does the NRSV or the NAB, "reading to the people." The instruction is not for ministers to be well read, presumably in the Bible and other literature, though this in itself is not bad advice. The Pastor's instruction refers to the public, pastoral ministry to others, as is made clear by its bracketing with "exhorting" and "teaching." Reading in the ancient world, even in private, was aloud, but the Pastor is not talking about the minister's personal study. Very few people had their own copies of Scripture, or even parts of it. In synagogue and church, the content of the

Bible was appropriated by hearing it read aloud in the community context of worship and study. It was in this community setting that believers learned the content of the Bible and appropriated its story as their own. The idea of individual believers with their own Bibles, silently reading for their own instruction or inspiration, would not emerge, or even become possible, until after the invention of printing in the fifteenth century. In 1 Timothy 4:13, the Pastor speaks of an essential dimension of ministry, the preaching and teaching of the Christian faith, the communication of the biblical story, content, and message to the congregation a minister is charged to guide and nourish in the faith. In the age of printed and digitized copies of the Bible, the text of Scripture is available in a way the Pastor could never have dreamed of, but the task of the minister has not changed. The ordained minister has the responsibility of facilitating biblical literacy in the congregation, and that not as a matter of personal piety but as equipment for Christian mission. "Until I arrive" means that in the absence of Paul, between the death of the apostles and the parousia, the essential nature of ministry includes preaching, teaching, and communicating the content of Scripture, inculcating its story (not just "stories") and imagery into the bloodstream of the body of Christ, with the goal that the "strange new world of the Bible" becomes the default setting for both the church and its individual members. Printing and electronic technology can be wonderful aids in the fulfillment of this task, but the Pastor's vision of the gathered congregation listening to extended sections of the story of the people of God remains the framework within which the church's Bible study takes place. The Scripture is God's gift to the church, which means serious Bible study cannot be limited to the ordained minister. The church's preachers and teachers are charged with helping the believing congregation to see all Bible study—individual, classes and small groups, congregational worship—within the encompassing image projected by 1 Timothy 4:13 of extensive passages of Scripture being read aloud to the congregation.

> "All scripture is inspired by God and is useful for teaching, for reproof, for correction, and for training in righteousness, so that everyone who belongs to God may be proficient, equipped for every good work." (2 Tim 3:16–17)

The Pastor has a high view of the role of the Bible in the life of the church, in this sense a "high view of Scripture." He is not, however, a participant in the later debates of the church, especially in the modern fundamental-ist/liberal controversy about the nature of biblical inspiration. This text does not instruct readers on a particular doctrine of the inspiration of the Bible. The question he addresses is not, "Is the Bible inspired?" but "How does the Spirit work?" The Pastor's response to this question is clear: as the Spirit works through the church's ordained ministry's teaching, reproving, correcting, training in righteousness, so the Spirit works through the Scripture, which functions in the same way to strengthen the church. He declares that the Scripture, all Scripture, is *theopneustos*, a word found only here in the Bible, which means God-breathed, in-spirited-by-God, given life and breath by God. The image is reminiscent of the creation story—God breathes life into the clay figure, and Adam becomes a living being—or the new-creation image of the church as the body of Christ, the second Adam, given life by the Spirit that God breathes into it (1 Cor 12). In neither case is it a matter of conferring infallibility on humanity or the church, but of affirming that the divine Spirit gives life to otherwise dead bodies (2 Cor 3:6, in context!). The Scripture is composed of words inscribed on a page, which in themselves are ink markings on paper or bits of electronic data on the hard drive or computer screen—mere dead letters—but they are brought to life and made agents of the life-giving power of God by God's breathing God's own life into them. In the Pastor's situation, however, the point is not to say something about the Bible but to say something about the Spirit. The Holy Spirit is at work in the life of the church, but not in unruly, random, arbitrary ways. Just as the Spirit works through authorized ministers to instruct the church and keep it on the proper path, so the Spirit breathes its God-breathed life into the church through the reading of Scripture aloud during congregational worship.

The reading of Scripture in the church is closely related to preaching and teaching (1 Tim 4:13). Scripture communicates the life (breath, word) of God when proclaimed, taught, and interpreted by the church's preachers and teachers, who do this work "with the help of the Holy Spirit living in us" (2 Tim 1:14). The Scripture is always interpreted Scripture, and that not only by the specific comment and exposition in sermon, lesson, or conversation. Scripture is interpreted in every act of "the public reading of Scripture," even when read without comment or exposition. The lector's selection, emphasis, punctuation, expression, body language, and tone of voice, as well as the particulars of the context into which the text is read, inevitably, and often helpfully, interpret the Scripture as the living Word of God. We will comment briefly on the one example in which the Pastor explicitly claims to interpret the Scripture to instruct the church.

"Let the elders who rule well be considered worthy of double honor, especially those who labor in preaching and teaching; for the scripture says, 'You shall not muzzle an ox while it is treading out the grain,' and, 'The laborer deserves to be paid.'" (1 Tim 5:17–18)

The role, status, and functions of the emerging class of "paid clergy" were a disputed point in the Christianity of Roman Asia. The Pastor quotes the instruction of Deuteronomy 25:4 about the care of farm animals, interpreting and applying it to the contested issue of the status and financial support of Christian ministers. Of course, he did not hit upon this interpretation by chance—it had already been interpreted in this sense by Paul in his defense of payment of church missionaries (1 Cor 9:9). For the Pastor, such interpretation, which may seem strange and arbitrary to us, is a matter of standing in the authentic tradition of the church, acknowledging the authority of the apostle, which, he claims, settles the issue at hand. We also note that a proverbial saying is combined with the citation of Scripture. This proverb, also found in Matthew 10:10/Luke 10:7 (= Q) in slightly different forms, is in each case cited in support of Christian preachers. It is unclear whether the proverb is included along with the citation from Deuteronomy as what "the Scripture says," but most interpreters consider it unlikely that the Pastor is citing Q, Matthew, or Luke as Scripture. In any case, the citation of Scripture is based on tradition, Pauline tradition and the oral tradition that included proverbial sayings that became the vehicle of Christian truth. Scripture and tradition are not the same, but they are inseparable. The God who gives the church the gifts of ministry and Scripture also gives the church the gift of tradition.

> I know whom I have believed
> and am persuaded that he is able
> to keep that which I have committed
> unto him against that day.

Some will recognize this refrain to a nineteenth-century gospel hymn, which expresses a true aspect of Christian faith: God is able to preserve what believers have entrusted to him.

This, however, is probably not the meaning of 2 Timothy 1:12, which more likely refers to what God has entrusted to Christian ministers: the deposit of faith they are responsible to keep and transmit to others.

The Gift of Tradition

Paul himself valued church tradition highly, handing on creedal, liturgical, and educational elements valuable for the life of the church. He used the conventional vocabulary for this, the verb "hand on/over" (*paradidōmi*, Rom 6:17; 1 Cor 11:23; 15:3) and the noun "tradition," what is handed on or over (*paradosis*, 1 Cor 11:2; Gal 1:14), as well as numerous items of tradition he valued and transmitted without specifically identifying them as such (e.g., Phil 2:6–11; Rom 1:3–4). The teachers in the Pauline school continued to hand on tradition but were not consistent in their use of Paul's own vocabulary. On the one hand, though the author of Colossians hands on key elements of tradition such as the magnificent christological hymn of Colossians 1:15–20 and the household code in 3:18–4:1, he uses the nomenclature of "tradition" only once, and in a negative sense, for the teaching of his opponents, which is only "human tradition . . . not according to Christ" (2:8). On the other hand, the author of 2 Thessalonians has Paul specifically identify authentic Christian life and witness as holding fast to the traditions Paul himself had taught (2 Thess 2:15), avoiding those people who do not adhere to the tradition they had received from Paul (3:6). All teachers in the Pauline school affirmed the necessity of abiding in the authentic tradition but did not express this conviction in a consistent vocabulary. Promoting the value of tradition is not bound to a particular terminology. Thus neither Ephesians nor the Pastorals, both advocates of adhering to the tradition, use the Pauline language of *paradidōmi/paradosis*. Though each of the Pastoral Letters is permeated with a variety of traditional materials, the Pastor's instruction focuses on the content and meaning of the term *parathēkē* (the "deposit, that which has been entrusted," 1 Tim 6:20; 2 Tim 1:12, 14) and the phrase *pistos ho logos* ("the saying is sure," i.e., faithful sayings, corresponding to the traditional faith, 1 Tim 1:15; 2:15–3:1; 4:8–9; 2 Tim 2:11–13; Titus 3:4–8).

Parathēkē: "Guard the Deposit Entrusted to You"

The Pastor may appear, on first impression, to be the kind of conservative who always avoids change, resisting the new paths into which the Spirit of God may be leading the church. The Pastor is indeed something of a traditionalist, but he also knows that people can be committed to tradition for the wrong reason ("I just like the way we have always done it"). *The Pastor is in fact an advocate of change, is himself a change agent in changing times.*

He knows that the church is not what it was in the days of the first followers of Jesus, and not the same as the Pauline churches first established in
Roman Asia in the first generation, just as he knows the church needs
to change as it moves into the next generation and writes the Pastoral Letters in Paul's name for precisely this reason. He is a champion of the new
leadership structures and firm theological statements the church needs to
keep the church steadfast in its mission, opposing both the sophisticated
developments of gnosticizing theology and the unregulated individualistic
spirituality threatening the church.

The anchor point for a changing church must be a firm grasp of the
tradition. The Pastor regards ministry in the same way Paul did. As Paul saw
his ministry as being entrusted with the gospel to which he must be faithful
(1 Thess 2:4), the treasure of the gospel in the clay jars of Paul (2 Cor 4:7),
so the Pastor sees himself and the ministers of his own time as having been
entrusted with the deposit of Christian faith that they are to study, preserve,
interpret, and pass on. The treasure, the mystery, is not esoteric, for the
minister's personal spiritual enrichment; it is to be passed on. The Pastor
should not be compared to the unfaithful slave in Jesus's parable who buried the treasure entrusted to him so he could present it later to his master,
unchanged, when the master returned (Matt 25:14–30; remember, the New
Testament uses the "slave" terminology for authorized ministers entrusted
with the master's business!). In the Pastor's view, the faithful minister of the
Word is like the "good and trustworthy (*pistos*!) slave," who received the
treasure and worked with it to produce more. He did not start from scratch,
with his own resources and ideas, but was faithful with what he had received.
We Christian ministers/slaves of Christ are not left alone with the treasure
of the gospel to do the best we can. We know that the treasure entrusted to
us is guarded not only by our own discipline and diligence but also by "the
Holy Spirit living in us" (2 Tim 1:14; "us" is not only in the individual but
also in the "us" of the Christian community). They can pray with the Paul of
2 Timothy 1:12 to the one who "is able to guard until that Day what has been
entrusted to me" (so the RSV, NAB, TEV, CEV, CEB).

Faithful Sayings: "The Saying Is Sure"

The faithful sayings are summary points of the faith, "creedal cameos,"[16] but
they are not creeds in the sense of definitive confessions of the faith. It is
difficult to imagine that the Pastor intends that the faithful sayings are to be

recited as part of the church's liturgy or required as confessional statements by those being baptized. They are pointers to the grand macronarrative that summarizes the church's faith, handles by which to grasp its deeper and broader substance, orientation points that display the Christian faith as not our invention, created by each new generation or situation, but that which is handed to us by previous generations of the faithful ministry of the faithful church.

"... His Steadfast Love Endures Forever"

Chesed, translated "mercy" in the KJV and NKJV, is more adequately rendered "steadfast love" (NRSV, ESV) or "faithful love" (NJB, CEV). The word does not refer to an inherent quality in God but to an act, the covenant-making act of God to which God remains faithful even if God's covenant partners in the church do not. *Chesed* is a matter of God's promise, made by the God who keeps his promises no matter what. God's *chesed* is unconditional, the basis of God's call for faithfulness to all members of the covenant people.

Each of the five faithful sayings is concerned with salvation. This does not mean merely going to heaven when we die, though the Pastor advocates a robust Christian hope of eternal life (1 Tim 1:16; 4:8; 6:12; 2 Tim 1:10; Titus 3:7). The faithful sayings point to the whole scheme of redemption, the saving plan fulfilled in the event of Jesus Christ. They are worthy of more careful study in order to hear what they have to say. Here, we note only one facet of each saying:

> 1 Timothy 1:15: "Christ Jesus came into the world to save sinners—of whom I am the foremost."

The saving significance of the Christ event as a whole is exemplified in the case of Paul.

> 1 Timothy 2:15–3:1: "She will be saved through childbearing."

This seems to be part of a larger unit concerned with conduct of men and women in public worship.[17] It is absurd to suggest that the Pastor believed that childless women cannot go to heaven, or that the Pastor supposed this to be a key article of Christian faith. This difficult saying is directed to what the Pastor perceives as a serious problem: young widows who want to live at the church's expense as some sort of pastoral visitors or teachers (see above). Salvation for such women is not to find a church job. In his view, the church and world do not need unqualified women (or men) attempting to be ministers and misrepresenting the church to the world. Young widows need to exhibit to the world the true character of the suspect Christian community by becoming mothers of Christian children and managers of Christian families. (Reminder: we are not here advocating this view as normative for our time and may well decide to reject it as misguided and misleading for any time. Before deciding what such texts might mean for us today, we must listen to the Scripture on its own terms.)

> 1 Timothy 4:7b–8: "Train yourself in godliness, for, while physical training is of some value, godliness is valuable in every way."

"Godliness" is *eusebeia*, used in the LXX for "awesome respect accorded to God."[18] The profession of Christian ministry calls for discipline (the word, of course, is related to "discipleship"), training for service as Olympic athletes do.

> 2 Timothy 2:11–13:
> "The saying is sure:
>> If we have died with him, we will also live with him;
>> if we endure, we will also reign with him;
>> if we deny him, he will also deny us;
>> if we are faithless, he remains faithful—
>> for he cannot deny himself."

This compact, poetic "faithful saying" portrays the life of discipleship and ministry as dying, living, and reigning with Christ. As in Paul's letters and in the later deutero-Pauline letters, being a disciple is not conceived only as following the teachings of Jesus, but of having one's life incorporated into the Christ event, sharing Christ's cross, resurrection, and reign (cf. Rev. 3:21). In this text, we have both the call to faithfulness and the assurance that God's faithfulness remains firm even when ours wavers; this brings to mind the repeated refrain that echoes in the background of the Psalter, "his steadfast love endures forever" (e.g., twenty-six times in Ps 136).

> Titus 3:4–8: "When the goodness and loving kindness of God our Savior appeared, he saved us, not because of any works of righteousness that

we had done, but according to his mercy, through the water of rebirth and renewal by the Holy Spirit. This Spirit he poured out on us richly through Jesus Christ our Savior, so that, having been justified by his grace, we might become heirs according to the hope of eternal life."

This compact summary faithfully preserves the Pauline doctrine of salvation by grace, blending it with the understanding of the believer's new birth current by the Pastor's time in the Johannine (John 1:13; 3:3–8; 1 John 2:29; 3:9; 4:7; 5:1), Petrine (1 Pet 1:3, 23; 2:2), and Jacobite (James 1:15, 18) traditions. Despite the Pastor's concentrated focus on Paul, he preserves and affirms elements of tradition he shares with the wider church.

> "Tradition is not a veneration of the ashes, but a handing on of the fire."
> —Austrian Jewish composer Gustav Mahler
>
> "Tradition tells us who we are, and what God requires of us."
> —Tevye, *Fiddler on the Roof*

The latest document of the Pauline school concludes with the same understanding of ministry as the earliest document with the appeal to the preachers and teachers reading it to "Guard the good treasure entrusted to you" (2 Tim 1:14; cf. 1 Thess 2:4). To be a minister, a preacher and teacher of the faith, is to be a living link in this chain of living tradition. "Be strong in the grace that is in Christ Jesus; and what you have heard from me through many witnesses entrust to faithful people who will be able to teach others as well" (2 Tim 2:1–2). This is the same understanding of tradition drawn from the Jewish roots of the community of faith. God has placed baptized believers in Jesus Christ in the church that is nourished by a grand tradition that includes the Scripture and men and women qualified and authorized to guide us to within hearing distance of the Word of God to us, the church, and the world.

Epilogue

Two travelers walk along the road together, engaged in serious and friendly conversation. It turns out they had both been wrong. They are disappointed. Shattered. They had met a young man, a life-changer and world-changer. They had believed in him and his cause, had believed that the world could be different. He had given them hope. The road they were on was going someplace. Now he was dead, done in by the world he had tried to make a better place. They still had his teaching, his example, but now his vision of what he had called the "kingdom of God" would have to join the many other shattered dreams along the road. "We had hoped," they say, but now he is dead. "The saddest words of tongue or pen are these—it might have been." Would it have been better never to have hoped, never even to have asked where the road was going? Now, it's too late.

As they approach a village where they would share the evening meal, a third traveler joins their conversation. A pleasant chap, though not very up to date, not even aware of recent events in the capital. During the meal, he speaks directly to them, as though he had always known them. Then he disappears. They return to the city, and in their efforts to tell their fellow disciples what had happened, they say things like, "Were not our hearts burning within us while he was talking to us on the road, while he was opening the Scriptures to us?" and "He was made known to us in the breaking of bread." While they are trying to tell this good news, Jesus himself stands among them and says to them, "Peace be with you. . . . You will be my witnesses in Jerusalem . . . to the ends of the earth." Even when it's too late, it's not too late.

It turns out, there is only one road. It is going someplace, and there is One who has been there and back. We didn't figure this out; it has been revealed to us, by One who once walked with us on the road, and still does. We are all on the same road, all children of the same Father, the Creator, who stands at the beginning and end of the road, who is with us on the road, and will bring us and the whole creation to the Holy City.

In the meantime, a job to do . . .

Notes

FOREWORD

1. David L. Bartlett, *What's Good about This News? Preaching from the Gospel and Galatians* (Louisville: Westminster John Knox, 2003), 10.
2. Bartlett, *What's Good about This News?*, 11.
3. Peter Cook, *Tragically I Was an Only Twin*, ed. William Cook (London: Century, 2002), 126.

PROLOGUE

1. This is my elaboration of the brief parable in John Hick, *Faith and Knowledge*, 2nd ed. (Ithaca, NY: Cornell University Press, 1966), 177–78 and 195.

CHAPTER 1

1. Unless otherwise indicated, quotations from Scripture come from the New Revised Standard Version.
2. Daniel Migliore, *Faith Seeking Understanding: An Introduction to Christian Theology* (Grand Rapids: Eerdmans, 1991), 6.
3. See Migliore's fine chapter, "Humanity in the Image of God," in *Faith Seeking Understanding*, 120–38.
4. Elaborated in Leander Keck, *Who Is Jesus? History in the Perfect Tense* (Columbia: University of South Carolina Press, 2000), 55–58; Leander E. Keck, "Good News for Us Gentiles," in *Christ's First Theologian: The Shape of Paul's Thought* (Waco, TX: Baylor University Press, 2015), 75–88.
5. Udo Schnelle, *Apostle Paul: His Life and Thought*, trans. M. Eugene Boring (Grand Rapids: Baker Academic, 2005), 45.
6. Thomas G. Long, *Preaching from Memory to Hope* (Louisville: Westminster John Knox, 2009), passim.

CHAPTER 2

1. The "my" in "my gospel" is not a possessive pronoun, nor does it suggest a claim that Paul devised the gospel himself. It does acknowledge that, like every preacher in every sit-

uation, he thinks through the distinctive form and content of the one gospel of Jesus Christ for his particular time and place. For my own explication of the events between Paul's conversion and the writing of 1 Thessalonians, see M. Eugene Boring, *An Introduction to the New Testament: History, Literature, Theology* (Louisville: Westminster John Knox, 2012), 182–207.

2. The additional instances of "beloved" in the NRSV (4:10; 5:4, 14, 25) represent the translators' interest in gender-inclusive language. In these cases, the Greek text has *adelphoi*, "brothers [and sisters]," as in 1:4; 2:1, 9, 14, 17; 3:7; 4:1, 9, 10, 13; 5:1, 12, 26.

3. Cf. Michael Wolter, *Paul: An Outline of His Theology*, trans. Robert L. Brawley (Waco, TX: Baylor University Press, 2015), 22, 347, and passim. This is the emphasis of the "new perspective on Paul." See, e.g., the works of Dunn and Wright, and Scot McKnight and Joseph B. Modica, eds., *The Apostle Paul and the Christian Life: Ethical and Missional Implications of the New Perspective* (Grand Rapids: Baker Academic, 2016), and the bibliographies they provide.

4. Leander Keck, "The Jewish Paul among the Gentiles," in *Christ's First Theologian: The Shape of Paul's Thought* (Waco, TX: Baylor University Press, 2015), 54.

5. The only exception is the one-page letter of Jude, where vocabulary statistics are skewed by the brevity of the letter. The holiness vocabulary is found ten times in 1 Thessalonians: *hagios* ("holy," 1:5, 6; 3:13; 4:8; 5:26); *hagiosmos* ("holiness," 4:3, 4, 7); *hagiazō* ("sanctify," 5:23); *hagiōsynē* ("holiness," 3:13).

6. Eduard Thurneysen, "Schrift und Offenbarung," *Zwischen den Zeiten* 2, no. 6 (1924): 3–30 (translation mine).

7. Leander Keck, "Good News for Us Gentiles," in *Christ's First Theologian*, 198.

8. The following paragraphs are an expanded and modified version of a section of Boring, *An Introduction to the New Testament*, 465–66.

9. A. M. Hunter, *Paul and His Predecessors* (Philadelphia: Westminster, 1961), 10–11. More recent scholars (such as James D. G. Dunn, cited in the sidebar) who share Hunter's interest and perspective on this issue and assume that Paul knew a lot about what the historical Jesus did and said and taught it in the churches he founded, acknowledge that the letters themselves tell us "next to nothing" about Jesus's life and ministry. The matter has been thoroughly explored in books, articles, and scholarly monographs such as David Aune, "Jesus Tradition and the Pauline Letters," in *Jesus in Memory: Traditions in Oral and Scribal Perspectives*, ed. Werner Kelber and Samuel Byrskog (Waco, TX: Baylor University Press, 2010), 63–86; Frans Neirynck, "Paul and the Sayings of Jesus," in *L'Apôtre Paul: personnalité, style et conception du ministère*, ed. Albert Vanhoye, Bibliotheca Ephemeridum Theologicarum Lovaniensium 100 (Leuven: Leuven University Press, 1986), 265–321; A. J. M. Wedderburn, *Paul and Jesus: Collected Essays*, Journal for the Study of the New Testament Supplement Series 37 (Sheffield: JSOT Press, 1989), and the bibliography they provide. The conclusion can be checked, of course, by any reader who works through the Pauline corpus with this question in mind.

10. In all the letters, the only candidate for reference to such an event in the pre-Easter life of Jesus is 2 Pet 1:18, which refers to hearing a voice from heaven while with Jesus "on the holy mount." This is often understood as a reference to the transfiguration, but the original story may well have referred to a post-Easter experience. See commentaries on the Synoptics and 2 Peter.

11. Oscar Cullmann, "The Tradition," in *The Early Church*, ed. A. J. B. Higgins (London: SCM, 1956), 59–104.

12. One of the few exceptions is Stanley E. Porter, *When Paul Met Jesus: How an Idea Got Lost in History* (Cambridge: Cambridge University Press, 2015), who argues Paul met Jesus not once but several times, beginning in Galilee, and followed him to Jerusalem, where the two had several encounters. Like previous similar claims, Porter's thesis has found little resonance in the academic community.

13. The conclusion of Victor Furnish's *The Jesus-Paul Debate: From Baur to Bultmann* (Manchester: John Rylands Library, 1965), 381, succinctly expresses the view with which most Pauline scholars still agree.

14. See, for example, with varying emphases and nuances, James D. G. Dunn, "How Much Did Paul Know or Care about the Life of Jesus," in *The Theology of Paul the Apostle* (Grand Rapids: Eerdmans, 1998), 183–85; Luke Timothy Johnson, *The Real Jesus: The Misguided Quest for the Historical Jesus and the Truth of the Traditional Gospels* (New York: HarperCollins, 1996), 117–22; Gordon D. Fee, *The First Epistle to the Corinthians*, New International Commentary on the New Testament, revised and enlarged ed. (Grand Rapids: Eerdmans, 1987), 322–27.

15. E.g., Martin Hengel, "Eye-Witness Memory and the Writing of the Gospels," in *The Written Gospel*, ed. Markus Bockmuehl and Donald A. Hagner (Cambridge: Cambridge University Press, 2005), 75; Peter Stuhlmacher, *Biblical Theology of the New Testament*, trans. and ed. Daniel P. Bailey, with the collaboration of Jostein Ådna (Grand Rapids: Eerdmans, 2018), 333–38, who also argues that Paul presupposed the firm catechetical tradition in the churches about the life and teaching of Jesus, and thus did not need to repeat it in the letters.

16. Cf. Victor Paul Furnish, *Theology and Ethics in Paul*, 2nd ed., New Testament Library (Louisville: Westminster John Knox, 2009), 55.

17. Keck, "Good News for Us Gentiles," 198.

18. Keck, "Good News for Us Gentiles," 199.

19. John Knox, *Chapters in a Life of St. Paul* (London: Adam & Charles Black, 1950), 130.

20. See M. Eugene Boring, "Matthew: Introduction, Commentary, and Reflections," in *The New Interpreter's Bible*, ed. Leander Keck (Nashville: Abingdon, 2002), 8:185–96.

21. Paul uses some form of *pisteuō, pistis, pistos* 142 times, more than 30 times with reference to the identity of church members, in all the undisputed letters except the brief Philemon. "Disciple" is the term for this in the Gospels and Acts, and "Christian" is occasionally used in Acts and 1 Peter. Neither word is found in Paul. For him, "believer" is the Christian's identity.

22. C. H. Dodd, *The Apostolic Preaching and Its Developments* (London: Hodder & Stoughton, 1960).

23. See commentaries on 1 Thess 4:11; 5:14. Evidence and argument for the view here presented are found in M. Eugene Boring, *1 and 2 Thessalonians: A Commentary*, New Testament Library (Louisville: Westminster John Knox, 2015), 149–54.

24. N. T. Wright, *The Resurrection of the Son of God*, vol. 3 of *Christian Origins and the Question of God* (Minneapolis: Fortress, 2003), 216.

25. Some of the content of this paragraph is adopted and adapted from Boring, *1 and 2 Thessalonians*, 82–83.

26. Cf. Leander Keck, *Paul and His Letters*, Proclamation Commentaries (Philadelphia: Fortress, 1979), 78.

213

CHAPTER 3

1. Scholars as different as Rudolf Bultmann and James D. G. Dunn approach Paul's theology through Romans. Bultmann's *New Testament Theology*, the agenda-setter for New Testament theologians of the past generation, has recently been reprinted with an outstandingly helpful introduction to the subject as a whole and Bultmann's role in it: Rudolf Bultmann, *Theology of the New Testament*, with a new introduction by Robert Morgan (Waco, TX: Baylor University Press, 2007), 1:190: Paul's "basic theological position [is] more or less completely set forth in Romans." See the thorough rationale in James D. G. Dunn, *The Theology of Paul the Apostle* (Grand Rapids: Eerdmans, 1998), esp. 19–26.

2. Such outlines are for the convenience of the reader. The text itself, of course, interweaves the themes throughout. Even the major division between the "indicative"-"kerygmatic" part 1 (chaps. 1–11) and the "imperative"-"ethical" part 2 (chaps. 12–16) is porous.

3. Leander Keck, *Romans*, ed. Victor Paul Furnish, Abingdon New Testament Commentaries (Nashville: Abingdon, 2005), 348: this is "the most radical understanding of sin in the New Testament, because its function is to inhibit the believer from continuing to understand sin as transgression. For the believer, it is not the law that finally identifies what is sin, but acting on a basis other than faith. . . . Still, one wonders why he did not say that whatever is not from love is sin."

4. The Johannine theologians later make clear that the revelation that climaxed in Christ is the definitive revelation of the universal light of God available to all human experience.

5. Repentance (*metanoia*) means a reorientation and transformation of the mind. On body, soul, mind, and heart as each representing the whole person rather than separate "parts," see Bultmann's classic treatment, *Theology of the New Testament*, 1:190–226.

6. Serene Jones, "What's Wrong with Us? Human Nature and Human Sin," in *Essentials of Christian Theology*, ed. William C. Placher (Louisville: Westminster John Knox, 2003), 142, 145.

7. John H. Leith, *Basic Christian Doctrine* (Louisville: Westminster John Knox, 1993), 105.

8. Leith, *Basic Christian Doctrine*, 135. Many moderns are uncomfortable or disdainful of the traditional doctrine of "total depravity," but Leith points out that this theology of human existence does not mean there are no good in people, but (1) every dimension of the human self is corrupted and tainted by sin, and (2) we can't just resolve to extricate ourselves from our sinful condition. *Basic Christian Doctrine*, 107. This is basic to the theology not only of Paul but also of Jesus and the Gospels.

9. Contra, e.g., the CEV translation, "Now we see how God does make us acceptable to him. The Law and the Prophets tell how we become acceptable, and it isn't by obeying the Law of Moses."

10. The various efforts to remedy this situation by more correct translations have not achieved wide acceptance. Cf., e.g., Kendrick Grobel's suggestion of "rightwise" in Bultmann, *Theology of the New Testament*, 1:253, and Leander Keck's use of "rectitude," "rectify," in Keck, *Romans*, 35, 52, and passim.

11. Martin Buber, *I and Thou* (Edinburgh: T&T Clark, 1958), 82–83.

12. Reinhold Niebuhr, *The Nature and Destiny of Man*, 2 vols. (New York: Scribner's Sons, 1964 [1941]), 1:142–43. Or as put by Colin Gunton, *The Actuality of Atonement* (Grand

Rapids: Eerdmans, 1989), 84: "God is revealed by the cross as one who bears the power of the demonic rather than punishes those who have fallen into its power."

13. Joe R. Jones, *A Grammar of Christian Faith: Systematic Explorations in Christian Life and Doctrine*, 2 vols. (Lanham, MD: Rowman & Littlefield, 2002), 2:349.

14. The issue has been vigorously debated among Pauline scholars in recent years, generating a massive bibliography. For summaries of the discussion, and bibliography listing advocates of each side of the issue, see Richard B. Hays, "Pistis and Pauline Christology," in *Looking Back, Pressing On*, ed. E. Elizabeth Johnson and David M. Hay, Pauline Theology (Atlanta: Scholars Press, 1997), 35–60; James D. G. Dunn, "Once More, Pistis Cristou," in Johnson and Hay, *Looking Back, Pressing On*, 61–91; Robert Jewett, *Romans: A Commentary*, Hermeneia (Minneapolis: Fortress, 2007), 277–78.

15. Keck, *Romans*, 124–25.

16. On the rediscovery of the potency of Paul as apocalyptic theologian, see especially Ernst Käsemann, *Commentary on Romans*, trans. Geoffrey W. Bromiley (Grand Rapids: Eerdmans, 1980); J. Louis Martyn, *Galatians: A New Translation with Introduction and Commentary*, Anchor Yale Bible 33A (New York: Doubleday, 1997); and the essays in Beverly R. Gaventa, ed., *Apocalyptic Paul: Cosmos and Anthropos in Romans 5–8* (Waco, TX: Baylor University Press, 2013), and the bibliography they present.

17. This paragraph and the next borrow and adapt content from M. Eugene Boring, *Introduction to the New Testament: History, Literature, Theology* (Louisville: Westminster John Knox, 2012), 310–12.

18. Karl Barth, *Christ and Adam: Man and Humanity in Romans 5*, trans. T. A. Smail (New York: Collier Books, 1962), 74–75, 107–9.

19. See the slender second volume of Paul Tillich's *Systematic Theology: Existence and the Christ* (Chicago: University of Chicago Press, 1957), 118–38.

20. The LXX translators were bothered by the cultural associations of *doulos* and *douleia*, the standard words for "slave" and "slavery," and tended to avoid them, using instead *pais* (boy, girl, child).

21. One of many illustrations: when Joseph sent to bring his father Jacob and all his family to Egypt, Jacob/Israel sent Judah ahead of him "to point the way" (Gen 46:28 in *Tanakh: The Holy Scriptures; The New JPS Translation according to the Traditional Hebrew Text*); the verb form of the word for Torah is used. Giving Torah is pointing the *way* for *Israel* to live in a world that worships other gods.

22. Gerd Theissen, *The Religion of the Earliest Churches: Creating a Symbolic World*, trans. John Bowden (Minneapolis: Fortress, 1999), 211–30. Though Theissen himself seems to succumb to the popular oversimplification that "in Paul a religion of grace often takes the place of a religion of the law" (211), he later summarizes his own view better: "The picture sketched out above does not contrast Jewish righteousness by works with a Christian religion of grace, but says that the tension between a religion of grace and righteousness by works is to be found within Judaism itself . . . this aporia was not 'resolved' in Christianity either" (213).

23. See, e.g., Dunn, *Theology of Paul*, 359.

24. In the interests of inclusive language, some translations and discussions obscure the fact that Paul uses the same word for Jesus as Son of God and believers as sons and daughters of God, *huios* (8:3, 14, 19; *huiosthesia*, "adoption," in 8:15, 23, is also a form of the word *huios*, i.e., "having the status of a son"). In the biblical tradition formative for Paul,

huios has the connotations of "agent" and "heir," which the gender-inclusive "child" does not have. Paul, of course, does not intend to restrict the imagery to males and uses *teknon*, "child," as equivalent (8:17, 21).

25. For a more comprehensive discussion of Paul's understanding of the Spirit, see below at 1 Cor 12.

26. See William C. Placher, ed., *Essentials of Christian Theology* (Louisville: Westminster John Knox, 2003), 139; Reinhold Niebuhr, *Moral Man and Immoral Society* (New York: Scribner's Sons, 1960); Langdon Gilkey, *Message and Existence: An Introduction to Christian Theology* (New York: Seabury, 1979), 112.

27. Morton Scott Enslin, *The Ethics of Paul* (New York: Harper & Brothers, 1930), 4. This truism, always known among Jews, has recently become more generally known among Christians and other non-Jews in the wake of E. P. Sanders, *Paul and Palestinian Judaism: A Comparison of Patterns of Religion* (Philadelphia: Fortress, 1977); see the author's summary, 419–28. This insight has long been known by careful Christian scholars. Typical Protestant exegesis has read Rom 10:3 as identical with Phil 3:9, which does contrast "the righteousness from God based on faith" with "a righteousness of my own that comes from the law." But not only is this a different context dealing with a different issue, the crucial *ek* (from) of Philippians is missing from Romans, which deals with God's own righteousness, God's way of dealing with humankind, not with an imputed righteousness from God. See Keck, *Romans*, 246–47.

28. On the general structure of Pauline theology/ethics, see above on 1 Thessalonians. Here, we concentrate on the particular foci of Rom 12–15.

29. See, e.g., 1 Cor 6–7, which includes, "To the married I give this command—not I but the Lord. . . . To the rest I say this (I, not the Lord) . . . each of you should live as a believer in whatever situation the Lord has assigned to you, just as God has called you. This is the rule I lay down in all the churches. . . . I have no command from the Lord, but I give a judgment as one who by the Lord's mercy is trustworthy. . . . In my judgment . . .—and I think that I too have the Spirit of God." Paul speaks as an apostle, which other believers cannot do, but in Rom 12 he models the obligation of all to participate, with their renewed minds, in discerning the will of God for God's people.

30. Udo Schnelle, *The Human Condition: Anthropology in the Teachings of Jesus, Paul, and John*, trans. O. C. Dean Jr. (Minneapolis: Fortress, 1996), 97.

31. Ernst Käsemann, "Principles of the Interpretation of Romans 13," in *New Testament Questions of Today*, New Testament Library (London: SCM, 1969), 205.

32. Georg Strecker, *Theology of the New Testament*, trans. M. Eugene Boring (New York: de Gruyter, 2000), 201.

33. Käsemann, "Principles of the Interpretation of Romans 13," 214.

CHAPTER 4

1. This perspective is associated especially with Rudolf Bultmann and his students. See, e.g., Rudolf Bultmann, *Theology of the New Testament*, with a new introduction by Robert Morgan (Waco, TX: Baylor University Press, 2007), 2:95–236, "The Development toward the Ancient Church," and Käsemann, "Paul and Early Catholicism," 236–51. For helpful critiques, see Andrew T. Lincoln and A. J. M. Wedderburn, *The Theology of the Later Pauline Letters*, New Testament Theology (Cambridge: Cambridge University Press,

1993), 137–41, and Frances M. Young, *The Theology of the Pastoral Letters*, New Testament Theology (Cambridge: Cambridge University Press, 1994), 74, 96–97, 146 and passim, and the bibliography they provide.

2. See Margaret Y. MacDonald, *The Pauline Churches: A Socio-Historical Study of Institutionalization in the Pauline and Deutero-Pauline Writings*, Society for New Testament Studies Monograph Series 60 (Cambridge: Cambridge University Press, 1988), and the bibliography she provides.

3. For the texts with introduction and commentary, see Edgar Hennecke and Wilhelm Schneemelcher, eds., *New Testament Apocrypha*, 2 vols. (Philadelphia: Westminster, 1963, 1964). For the gnostic appropriation of Paul, see especially Elaine H. Pagels, *The Gnostic Paul: Gnostic Exegesis of the Pauline Letters* (Philadelphia: Fortress, 1975).

4. For elaboration of the approach, my own perspective on its value, and further bibliography, see M. Eugene Boring, "Narrative Dynamics in First Peter: The Function of Narrative World," in *Reading 1 Peter with New Eyes: Methodological Reassessments of the Letter of First Peter*, ed. Robert L. Webb and Betsy Bauman-Martin, Library of New Testament Studies (Edinburgh: T&T Clark, 2007), 7–40, and M. Eugene Boring, *1 Peter*, Abingdon New Testament Commentaries (Nashville: Abingdon, 1999), especially appendix 1, "The Narrative World of First Peter," 183–201.

5. "Jew," "Jewish," and "Judaism" are all absent from Ephesians, though these terms were common parlance in religious circles in the author's context in Roman Asia, as documented not only by the Pauline tradition (including his template—cf. Col 3:11) but also by the neighboring Johannine community's tradition (seventy-seven times in Revelation and in John's Gospel). Ephesians prefers the older, more biblical, and more theologically comprehensive term "Israel," to which both Judaism and the church belong. In this summary, I have retained the conventional vocabulary.

6. Fred B. Craddock, *The Pre-existence of Christ in the New Testament* (Nashville: Abingdon, 1968).

7. Larry W. Hurtado, *God in New Testament Theology*, Library of Biblical Theology (Nashville: Abingdon, 2010); Larry W. Hurtado, *Lord Jesus Christ: Devotion to Jesus in Earliest Christianity* (Grand Rapids: Eerdmans, 2003).

8. Andrew T. Lincoln in Lincoln and Wedderburn, *Later Pauline Letters*, 138.

9. See further in Paul S. Minear, *Images of the Church in the New Testament* (Philadelphia: Westminster, 1960), and the major New Testament theologies listed in the bibliography at the end of this volume.

10. Markus Barth, *The Broken Wall: A Study of the Epistle to the Ephesians* (Philadelphia: Judson, 1959).

11. Cf. Thomas G. Long, *Testimony: Talking Ourselves into Being Christian* (San Francisco: Jossey-Bass, 2004).

12. Jesus is the example for believers in that he "made the good confession" before Pontius Pilate (1 Tim 3:16). The only contact with the tradition of Jesus's sayings is "The laborer deserves to be paid" (cf. Matt 10:10/Luke 10:7), cited in support of the emerging "order" of "paid clergy," but it is cited as a proverbial saying rather than attributed to Jesus or a written gospel. It is unclear whether it is included as "Scripture" with Deuteronomy 25:4, which had been cited by Paul, also in support of paid ministers (1 Cor 9:9).

13. See Udo Schnelle, *Theology of the New Testament*, trans. M. Eugene Boring (Grand Rapids: Baker Academic, 2009), 584.

14. H. Richard Niebuhr, *Christ and Culture* (New York: Harper & Brothers, 1951). This book was reissued in 2001 as the expanded fiftieth anniversary edition with a new foreword by Martin E. Marty, a new preface by James M. Gustafson, and an introductory essay by the author.

15. As Jesus was appointed by God (Acts 3:20; 17:31), and as apostles were appointed by Jesus (Mark 3:14; John 15:16; cf. Acts 26:16), so the apostles appointed their assistants and congregational leaders, including elders in each church (Acts 6:3; 14:23).

16. Raymond F. Collins, *I & II Timothy and Titus: A Commentary*, New Testament Library (Louisville: Westminster John Knox, 2002), 43.

17. It is not clear whether the designation "faithful saying" in 3:1a points to the preceding or following paragraph, which deals with bishops and elders. In either case, 1:15 is one of the most difficult texts in the Pastorals for modern readers to understand in its own context and to perceive as something central to Christian faith and life, then or now.

18. Frederick W. Danker et al., *Greek-English Lexicon of the New Testament and Other Early Christian Literature*, 3rd ed. (Chicago: University of Chicago Press, 2000), 413.

Bibliography

Among the numerous online resources available for biblical study, the following may be consulted for the study of this book:

thepaulpage.com
NTgateway.com

General

Boring, M. Eugene. *Hearing John's Voice: Insights for Teaching and Preaching*. Grand Rapids: Eerdmans, 2019.

———. *An Introduction to the New Testament: History, Literature, Theology*. Louisville: Westminster John Knox, 2012.

Boring, M. Eugene, and Fred B. Craddock. *The People's New Testament Commentary*. Louisville: Westminster John Knox, 2004.

Brown, Raymond E. *An Introduction to the New Testament*. New York: Doubleday, 1997.

Bultmann, Rudolf. *Theology of the New Testament*. Translated by Kendrick Grobel. With a new introduction by Robert Morgan. 2 vols. New York: Scribner's Sons, 1951.

Childs, Brevard S. *Biblical Theology of the Old and New Testaments: Theological Reflection on the Christian Bible*. Minneapolis: Fortress, 1992.

Feldmeier, Reinhard, and Hermann Spieckermann. *God of the Living: A Biblical Theology*. Waco, TX: Baylor University Press, 2011.

Holladay, Carl R. *A Critical Introduction to the New Testament*. Nashville: Abingdon, 2005.

Hurtado, Larry W. *God in New Testament Theology*. Library of Biblical Theology. Nashville: Abingdon, 2010.

Minear, Paul S. *The Kingdom and the Power: An Exposition of the New Testament Gospel*. Louisville: Westminster John Knox, 1950.

Schnelle, Udo. *The History and Theology of the New Testament Writings*. Translated by M. Eugene Boring. Minneapolis: Fortress, 1998.

———. *Theology of the New Testament*. Translated by M. Eugene Boring. Grand Rapids: Baker Academic, 2009.

Stuhlmacher, Peter. *Biblical Theology of the New Testament*. Translated and edited by Daniel P. Bailey, with the collaboration of Jostein Ådna. Grand Rapids: Eerdmans, 2018.

Theology: Systematic, Biblical, Pauline

Barrett, C. K. *Paul: An Introduction to His Thought*. Louisville: Westminster John Knox, 1994.

Bassler, Jouette M., ed. *Pauline Theology I: Thessalonians, Philippians, Galatians, Philemon*. Minneapolis: Fortress, 1991.

Becker, Jürgen. *Paul: Apostle to the Gentiles*. Louisville: Westminster John Knox, 1993.

Beker, Johan Christiaan. *Paul's Apocalyptic Gospel: The Coming Triumph of God*. Philadelphia: Fortress, 1982.

Boring, M. Eugene. *Hearing John's Voice: Insights for Teaching and Preaching*. Grand Rapids: Eerdmans, 2019.

———. "The Language of Universal Salvation in Paul." *Journal of Biblical Literature* 105 (1986): 269–92.

Brunner, Emil. *The Word and the World*. London: SCM, 1931.

Buber, Martin. *I and Thou*. Edinburgh: T&T Clark, 1958.

Craddock, Fred B. *The Pre-existence of Christ in the New Testament*. Nashville: Abingdon, 1968.

Cullmann, Oscar. "The Tradition." In *The Early Church*, edited by A. J. B. Higgins, 59–104. London: SCM, 1956.

Dunn, James D. G. *The Theology of Paul the Apostle*. Grand Rapids: Eerdmans, 1998.

Feldmeier, Reinhard, and Hermann Spieckermann. *Menschwerdung*. Topoi Biblischer Theologie. Tübingen: Mohr Siebeck, 2018.

Furnish, Victor Paul. *The Jesus-Paul Debate: From Baur to Bultmann*. Manchester: John Rylands Library, 1965.

Gaventa, Beverly R., ed. *Apocalyptic Paul: Cosmos and Anthropos in Romans 5–8*. Waco, TX: Baylor University Press, 2013.

Gunton, Colin. *The Actuality of Atonement.* Grand Rapids: Eerdmans, 1989.

Hays, Richard B. *The Faith of Jesus Christ: An Investigation of the Narrative Substructure of Galatians 3:1–4:11.* 2nd ed. Grand Rapids: Eerdmans, 2002.

Hunter, A. M. *Paul and His Predecessors.* Philadelphia: Westminster, 1961.

Hurtado, Larry W. *God in New Testament Theology.* Library of Biblical Theology. Nashville: Abingdon, 2010.

———. *Lord Jesus Christ: Devotion to Jesus in Earliest Christianity.* Grand Rapids: Eerdmans, 2003.

Johnson, E. Elizabeth, and David M. Hay, eds. *Looking Back, Pressing On.* Vol. 4 of *Pauline Theology.* Society of Biblical Literature Symposium Series. Atlanta: Scholars Press, 1997.

Jones, Joe R. *A Grammar of Christian Faith: Systematic Explorations in Christian Life and Doctrine.* 2 vols. Lanham, MD: Rowman & Littlefield, 2002.

Jones, Serene. "What's Wrong with Us? Human Nature and Human Sin." In *Essentials of Christian Theology,* edited by William C. Placher, 133–57. Louisville: Westminster John Knox, 2003.

Käsemann, Ernst. *Perspectives on Paul.* Philadelphia: Fortress, 1971.

Keck, Leander. "Good News for Us Gentiles." In *Christ's First Theologian: The Shape of Paul's Thought,* 195–206. Waco, TX: Baylor University Press, 2015.

———. "The Jewish Paul among the Gentiles." In *Christ's First Theologian: The Shape of Paul's Thought,* 43–62. Waco, TX: Baylor University Press, 2015.

———. "Paul and Apocalyptic Theology." In *Christ's First Theologian: The Shape of Paul's Thought,* 195–206. Waco, TX: Baylor University Press, 2015.

———. *Paul and His Letters.* Proclamation Commentaries. Philadelphia: Fortress, 1979.

Keck, Leander, and Victor Paul Furnish. *The Pauline Letters.* Interpreting Biblical Texts. Edited by Lloyd R. Bailey Sr. and Victor Paul Furnish. Nashville: Abingdon, 1984.

Knox, John. *Chapters in a Life of St. Paul.* London: Adam & Charles Black, 1950.

Leith, John H. *Basic Christian Doctrine.* Louisville: Westminster John Knox, 1993.

Long, Thomas G. *Preaching from Memory to Hope.* Louisville: Westminster John Knox, 2009.

————. *Testimony: Talking Ourselves into Being Christian*. San Francisco: Jossey-Bass, 2004.

Long, Thomas G., Beverly Roberts Gaventa, and David L. Petersen, eds. *The New Interpreter's One-Volume Commentary*. Nashville: Abingdon, 2010.

Martyn, J. Louis. *Theological Issues in the Letters of Paul*. Nashville: Abingdon, 1997.

McKnight, Scot, and Joseph B. Modica, eds. *The Apostle Paul and the Christian Life: Ethical and Missional Implications of the New Perspective*. Grand Rapids: Baker Academic, 2016.

Migliore, Daniel. *Faith Seeking Understanding: An Introduction to Christian Theology*. Grand Rapids: Eerdmans, 1991.

Minear, Paul S. *Images of the Church in the New Testament*. Philadelphia: Westminster, 1960.

Niebuhr, H. Richard. *Christ and Culture*. New York: Harper & Brothers, 1951.

Niebuhr, Reinhold. *The Nature and Destiny of Man*. 2 vols. New York: Scribner's Sons, 1941.

Placher, William C., ed. *Essentials of Christian Theology*. Louisville: Westminster John Knox, 2003.

Roetzel, Calvin J. *The Letters of Paul: Conversations in Context*. 6th ed. Louisville: Westminster John Knox, 2015.

————. *Paul: The Man and the Myth*. Minneapolis: Fortress, 1999.

Sanders, E. P. *Paul and Palestinian Judaism: A Comparison of Patterns of Religion*. Philadelphia: Fortress, 1977.

Schnelle, Udo. *Apostle Paul: His Life and Thought*. Translated by M. Eugene Boring. Grand Rapids: Baker Academic, 2005.

Stuhlmacher, Peter. *Biblical Theology of the New Testament*. Translated and edited by Daniel P. Bailey, with the collaboration of Jostein Ådna. Grand Rapids: Eerdmans, 2018.

Thurneysen, Eduard. "Schrift und Offenbarung." *Zwischen den Zeiten* 2, no. 6 (1924): 3–30.

Wedderburn, A. J. M. *Paul and Jesus: Collected Essays*. Journal for the Study of the New Testament Supplement Series 37. Sheffield: JSOT Press, 1989.

Wolter, Michael. *Paul: An Outline of His Theology*. Translated by Robert L. Brawley. Waco, TX: Baylor University Press, 2015.

Wright, N. T. *Paul and the Faithfulness of God*. Vol. 4 of *Christian Origins and the Question of God*. Minneapolis: Fortress, 2013.

————. *Paul in Fresh Perspective*. Minneapolis: Fortress, 2005.

———. *The Resurrection of the Son of God.* Vol. 3 of *Christian Origins and the Question of God.* Minneapolis: Fortress, 2003.

1 Thessalonians

Boring, M. Eugene. *1 and 2 Thessalonians: A Commentary.* New Testament Library. Louisville: Westminster John Knox, 2015.

Donfried, Karl P., and I. Howard Marshall. *The Theology of the Shorter Pauline Letters.* New Testament Theology. Cambridge: Cambridge University Press, 1993.

Fee, Gordon D. *The First and Second Letters to the Thessalonians.* New International Commentary on the New Testament. Grand Rapids: Eerdmans, 2009.

Furnish, Victor Paul. *1 Thessalonians, 2 Thessalonians.* Abingdon New Testament Commentaries. Nashville: Abingdon, 2007.

Gaventa, Beverly Roberts. *First and Second Thessalonians.* Interpretation: A Bible Commentary for Teaching and Preaching. Louisville: Westminster John Knox, 1998.

Malherbe, Abraham J. *The Letters to the Thessalonians: A New Translation with Introduction and Commentary.* Anchor Yale Bible 32B. New York: Doubleday, 2000.

Roetzel, Calvin. "The Grammar of Election in Four Pauline Letters." In *1 & 2 Corinthians,* vol. 2 of *Pauline Theology,* edited by David M. Hay, 211–34. Minneapolis: Fortress, 1993.

Still, Todd D. *Conflict at Thessalonica: A Pauline Church and Its Neighbours.* Journal for the Study of the New Testament Supplement Series. Sheffield: Sheffield Academic, 1999.

Romans

Achtemeier, Paul J. *Romans.* Interpretation: A Bible Commentary for Teaching and Preaching. Atlanta: John Knox, 1985.

Barth, Karl. *The Epistle to the Romans.* Translated by Edwyn C. Hoskyns. London: Oxford University Press, 1933.

Gaventa, Beverly R. *When in Romans: An Invitation to Linger with the Gospel according to Paul.* Waco, TX: Baylor University Press, 2016.

Grieb, A. Katherine. *The Story of Romans: A Narrative Defense of God's Righteousness*. Louisville: Westminster John Knox, 2002.

Jewett, Robert. *Romans: A Commentary*. Hermeneia. Minneapolis: Fortress, 2007.

Käsemann, Ernst. *Commentary on Romans*. Translated by Geoffrey W. Bromiley. Grand Rapids: Eerdmans, 1980.

Keck, Leander. *Romans*. Abingdon New Testament Commentaries. Edited by Victor Paul Furnish. Nashville: Abingdon, 2005.

Long, Thomas G. "Preaching Romans Today." *Interpretation* 58, no. 3 (July 2004): 265–76.

Wright, N. T. "The Letter to the Romans." In *The New Interpreter's Bible*, edited by Leander Keck, 393–770. Nashville: Abingdon, 2002.

The Emerging Church in the Pauline Tradition

Household Codes

Balch, David L. "Household Codes." In *Greco-Roman Literature and the New Testament: Selected Forms and Genres*, edited by David E. Aune, 25–50. Society of Biblical Literature Sources for Biblical Study 21. Atlanta: Scholars Press, 1988.

Boring, M. Eugene. "Christian Existence and Conduct in the Given Structures of Society." In *1 Peter*, 102–28. Abingdon New Testament Commentaries. Nashville: Abingdon, 1999.

Crouch, James E. *The Origin and Intention of the Colossian Haustafel*. Göttingen: Vandenhoeck & Ruprecht, 1972.

Young, Frances. "Duties in the Household of Faith or What about Church Order." In *The Theology of the Pastoral Letters*, 97–121. New Testament Theology. Cambridge: Cambridge University Press, 1994.

Ephesians

Barth, Karl. *The Epistle to the Ephesians*. Translated by Ross M. Wright. Grand Rapids: Baker Academic, 2017.

Barth, Markus. *The Broken Wall: A Study of the Epistle to the Ephesians*. Philadelphia: Judson, 1959.

Best, Ernest. *A Critical and Exegetical Commentary on Ephesians*. International Critical Commentary. Edinburgh: T&T Clark, 1998.

Fowl, Stephen E. *Ephesians: A Commentary*. New Testament Library. Louisville: Westminster John Knox, 2012.

Lincoln, Andrew T., and A. J. M. Wedderburn. *The Theology of the Later Pauline Letters*. New Testament Theology. Cambridge: Cambridge University Press, 1993.

Perkins, Pheme. *Ephesians*. Abingdon New Testament Commentaries. Nashville: Abingdon, 1997.

The Pastorals

Collins, Raymond F. *I & II Timothy and Titus: A Commentary*. New Testament Library. Louisville: Westminster John Knox, 2002.

Marshall, I. Howard. *The Pastoral Epistles*. International Critical Commentary. Edinburgh: T&T Clark, 1999.

Young, Frances M. *The Theology of the Pastoral Letters*. New Testament Theology. Cambridge: Cambridge University Press, 1994.

Index of Names and Subjects

Index of Scripture and Other Ancient Sources